PREACHING AT THE DOUBLE FEAST

Homiletics for Eucharistic Worship

Edited by

Michael Monshau, O.P.

Contributors

Linda L. Clader
Sergius Halvorsen
Michael Monshau, O.P.
Mary Alice Mulligan
Mary Ann Wiesemann-Mills, O.P.

LITURGICAL PRESS
Collegeville, Minnesota

www.litpress.org

Cover design by David Manahan, O.S.B. Photo by Jenny Home, iStockphoto.com.

1   2   3   4   5   6   7   8   9

Library of Congress Cataloging-in-Publication Data

Preaching at the Double Feast : homiletics for Eucharistic worship / edited by Michael Monshau ; contributors, Linda L. Clader . . . [et al.].
    p. cm.
    Includes bibliographical references and index.
    ISBN-13: 978-0-8146-2780-8 (alk. paper)
    ISBN-10: 0-8146-2780-3 (alk. paper)
    1. Lord's Supper (Liturgy).   2. Lord's Supper—Catholic Church.   3. Communion sermons.   4. Preaching.   I. Monshau, Michael.   II. Clader, Linda L., 1946– .   III. Title.

BX2215.3.P74 2006
251—dc22

2006002343

*To the Dominican novices and student brothers
of the Province of the Most Holy Name of Jesus
whom I have served as
professor, religious formator, and religious superior.
It has all been a labor of love.*

Ecce quam bonum et quam jucundum
habitare fratres in unum *(Ps 133)*.

M.M.

CONTENTS

INTRODUCTION

This work adds critical new perspective to current conversations in homiletics.

The term "Double Feast" is introduced in this volume to identify the liturgical structure of those churches for which normative liturgical worship features the rites of the two tables of the Word (the proclamation of the Scriptures and the preaching) and of the Eucharist (Holy Communion).[1] The majority, though by no means all, of Protestant liturgies, are frequently "Single Feast" events, that is, non-eucharistic Word-centered worship services. In terms of time, to say nothing of content and structure, it stands to reason that the preaching event at a Single Feast liturgy is going to be constructed differently from the preaching event of a eucharistic liturgy.

When challenged to reflect upon the teaching of preaching, today's homileticians widely agree that most of the contemporary wisdom about preaching has been learned from men of various mainline Protestant traditions; hence the primary voices forming successive generations of preachers, and to whom we are most grateful, have been males of Single Feast traditions. It is time to complement those worthy voices with input from women as well as men, a corrective fortunately already well in progress albeit new. Furthermore, the Double Feast churches have much to add to contemporary understandings of the preaching dynamic. In response to these needs, this volume presents the work of five homileticians, three women and two men, all representing Double Feast churches.

Father Sergius Halvorsen, Ph.D., of the Orthodox Church in America, has contributed a chapter entitled "The Context of the Eucharistic

---

[1] Of course, it is understood that the liturgical praxis of all the churches represented by this nomenclature includes a wide variety of non-eucharistic worship events as well as the Sunday eucharistic worship.

Liturgy," in which he examines preaching within the context of the Eastern Orthodox eucharistic liturgy. This contribution, complementing the wisdom of the tradition with contemporary voices, adds the critically important but often missing Eastern Orthodox voice to the homiletic discussion table. Rev. Mary Alice Mulligan, Ph.D., of the Christian Church (Disciples of Christ), has entitled her work "Teaching Disciples to Preach in the Service of Word and Table." In this consideration of the theological claims upon preaching and homiletic method informed by her obviously extensive pastoral background, Dr. Mulligan presents a homiletic method of value to an audience far transcending her mainline American Protestant context, and all Double Feast preachers will be indebted to her genius. Sister Mary Ann Wiesemann-Mills, O.P., D.MIN., a member of the Akron Dominican congregation of Catholic Sisters, reveals her multi-faceted approach to preaching (as spirituality, homiletic theory, theological task, exegetical mission, and challenge to the imagination), as well as her command of pedagogy and adult learning models in her chapter entitled "Preaching in the Context of 'Doing the Liturgy.'" The Rev. Linda L. Clader, Ph.D., representing the Episcopalian perspective, has attended to the task of preparation for the vocation of the preacher in her creative contribution entitled "The Formation of a Eucharistic Preacher." Father Michael Monshau, O.P., Ph.D., editor of this volume and Catholic priest, prepared a chapter entitled "A Catholic Conversation about Preaching," in which he presents a chronological method for homily formation for a Double Feast preacher.

Each chapter follows a different format. Originally we considered the utilization of a template to govern the formation of each chapter. Following a certain amount of time and energy devoted to the construction of such a template, we realized that such a structure could compromise the freedom each of us required to enflesh our homiletic according to our unique contexts. Since the genius of this book is that it provides varying insights into a common task, it was decided not to incorporate any ingredients (like a template) that would inhibit freedom of expression. Hence, this work is an eclectic collection of five homiletic methods gathered together because of their unique role within the world of Christian preaching: preaching at the Double Feast.

Michael Monshau, O.P.
Berkeley, California
June 2005

Michael Monshau, O.P.

A CATHOLIC CONVERSATION ABOUT PREACHING

Any attempt to construct a homiletic from a Catholic perspective must be built upon the church's relationship to the ancient and normative two-fold liturgical structure of word and sacrament restored at Vatican II. This twentieth-century restoration has reclaimed for the contemporary church a liturgical praxis that nourishes the faithful at two tables, the table of the Word and the table of the Eucharist; hence, liturgy becomes a "Double Feast."

In its conciliar restoration of the Double Feast structure, the Church recognized the integral nature of the word at liturgy, which in turn affected a preaching renewal within the church's worship patterns. Although the call to reclaim the word/sacrament structure actually heralded Catholicism's return to its own ancient traditions, it called for a dynamic so radically different from the common practice of the time that it seemed as if this directive were breaking new ground rather than reclaiming authentic tradition.

The liturgical word-event had been severely compromised in the pre-Vatican II church. The Scripture readings themselves were not necessarily proclaimed in the vernacular and preaching could be omitted when the ordained celebrant chose to do so. The obligation that the Church placed upon its congregants to participate at Mass each Sunday could be fulfilled even if one had arrived after the conclusion of the entire Liturgy of the Word. Outside of specially scheduled preaching events such as parish missions or retreats, preaching occurred only rarely at eucharistic liturgies on weekdays. In effect, the sermon was not considered to be an integral ingredient of worship, but rather was regarded as a pastoral excursus from

1

the movement of the liturgy itself. Moreover, it was a dispensable excursus. This constituted a betrayal of Catholicism's heritage of the word.

The origins of the word/action structure for Christian worship are found in the Jewish context out of which Christianity emerged. In Hebrew antiquity, a person's words were not typically understood to have been separate from the speaker's own person. One's words were perceived to convey the expression of one's own self. Hence, the word of God in Scripture would have been recognized as the source of special power since God's words were understood to manifest the very presence of God's self. Worship events featured a celebration of God's word and a remembering of God's activities. Accordingly, people related to God through the divine word as it was delivered through the mouths of others from their number.

Domenico Grasso writes that

> the best known text about the efficacy of the Word of God may be found in Isaiah in the Old Testament: "For just as from the heavens the rain and snow come down and do not return there till they have watered the earth, making it fertile, and fruitful, giving seed to him who sows and bread to him who eats, so shall my word be that goes forth from my mouth; it shall not return to me void, but shall do my will, achieving the end for which I sent it" (Isa 55:10-11 NAB).[1]

The principle that God's own work is located within the divine word is evidenced in this text and it becomes paradigmatic for the manner in which the ancient Hebrews contextualized God's word. The expression *dāḇār Yahweh* represents the dynamic and effective force in God's word; that which God says comes to pass. By way of definition, the *Theological Dictionary of the New Testament* reads: "Only in the Hebrew *(dāḇār)* is the material concept with its energy felt so vitally in the verbal concept that the words appear as a material force which is always present and at work."[2] Subsequently, the definition continues: "The Word is seen to be a heavenly force which creatively accomplishes its work on earth";[3] "the power of God finds recognizable expression in the *(logos)*";[4] and "Since God's Word is power, it is infallibly accomplished. Its authenticity may

---

[1] Domenico Grasso, *Proclaiming God's Message* (Notre Dame: University of Notre Dame Press, 1965) 126.

[2] O. Procksch, "λεγω" in the *Theological Dictionary of the New Testament,* ed. Gerhard Kittel, trans. and ed. Geoffrey W. Bromiley, vol. IV (Grand Rapids: William B. Eerdmans Publishing Co., 1965) 93.

[3] Procksch, "λεγω," 98.

[4] Ibid., 94.

be known by the fact that it comes to pass" (Jer 28:9).[5] Still elsewhere the definition notes "As rain and snow cannot be unfruitful but soak into the earth and cause seeds to sprout, so the word of Yahweh cannot return to heaven without accomplishing its mission. It executes God's will and does what it was sent to do. . . . Every prophetic word is an effectual force. . . . The Word is seen to be a heavenly force which creatively accomplishes its work on earth."[6]

Within this context, it can be understood that human life is an obedient response to God's command "to be." Life is the continuation of the dialogue that God initiated when the command to exist was uttered; the fact of life assures that God's word will not return empty to its source. The fact of human life further provides the human dimension within God's continuing word in the world. The presence of God's word, therefore, is an event, a moment in which that word which God has spoken is affected. God's word is God's work. What God has uttered has come into being: when God called for the existence of light, matter, life, the immediate result was the very existence of light, matter, life.

Hence, when the ancient Hebrews attended to God's word, they recalled God's work in their midst and made anamnetic thanksgiving for that divine activity spoken as well as realized. Worship gatherings were events which marked the presence of God's word and commemorated God's work in the life of the worshiping community.

Even when understood in this powerful context, the word-event, however, did not stand alone in Jewish worship. In asserting this point, Lucien Deiss writes:

> [The Word-event was experienced in conjunction] with the sacrificial ritual to such an extent that the "blood of the covenant" is inconceivable apart from the proclamation of the word and its acceptance by the people: "Moses came to the people and related all the words and ordinances of the Lord" (24:3). The people with one voice shouted their acceptance. Then "Moses wrote down all the words of the Lord" (24:4). Finally, when the altar had been readied and the victims immolated, "taking the book of the covenant, he read it aloud to the people who answered, 'All that the Lord has said, we will heed and do,' then he took the blood and sprinkled it on the people, saying 'This is the blood of the covenant which the Lord has made with you, in accordance with all these words of his'" (Exod 24:7-8).[7]

---

[5] Ibid., 98.

[6] Ibid.

[7] Lucien Deiss, *God's Word and God's People*, trans. M. J. Connell (Collegeville, MN: Liturgical Press, 1976) 258.

When the ancient Hebrew people worshiped, they related to God through God's word and they also enacted ritual. Given that this narrative describes Moses reading the word of God to the assembled nation prior to offering those sacrifices designated for immolation, the two-part structure of word and cult, which will remain invariably present in Jewish worship, is already in place at this time. Accordingly, those who were later served by the ministry of Jesus would have been familiar with and well rooted in the word/cult structure of divine worship.

THE WORD/TABLE STRUCTURE IN THE CHRISTIAN SCRIPTURES

Certain New Testament texts provide helpful descriptions of the elements of worship: Eucharist; readings; preaching and instruction; the offerings of prayers of thanksgiving and intercession; the use of psalms, hymns, and canticles; and evidence of the charismatic gifts of prophecy, tongues, and interpretation.

Perhaps the most critical approach to this examination into the Christian Scriptures is to situate the context of the *dābār* Yahweh as it continues to evidence itself in primitive Christianity. Anthony J. Tambasco has written:

> In the NT the qualities of the word of God as living and effective are maintained, but they are deepened and focused on the person of Jesus himself. The word is related to Jesus as he extends the prophetic vocation in his own life (Mt 12:41; Mk 6:4). His proclamation is often referred to as the word of God (Lk 5:1). His preaching is seen as powerful and efficacious, often translated into signs and wonders (Mt 8:16), and accompanied by the Spirit who enables the teaching of Jesus to now become the "good news" (Lk 4:18). However the fullest statement of the NT on the word of God comes with the deepening of the process of personification and the appreciation of Jesus as the very word of God incarnate (Jn 1:14). John's use of the Greek term *logos* draws more from the Hebrew *dābār* than it does from the Hellenistic philosophical understanding of the term as intellectual abstraction. Jesus is "word of life" and the dynamic self-disclosure of God is most fully experienced in what "we have seen with our eyes" and "touched with our hands," the human reality of Jesus (1 Jn 1:1).[8]

---

[8] Anthony J. Tambasco, "Word of God" in *The New Dictionary of Theology*, Joseph A. Komonchak, Mary Collins, and Dermot A. Lane, eds. (Wilmington, DE: Michael Glazier, Inc., 1987) 1096.

As the very Word of God, Jesus the Christ continues effecting the event of the divine presence in the midst of creation. Just as God's command for light in the Old Testament resulted in light, so do the words of Christ effect what they intend. When Jesus said, "be healed," healing occurred; when Jesus announced reconciliation, the divisive reality of sin was simultaneously annihilated within the person being addressed.

The authoritative power of Christ's healing word is manifested superbly in the narrative of the centurion at Capernaum (Matt 8:5-13). Here Jesus uniquely heals at a distance through his word alone. The typical use of the imposition of hands or other physical contact, or his direct address to the person being healed is absent in this event. All that is required for Christ's power to become manifest at this moment is the utterance of his authoritative and healing word. Christ notes and affirms the faith of the centurion who has recognized God's activity in the word of Christ, "Truly I tell you, in no one in Israel have I found such faith" (8:10b).[9] What is the remarkable faith that Jesus is affirming here? It is faith in his word. Hence in Jesus Christ, the effective word of God continues to make present God's own work. This phenomenon is paradigmatic for Christians just as it was for the ancient Hebrews.

Accordingly, Christian worship is rooted in the same word tradition as are Jewish structures; consequently, one naturally expects to discover that the ritual form of Christian worship contains the word/rite structure already evidenced in the Jewish context.

The three Synoptic institution narratives (Matt 26:26-30; Mark 14:22-26; Luke 22:14-22), as well as the Pauline passage (1 Cor 11:23-26), all convey the eucharistic heritage that Christ bequeathed to his followers. The narrative of the Last Supper in the Synoptic accounts reveals the word and table structure: Christ's instructive words and the sharing of the bread and cup are both present. Whereas in Corinthians, Paul does not communicate any of Jesus' instruction that night and whereas John's lengthy set of teachings does not include the actual sharing of the bread and cup, neither of these texts denies the presence of the missing dimension; they simply do not mention it as they describe that aspect of the event which they wish to emphasize. At the same time, the Synoptic texts all reveal that both aspects of the structure under scrutiny were present. Other essential material is found in the sixth chapter of the Fourth Gospel, as well as in its Last Supper narrative (John 13–16), despite the fact that it excludes the institution itself.

[9] Quoted Scriptural texts here and throughout this chapter, unless otherwise noted, are taken from the New Revised Standard Version.

Additionally, the miraculous feedings and the post-Resurrection meal accounts are indispensable to any understanding of the early church's eucharistic context. They all feature the teaching of Jesus. An invitation from Jesus to sit at table always features communication by word with the Lord; in fact, Jesus uses meal events and the miraculous feedings as especially opportune moments to communicate his message.

The Book of Acts reveals what are to endure as fundamental aspects of Christian worship: instruction, preaching, prayer, and the breaking of the bread (cf. Acts 2:42ff.). These worship accounts from the annals of the earliest church reveal the two-part structure featured in their primitive liturgical events.

The Road to Emmaus account (Luke 24:13-35) relates that after Jesus, Cleopas, and the anonymous companion spent the better part of an afternoon engaged in a word-event, they sat down at table for a sharing of bread, an event which features the easily recognizable fourfold eucharistic structure of taking, blessing, breaking, and giving. In that table sharing, the two disciples recognized the Lord and then, in hindsight, later realized that they could well also have recognized him in the words he had spoken. Cleopas and his friend had been nourished by Christ's word as well as at table in the company of Christ.

The two-fold worship structure is again found in Acts 2:42-47, which describes primitive Christian life, the community's concern for its needy members, the peace of the community, its life of charity, and its living witness as a kind of word-event in action. The literal word-event of the apostles' instruction is followed in this informal account by the breaking of bread and prayer. This text uncovers that the earliest Christians attracted other followers to Christ simply by having ". . . devoted themselves to the apostles' teaching and fellowship, to the breaking of bread and the prayers" (Acts 2:42). This text is significant to the contemporary church's understanding that Christian praxis is itself gospel proclamation. For the primitive church, the silent proclamation of the word by praxis was indeed a word-event which was critically important to the church's kerygmatic preaching, but even in this description, the two-fold liturgical activity is present.

Another pertinent example is found in Acts 20:4-12, which depicts Paul's preaching at Troas the evening that the young Eutychus fell from the windowsill. The pericope opens with 20:7, which reads "On the first day of the week, when we met to break bread, Paul was holding a discussion with them." The expression "on the first day of the week" is already understood in the earliest days of the church to imply reference to the weekly eucharistic gathering of the faithful. Behm states that ". . . within the context of the Pauline mission, the breaking of the bread, which is on the Lord's Day in Acts 20:7, is a cultic meal."[10] Of course, our contemporary inability to clarify the distinctions between two Christian religious meal-types of the first century (the eucharistic sharing and the agape meal) commands our reservation. As to whether this passage describes an agape meal or a eucharistic gathering, I am disinclined to view this as an agape meal because of the late hour of the gathering. The ritual consumption of the eucharistic elements seems more likely than the consumption of the full meal which was the agape feast at an hour so late in the day that participants were falling asleep. However, more extensive analysis uncovers additional information.

In verse 11, after Paul has brought the dead Eutychus back to life, one reads that Paul "went upstairs, and after he had broken bread and eaten, he continued to converse with them until dawn." The verb for "broke" in the Greek text is κλάσας, which in the New Testament is only used for the breaking of bread, which itself is often of a religious ceremonial nature.[11] Of important note is the fact that this is the same verb used to describe the action of Jesus in the eucharistic institution narrative in all three Synoptic accounts as well as in the Pauline text. Consequently, when the clear presence of Paul's preaching at this event is considered in light of the likelihood that those assembled in the upstairs room at Troas were gathered for Eucharist, another credible New Testament defense for the word and table structure of early Christian worship is established. Although this theory is more clearly supported if this event can be proven to have been eucharistic, it is not essential to what is being posited here. Since the "non-eucharistic" agape meal was itself a ritual event attended by Christians desirous of remembering and celebrating the Christ-event in their communal lives, even without Eucharist this event suggests that when gathered in a worshipful context, first generation Christians heard the word proclaimed and broke bread.

Pauline literature asserts that the table sharing cannot be separated from the word event because the table sharing is itself a proclamation of the Word. This is most strongly evidenced in 1 Corinthians 11:26, in which Paul teaches "For as often as you eat this bread and drink the cup,

---

[10] Procksch, "λεγω," 730.

[11] Walter Bauer, *A Greek-English Lexicon of the New Testament and Other Christian Literature*, 2nd ed., rev. and augmented by F. Wilbur Gingrich and Frederick W. Danker (Chicago: University of Chicago Press, 1979) 433. Kurt Aland, *et al.*, eds., *The Greek New Testament*, 3rd ed. (Stuttgart: United Bible Societies, 1983), Dictionary Appendix p. 100.

you proclaim the Lord's death until he comes." Interestingly enough, his word for "proclaim" is "kerygma," which is the proclamation of the Lord's Passover Mystery. The proclamation of the word which has been announced through the Scripture readings and preaching is not a separate event from the proclamation of the same word which happens through the sharing of the Eucharist. Hence, Paul associates the table-event with the proclamation of the word as two parts of one united activity.

Despite the fact that the Christian Scriptures neither claim to report careful liturgical outlines nor do they provide them, the material examined here suggests that the word and table structure functioned normatively in the worship of the early church and reflected the two-part worship structure Christians had inherited from their Jewish roots. Subsequently, this same two-fold structure appears consistently in the post-apostolic liturgical orders.

THE WORD/SACRAMENT STRUCTURE IN THE EARLY CHURCH

The Church Fathers provide explicit evidence that Christians broke open the word at the same gatherings at which they broke bread and shared the cup. Obviously, effective preaching of the word was essential during this formative period in the life of the church when its evangelical and pedagogical responsibilities were so essential to the continued life of the nascent ecclesial community. The church of those first centuries was heavily concerned with adult converts and their needs for instruction as they prepared for baptism as well as their eventual need for post-baptismal instruction—*mystagogia*. Therefore, an earnest ministry of the Word occurred at eucharistic assemblies. Bernard Cooke writes:

> [T]he assembly of Christians for the eucharistic celebration was *the* occasion for the continuing catechetical formation of their faith. Such instruction of their faith was intrinsic to the action, a clarification of the very mystery they were enacting and the very word they were therein hearing; it was not something extra brought in to profit by the fact that people were present. What was most instructive was the very action itself, and the purpose of the homily was to indicate the "revelation" contained in that particular day's liturgy, to draw from it the lessons appropriate to the assembled community.[12]

---

[12] Bernard Cooke, *Ministry to Word and Sacraments* (Philadelphia: Fortress Press, 1976) 246–47).

It was during this period of church history from which are drawn some extant statements about the dignity of the word in Christian life and worship. These statements clarify the theological underpinnings to the word and table structure which other sources reveal to have been present at worship in this period. For instance, in the middle of the third century, Origen preached:

> I wish to admonish you with examples from your religious practices. You, who are accustomed to take part in divine mysteries know, when you receive the body of the Lord, how you protect it with all caution and veneration lest any small part fall from it, lest anything of the consecrated gift be lost. For you believe, and correctly, that you are answerable if anything falls from there by neglect. But if you are so careful to preserve his body, and rightly so, how do you think that there is less guilt to have neglected God's word than to have neglected his body?[13]

Elsewhere, St. Jerome

> . . . applies the biblical word to the Eucharist and describes the result as the question of two foods given by God for the soul: "If the flesh of Christ is true food and His blood true drink, we have in this life the only good, that of eating this flesh and drinking this blood, not only in the mystery of the Eucharist, but also in reading Scripture."[14]

Not surprisingly, when St. Augustine engaged this subject, he provided theological reflection upon the nature of the sacraments themselves (including the Eucharist), and he reflected upon the relationship between word and sacrament. In his well-known *Sermon 80* on the Fourth Gospel, he wrote: "The word is added to the element, and it becomes a sacrament, as it were a visible word."[15] This statement reveals that, according to Augustine, sacraments (and therefore Eucharist) involve elements, activity, and a proclamation of the word of God. The word dimension to this dynamic further tends to identify the observance of the sacrament with worship, since the proclamation of the word is consistently featured in Christian worship ever since the primitive era of the church. For Augustine, sacraments are not only rituals that

---

[13] Origen, *Homilies on Genesis and Exodus,* vol. 71 of *The Fathers of the Church,* ed. Hermigild Dressler, *et al.,* trans. Ronald F. Heine (Washington, DC: Catholic University of America Press, 1981) 380–81.

[14] Grasso, *Proclaiming God's Message,* 130.

[15] Augustine, Bishop of Hippo, *Homilies on the Gospel According to St. John, and His First Epistle,* vol. II, Homily LXXX (Oxford: John Henry Parker, 1849) 827.

point to faith and convey grace, but they are *verbum visibile;* that is to say, they are observable proclamations of the Gospel. When synthesized, Augustine's various writings identify sacraments as external and observable sign/symbols related to God, joined with the word of God, having spiritual efficacy in the life of the recipient and somehow expressive of the recipient's relationship to the community of believers; that is to say, sacraments point to faith, convey grace, are ecclesial, and always feature the word of God as an essential ingredient. One does not experience sacrament without the word in Augustine's system.

This sampling of representative sources evidences the early church's regard for the dignity of the word of God in Scripture. Such evidence, however, is not the equivalent of indisputable and specific proof that the scriptural word, proclaimed and preached, comprised an essential aspect of the eucharistic liturgy of the time. The earliest extant post-biblical document that does this is Justin Martyr's *First Apology,* which dates to the middle of the second century (ca. 155). The pertinent passage from this significant text reads:

> And on that day which is called Sunday, there is an assembly in the same place of all who live in the cities, or in country districts; and the records of the Apostles, or the writings of the Prophets, are read as long as we have time. Then the reader concludes: and the President verbally instructs and exhorts us, to the imitation of these excellent things; then we all together rise and offer up our prayers; and, as I said before, when we have concluded our prayer, bread is brought, and wine, and water; and the President, in like manner, offers up prayers and thanksgivings, with all his strength; and the people give their assent by saying Amen: and there is . . . partaking by everyone, of the Eucharistic elements; and to those who are not present, they are sent by the hands of the deacons.[16]

This text provides evidence that by this period in time (ca. 155 A.D.), the word and table structure was an element of Christian worship. Subsequent documents reveal that this structure was the norm for the primary worship event of the Christian community. This is not to say that whenever Christians gathered, they gathered for Eucharist; in particular the *Apostolic Tradition* and the *Diary of Egeria* indicate that many other kinds of rituals and worship events which were not eucharistic were also conducted. Evidence does reveal, however, that whenever Christians did

---

[16] Justin Martyr, *The Works Now Extant of St. Justin the Martyr, A Library of Fathers of the Holy Catholic Church Anterior to the Division of the East and West* (Oxford: J. H. and Jas. Parker, 1861) 52.

gather for Eucharist, they did not approach the table without also feeding upon the word of God (either before or after).

Similarly, the *Apostolic Constitutions* (ca. 400 A.D.) reveals that the liturgical structure in question was commonplace. It is quite revealing that the account of the Eucharist in Book II of this text begins with a rather detailed description of the Liturgy of the Word with which the eucharistic celebration began. It states:

> Let the reader, standing on a high place in the middle, read the books of Moses, of Joshua the son of Nun, of the Judges and of the Kings and of the Chronicles and those written after the return from the captivity; and besides these, the books of Job and Solomon and of the sixteen prophets. After two lessons have been read, let some other person sing the hymns of David, and let the people join in singing the refrains. Afterwards, let our Acts be read, and the epistle of Paul, our fellow worker, which he sent to the churches under the direction of the Holy Spirit; and after that let a presbyter or a deacon read the gospels, those which I, Matthew and John have delivered to you, and those which the fellow workers of Paul, Luke and Mark, compiled and left to you. And while the gospel is read, let all the presbyters and deacons and the whole people, stand in profound silence, for it is written: "be silent and hear O Israel," And again: "But do you stand there and listen." Next let the presbyters, each in turn, not all together, exhort the people, and lastly the bishop, as captain of the ship.[17]

In her diary, the fourth–fifth-century nun Egeria frequently identified the reading of Scripture or the preaching as the initial segment of the various eucharistic assemblies in which she participated. In Chapter 25, Egeria writes:

> Since it is Sunday, at dawn they assemble for the liturgy in the major church built by Constantine and located on Golgotha behind the cross; and whatever is done all over customarily on Sundays is done here. Indeed it is the practice here that many priests who are present and are so inclined may preach; and last of all, the bishop preaches.[18]

It is clear from the ancient sources that although Christians did not always share Eucharist when they gathered prayerfully, their eucharistic gatherings were events at which sacred writings, the reading of letters

---

[17] W. Jardine Grisbrooke, ed., trans., *The Liturgical Portions of the Apostolic Constitutions: A Text for Students* (Bramcote, Eng.: Grove Books Ltd., 1990) 15.

[18] Johannes Quasten, Walter Burghardt, and Thomas Comerford Lawler, eds., *Egeria: Diary of a Pilgrimage* in *Ancient Christian Writers,* no. 38, trans. George E. Gingras (New York: Paulist Press, 1970) 93.

from church teachers, and evangelical documents were read aloud followed by preaching or exhortation by church leaders. Sufficient evidence does not exist to create a complete picture of the primitive Christian liturgy. Furthermore, it is important to remember that no *urtext* or other sort of common outline for primitive eucharistic worship is likely ever to have existed. What is sufficient is the available material which evidences the word and table structure as the norm, theologically and practically, for the primitive Church's worship when that worship featured the celebration of the Eucharist. It is this norm that the Catholic Church at the Second Vatican Council reclaimed as the norm for its contemporary eucharistic praxis.

THE STATUS OF THE WORD/SACRAMENT STRUCTURE THROUGH THE REFORMATION

Despite the firm grounding the word and table structure was given in the primitive church extending well into the Patristic period, this structure unfortunately was not to enjoy enduring status through the next millennium. Thus, during the one thousand year period which began late in the Patristic period and lasted until the Reformation, it was to develop that at liturgy Christians were not always nourished on the word (nor sometimes on the Eucharist, nor perhaps on either, depending upon circumstances) when they convened themselves for the eucharistic liturgy.

In justice, it must be acknowledged that when the serious decline of liturgical preaching is noted for this period of history, it is incorrect to conclude that no good preaching was being provided. In addition, it is erroneous simply to imagine that whatever preaching did occur was no longer featured within the Mass. Paradoxically, this period of the decline of liturgical preaching as it is presented here began to evolve precisely during that unique era known as the "Golden Age of Preaching," when such celebrated preachers as John Chrysostom, Ambrose, Augustine, and the Cappadocian Fathers (Basil the Great, Gregory of Nyssa, and Gregory Nazianzen) dotted the landscape. Furthermore, in the third and fourth centuries, the proper concern for effective preaching led to the application of the principles of classical rhetoric to Christian preaching. This was a period during which much discussion about preaching and its proper execution was entertained, with Augustine's *De Doctrina Christiana* featuring notably as this phenomenon began and extending to the eve of the Reformation, including a lengthy list of homiletic theoreticians featuring such random names as Theodulf of Orleans (eighth century); Paul the Deacon, Rabanus Maurus, and Alcuin (the time of Charlemagne); Guibert of Nogent (eleventh century); Allan of Lille (twelfth century); and Humbert of Romans, fifth master general of the Dominican Order, whose writing included *The Grace of Preaching*, which occasioned important discussions relative to the spirituality of the preacher.

Nonetheless, few scholars would entertain the inclination to identify this millennium as an ideal time for preaching, and yet the depth of the criticism of the preaching in this period has perhaps been excessive. Gregory Dix issues an important corrective that is helpful to consider before proceeding. In remarking upon the lack of authentic conversion among many of the mass converts in medievalism, Dix writes, "Perhaps when it got to church there was not enough preaching. The Reformers thought not, though there was certainly more than the Reformers said there had been, particularly after the Thirteenth Century."[19] Not only was there more preaching going on than the Reformers were willing to admit, but along with the legion of incompetent preachers of this period, some outstanding preachers featured into this lengthy period, including the mellifluous doctor, the great Bernard of Clairvaux (1090–1153); the founder of the Friars Preachers, Dominic Guzmán (1170–1221); the humble standard bearer of exhortative preaching, Francis of Assisi (1181?–1227); Peter Martyr of Verona (1206–1252); Humbert of Romans (1193–1277); John Wycliffe (ca. 1329–1384); and Vincent Ferrer (1350–1419), to name only several of those who merit inclusion in this distinguished list of preachers.

No, the crisis in preaching during this millennium was not substantially the result of the absence of sound preaching. Preaching was often neglected, but just as often, it seems to have been done remarkably well. The crisis in preaching for which this period is noted is rather the result of a curious combination of phenomena which all contributed to the overall decline in liturgical preaching at this point in history.

It is true, of course, that a monumental ingredient of the breakdown in liturgical preaching is that preaching was, indeed, *all too often* omitted. By the end of the sixth century, successive popes and other church leaders began to express interest, at least sporadically, in a systemic approach to the regularization of the church's liturgy. The motivation for such development was just as often due to political goals as it was to spiritual goals, but regardless of the motivation, movement along

---

[19] Gregory Dix, *The Shape of the Liturgy* (New York: Seabury Press Edition, 1982) 596.

lines of standardization was observable in many locations. Much of the formalization and symbolic dignity which became associated with the church and its liturgy following Constantine's Peace of the Church in 313 continued to develop; a good many critics of this period would say that this liturgical development grew to obnoxious proportions. Regardless of one's adjudication of the liturgical product of this situation, one is faced with the evidence that by the beginning of the eighth century (and in many cases much earlier), because of the degree to which liturgical structure had become elaborate, it was not uncommon for the presider to delete preaching from the eucharistic liturgy altogether as a time-economy measure. In his description of the elements of the liturgy in this period, Theodor Klauser notes the peculiar way in which the Liturgy of the Word concluded:

> But what, we may ask, has happened to that other basic element which together with the lections used to form a part of the original service of the Word, i.e. the sermon? In the [Gregorian] Ordo, this has been omitted altogether. It looks as if on account of the dimensions of the stational services, and equally by reason of the length of the service, which was already excessive without a sermon, the Pope had given up the practice of having a liturgical address at every Eucharist.[20]

Of course, this was long before the order of the liturgy was regulated for all places by central authority, and so it cannot be said that preaching was generally eradicated from the liturgy everywhere, and, as it has already been stated, good preaching did continue in many places. Nonetheless, the evidence provided above (which actually describes the papal liturgy, regarded by many as a standard by which local liturgies could be formed), which does not stand out as unique among other samples from this same era, reveals that liturgical preaching was frequently omitted.

Preaching suffered on other accounts as well. Most likely, the one factor that emerged during this thousand-year period, which most negatively influenced the role of preaching at the liturgy, was the medieval attentiveness to making the sacraments "real." In their day, the Scholastics led the discussions, which focused upon the cause and effect principle of the sacraments rather than today's emphasis upon pastoral effectiveness. John Schanz reflects upon this period by noting:

---

[20] Theodor Klauser, *A Short History of the Western Liturgy* (Oxford: Oxford University Press, 1969) 64.

Gradually, more emphasis came to be placed on the causal power of the sacraments and less on the word-power to evoke sacramental meaning and faith. Abuses crept in that led to an almost magical or mechanical use of sacraments as rituals that took effect *ex opere operato* (from the action itself that was performed), independently of the response of the participant.[21]

Inasmuch as preaching did not comprise part of the necessary formula for effecting the sacraments, the spiritual value of the preached word lost significance in the minds of many people. This eventuated a curious hybrid in church life. Priests were so preoccupied with the correct administration of the sacraments for validity, which was believed to result from the correct intention in harmony with the mere pronunciation of the required words and the performance of the designated acts (that is to say, the correct use of the appropriate matter and form), they no longer felt the words themselves had any communicative value for the assembly. Accordingly, the necessary formulaic words were almost always pronounced inaudibly or at least out of the hearing range of the assembled laity and in the Latin language with which people became increasingly unfamiliar as time passed. This breakdown in the liturgical recognition of the value of the communicative integrity of words negatively influenced the value given to the communicative integrity of the scriptural word, proclaimed and preached. The result was that quite typically, when preaching did occur, it might well be in the Latin tongue (although not always), just as the rituals of the liturgies and the scriptural readings were, therefore, becoming incomprehensible to most people, particularly the less affluent.

Unfortunately, even occasional attempts to improve the effectiveness of the preaching event sometimes had harmful effects upon the proclamation of the word. For example, to the degree that effective preaching did occur during this period, rather than being a scripturally based homily, it was all too often deformed into a thematic sermon covering assigned theological, catechetical, or even political topics. Preaching in many instances became preoccupied with commentaries on miracles, the attributes of the saints, devotion to the Virgin Mary, and the like. Such discourses rarely had any relationship to the scriptural readings of that day's liturgy. Far too often, when liturgical preaching did attempt to treat the Scriptures, the Scriptures were explained by the use of over emphasized allegorization or other woefully inadequate hermeneutical methods instead of by means of solid exegesis.

---

[21] John P. Schanz, *Introduction to the Sacraments* (New York: Pueblo Publishing Co., 1983) 70.

Another example of good intention actually resulting in further damage to liturgical preaching occurred in the thirteenth century when the mendicant friars began to provide better and more frequent preaching. Not all of the friars' preaching was liturgical, of course, but much of it was. Often, it was necessary to construct pulpits in the midst of the assembled congregants so that the preaching could be heard. This simple movement resulted in locating the pulpit outside of the physical space from which the rest of the liturgy was "conducted" (known as the "sanctuary" in Catholic parlance and as the "chancel" by most Protestants). Klauser assesses that "[t]his separation of the altar and the sermon both furthered and reflected the fact that the sermon was becoming thematically divorced from the liturgy."[22] Hence, it seems that even positive efforts at enhancing preaching ultimately played some part in negatively influencing the integrity of liturgical preaching. Accordingly, the pre-Reformation crisis in preaching was somewhat complex. However, it is unlikely that various combinations of these problems bear the entire responsibility for the problem. These breakdowns appeared without uniformity and delightful exceptions existed.

Edwin Dargan attributes certain other liturgical developments to the decline of effective preaching in this period. He writes:

> We should not fail also to take account of the growth of liturgy and forms of worship. While these preserved a prominent place for preaching in the services of the church their effect then, as too often since, was to make the spoken word of far less relative value than forms of worship. This tendency, while stronger in later times, was already powerful, and preaching was not vigorous and able enough to overcome the trammels of liturgy.[23]

There is a very significant point somewhat hidden in Dargan's comments. He notes precisely what we have been attempting to establish, namely, that while the liturgy always reserved a prominent place for preaching, preaching nonetheless diminished. This may seem self-contradictory, but it is true. Church regulations, to the degree that they did exist (and they were inconsistently applied and never uniform before the Council of Trent), typically did not fail to legislate for the proper place of preaching within worship events. It would be a very facile task, indeed, if one could simply assert that before the Reformation preaching had been virtually discarded by the church, but such was not the case.

---

[22] Klauser, *A Short History,* 149.

[23] Edwin Charles Dargan, *A History of Preaching,* vol. 1 (Grand Rapids: Baker Book House, 1954) 109–10.

What, then, did this ignominious breakdown in preaching look like that originally drew such condemnation from the Reformers and continues to do so from most contemporary liturgists, Catholic and Protestant alike? The problem was not poor nor even irregular preaching; it was the disintegration of the constitutive role of the preaching event within the liturgical structure itself.

This is the heart of the crisis in preaching in the midst of a milieu which sometimes featured extraordinary preaching events. Much of the good preaching that the people loved simply was not delivered as a liturgical act. A traditional Catholic way of categorizing preaching places preaching events into four categories: liturgical (preaching at formal liturgical events); occasional (preaching and exhortation at non-liturgical prayer gatherings, retreats, revivals, etc.); catechetical (occasions for teaching the riches of the faith tradition); and missionary (evangelical preaching to attract converts). Much of the successful preaching which can be identified during these years qualifies for identification under the latter three categories more than with the first category of liturgical preaching. A good case in point is the medieval preaching service known as Prone that was much cherished by the people. True, it was delivered in the middle of the Mass, but it was technically and officially extraneous to the Mass and was therefore aliturgical. Typically this service was delivered from a pulpit located outside of the chancel, thus creating a physical statement which paralleled liturgical (if unarticulated) theory, calling for a clear distinction between the action of the Mass itself and this pastorally sensible, but extraneous event. According to Herman Wegman, this unofficial preaching service within the Mass developed and grew to include a vernacular reading of the scriptural texts, a sermon, announcements, the recitation of prayers including the Creed, the Lord's Prayer, the Ave Maria, the decalogue, a blessing, confession of sins, and intercessions for the living and dead; hymns were sometimes included.[24] Wegman concluded:

> Adding all these elements together one discovers a complete service at the pulpit that had fully developed by the end of the Middle Ages, especially in Germany and Switzerland. This pulpit liturgy was known to the reformers and adopted by them.[25]

This, then, was the crux of the problem: the word and table structure had itself been dramatically compromised, if not obliterated. The

---

[24] Herman Wegman, *Christian Worship in East and West: A Study Guide to Liturgical History* (Collegeville, MN: Liturgical Press, 1990) 313.
[25] Ibid.

preaching event at liturgy in the Christian tradition is not merely a pastorally sensible technique. From biblical, theological, and historical perspectives, as has been evidenced already in this chapter, the word-event is a constitutive half of a two-part structure. The crisis which the Reformation addressed was not that liturgical preaching was poorly done, if it was done at all; the crisis was that liturgical preaching no longer enjoyed its proper essential role at liturgy. A preoccupation with the mysterious dynamics of God in a sacramental system which operated *ex opere operato* had developed in place at the expense of the presence of God in the power of the Word. This is what commanded the attention of the Reformers.

Thereafter, Rome was inclined to judge all tendencies which seemed to represent the mentality of the reformers with suspicion. Despite the fact that many Reformers (e.g., Luther, Calvin) pursued a balance between word and table, the Protestant movement was to become largely identified with the primacy of the word at worship at the expense of the eucharistic celebration (to the extent that a norm emerged among many dictating that if none of the congregants intended to receive the Eucharist at liturgy, there would be no service of the Eucharist performed at that particular liturgy). Conversely, Rome focused primarily on the Eucharist at liturgy and regarded the preaching event (as well as the developing Protestant custom of lay Scripture study) with suspicion. Both sides sustained profound losses regarding the word and sacrament structure for their liturgical worship. Contemporary liturgical work bears this premise out. Many mainline Protestant liturgists today are quite committed to the current emphasis placed upon eucharistic celebration (many mainline "prayer book" committees tend to regard the word/table structure as normative, even though current practice at most local churches seems not to feature weekly Eucharist), whereas the Catholic community is quite aware of the pressing need for continued growth in its appreciation of liturgical preaching. Both groups today typically understand there to have been something of a liturgical impoverishment in the past resulting from a lack of balance between the two parts of the structure.

Thus, by the sixteenth century the normative word and table structure of the liturgy had broken down in Catholicism, with a disproportionate (although not a total) emphasis placed upon the sacramental dimension.

THE ROLE OF THE WORD IN
THE TRIDENTINE EUCHARISTIC LITURGY

The Council of Trent (1545–1563), the official Catholic response to the Protestant Reformation, included in its goals the establishment of liturgical uniformity which would be all but universal. Because Trent nearly succeeded in its attempt to legislate uniformly for what can be identified as the entire Catholic Latin rite world, its liturgical, and more importantly, its homiletic reforms take precedence over all previous such attempts. In actuality, the Tridentine decrees on preaching are not that much at variance with the ideas of the Reformers nor of contemporary Christians: preaching was important; it was to be frequent (it was to be regular on Sundays and holy days); it was to occur within the context of the Mass (although not necessarily part of the liturgical structure itself).

The Council of Trent treated the subject of preaching twice in its deliberations, making clear that preaching was the prerogative and responsibility of the bishops as well as of all the ordained who held responsibility for the care of souls. The Council also stressed the importance of weekly preaching and it addressed preaching needs. Those needs betray the breakdown of the word and sacrament structure, for they explain that the virtues, articles of the faith, and other catechetical concerns are to be the object of the preacher's attentions.[26] Although their attitude toward scriptural integrity is not cavalier, it is not obvious that the Council capitulars were even aware of a difference between a sermon and a homily. The place of preaching, the person of the preacher (i.e. the office of preaching), and preaching's attendant regulations were elaborated upon at Trent, showing a great concern for authority and legislation. Lay preaching in church was adamantly forbidden, probably because the leaders of the Church believed that previous lay preaching had led to the disintegration of obedience that provided one of the ingredients for the "Protestant Revolt," as they would have termed it. More important distinctions were missed at Trent. As this quotation from Tridentine legislation at its Twenty-Fourth session reveals, the Council was unable to identify the integral liturgical structure which called for a proclamation of God's word in tandem with Eucharist. The sample reads:

---

[26] Trent, *Conc. Oec. Dec.*, Session Five, *"Decretum Secundum: super lectione et praedicatione"* (p. 643ff.); and Session Twenty-Four, Canon 4 (p. 739), Canon 7 (p. 740). Translation used: *Canons and Decrees of the Council of Trent*, ed. H. J. Schroeder (New York: Herder and Herder, 1941).

> In like manner shall they explain on all festivals or solemnities during the solemnization of the mass or the celebration of the divine offices, in the vernacular tongue, the divine commandments and the maxims of salvation, and leaving aside useless questions let them strive to engraft these things on the hearts of all and instruct them in the law of the Lord.[27]

Trent failed to call explicitly for the reform of preaching. The Council's method for implementing its directives relative to preaching was basically publishing the *Catechism of the Council of Trent* as well as its directives for the formation of priesthood candidates, including their needs for training in preaching. It is surprising, given the positive rhetoric that Trent used for preaching, that preaching did not take a definite turn at this point toward scripturally rooted homilies as integral to the structure of the eucharistic liturgy, but it did not. Certainly prominent preaching and strong preaching movements followed; Charles Borromeo and the Milanese preaching synods, and Ignatius Loyola and the Jesuits come immediately to mind. But a solid definition of homiletic preaching was wanting; the word and sacrament structure was no longer recognized as normative; and there was a preoccupation with canonical minimalism (that which was minimally required for validity in the execution of the sacraments). All of these factors eclipsed the church's need for a genuine renewal of homiletic preaching as a constitutive element of liturgy. Resultantly, the Church missed an opportunity pregnant with possibilities for genuine homiletic renewal.

During the four succeeding centuries, preaching's structural role at liturgy experienced a continuation of breakdown rather than a notable renewal. This is not to say that extraordinary and significant preaching movements did not emerge in various places and times, just as they had in the past; they did. The liturgical integrity of such preaching, however, was often severely deficient. James F. White comments on the status of the liturgical context of Catholic preaching during these centuries. Relative to the seventeenth century, he wrote: "Like music, much of the preaching in the baroque era was also aliturgical in having little or no connection with the mass of the day. . . . Preaching, when it occurred, often happened outside the mass altogether. . . ."[28] Noting eighteenth-century trends, he observed: ". . . preaching was by no means frequent in many parish churches, many having a sermon no more than once

---

[27] Schroeder, *Trent,* 197–98.
[28] James F. White, *Roman Catholic Worship: Trent to Today* (New York: Paulist Press, 1995) 43.

a month. . . . Part of the problem was the notion that preaching was basically a Protestant thing. . . ."[29] In the nineteenth century, White notes that the best in Catholic preaching occurred at parish missions and revivals and not at liturgy.[30]

Similarly, some remarkable preaching movements emerged during these centuries, but they, too, proved resistant to the notion of liturgical preaching and were quite typically movements of missionary, occasional, or catechetical preaching instead. The resultant pattern was that emphasis was given to the sacramental life of the church at the expense of liturgical preaching. This unbalanced status endured until the eve of the great Vatican Council II which reclaimed the primitive Double Feast structure of word and table for worship. Any attempt at constructing a contemporary Catholic liturgical homiletic must build upon this structure as normative, while also allowing for the consequences of the dramatic liturgical shift of the previous century.

This does not necessarily mean, as some liturgists conclude, that all preaching at the Eucharist must conclude in such a way as to provide segue from the ambo to the altar, but it does mean that the preaching event is only one part of a liturgical unity comprised of two parts. The ritual at the table is, without exception, the partner of the event at the ambo. Accordingly, Eucharistic preaching fits into a stricter time constraint (typically eight to twelve minutes) than does the non-eucharistic homily. We now turn our attention to the construction of a homiletic for this type of preaching event.

A CATHOLIC HOMILETIC

With the 1971 publication of his ground-breaking work, *As One without Authority,* homiletician Fred B. Craddock ushered homiletics into a new era of theorizing that has come to be known as the New Homiletic. Unique to the New Homiletic is its fundamental turn toward the hearer in the congregation (as compared, for example, to a fundamental orientation toward the material or doctrine to be communicated which might be a preoccupation of a preacher subscribing to Dulles' ecclesial model of the institution). With the New Homiletic, the preacher, in creating a homily, begins by assessing the context or current needs of the congregants and devising a vehicle for communicating those needs as

[29] Ibid., 66.
[30] Ibid., 89–90.

effectively as possible. Gradually, other conversation partners are drawn into the pre-writing phase of homily construction. It is in harmony with this pattern that the following first step or "prequel" to homily construction is crucial. Obviously, few preachers have the time or inclination to engage every single step of the following outline. The preacher would select those dynamics which seem helpful. From time to time, one might wish to try an individual suggestion which wouldn't normally appeal to the preacher; above all, the preacher ought to try to retain the order in which these suggestions are presented.

A. Approaching the Preaching Task: The "Prequel" of the Homily

Obviously, in preparing a homily, a number of significant ingredients precede the actual writing of the text. Were we merely discussing the construction of an individual homily, a simple list of these ingredients would suffice. However, here we are discussing a methodology of homiletics, that is to say, we are identifying how one addresses the task of preaching in general, and so greater care is required in explaining these steps.

1. Pray. The preaching task is a shared effort beyond God and the preacher.

2. Do congregational analysis. The first step in preaching is assessing the context of the congregation to whom the preaching will be delivered. This occurs on two levels. On one level, the preacher wants to understand the standing context of this congregation. To the degree that it is possible to do so, this means acknowledging neighborhood realities, socio-economic status, placement on various ideological and political indices, on-going projects, campaigns, struggles, or other phenomena in which this parish is involved and the like. It's understandable that here one is dealing with certain generalizations and certain red warning flags should pop up with any pastoral minister in the presence of generalization, but with certain appropriate cautions, such generalization can be helpful. The resident pastor would want to lend a listening ear to others who know the parishioners, since one's own perceptions are often nuanced.

On another level, the preacher turns to the immediate circumstances in the life of the congregation. What is happening this week in the world, the country, the city, the parish, an so on? Are any events this particular week impacting the hunger in the human hearts of this congregation for God's Word? Pastorally responsible preaching is constructed in response to the lives of the hearers.

3. Pray. What does God have to say about all of this?

4. Choose Scripture texts. In the Free Church tradition, this means literally what it says: the preacher must choose the Scripture text on which to preach. For the Catholic preacher, the task is somewhat nuanced. If the homily is to be delivered at a non-eucharistic worship, then one often does have to choose the Scripture text from which to preach, even if the choice to be made is for one text from a prescribed set of options. For preaching at Mass, however, and at various other rites for which the readings may be pre-determined, the preacher needs to choose which reading or readings to preach. At a Sunday Eucharist, for example, the readings assigned for the day have not all been chosen because of any natural harmony between them. The first reading and the Gospel generally have been matched to each other, while the second reading has been chosen in an entirely independent manner. Eventually, the psalm response and the alleluia verse may or may not complement the direction in which the preacher develops the texts. The preacher must choose the text to preach, and proceed with that choice.

5. Pray.

6. Read the biblical texts. The reading of the biblical texts constitutes an important step in the development of the preacher's internal relationship to them. There are times when a specific word, concept, or turn of phrase creates the nucleus of a strategy in the human imagination for preaching, and so the preacher might first want to engage the text as it will be proclaimed to the congregation at worship. This means that the first time the preacher reads the text to be preached, this initial encounter with that text should occur with the biblical translation which will be used at the liturgy. Concepts form and take on a life of their own, and so this is important. Following that, if the preacher is ministering in an acquired language, the text should be read in the preacher's own native tongue; there is no substitution for conceptualizing in one's first language. Finally, other scholarly translations, including the ancient biblical language, if one has the skills to do so, can be considered; this is a reliable technique for increasing one's understanding of a text.

7. Do personal exegetical work. After the texts have been studied, one's own exegetical work of the scriptural text(s) can begin. This is not yet the time to consult the exegetes and their commentaries.

8. Integrate the exegetical work. This is the moment to search for a match between the lessons inherent in the text(s) and the pastoral, catechetical, or doctrinal needs of the preacher's local congregation. Does an obvious marriage emerge?

9. Consult authoritative voices. More diverse meanings emerge for the text(s) when one becomes acquainted with what other authoritative voices have added. This includes the sermons from the Fathers of the Church, magisterial teachings, spokespersons for various theological and social critiques—especially those which fall outside one's own particular areas of interest—and other sermon collections. Members of religious institutes may often be guided by pronouncements their religious institute may have articulated on various significant issues; this is the correct place to consult those wisdom sources.

10. Consult Scripture commentaries. Note that this step does not occur earlier. Through the church's commissioning of one to preach at this particular worship event, the Holy Spirit has chosen this preacher—not a published Scripture scholar—to preach this particular homily. That means that the spirit and direction of the homily are to *come from the individual preacher.* Consultation of commentaries at this point is not for the purpose of doing the job of finding a direction or inspiring an idea for the homily. Rather, consulting a biblical commentary provides the preacher with a discussion partner for checking the scriptural integrity of one's exegesis and for supplementing one's understanding of the world of the text.

11. Begin constructing the preaching event.

B. The Construction Phase: Tools for Building the Homily

When people are asked to critique preaching they have heard, reliably they usually report quite similar things. For instance, to the question "What has caused bad preaching you have heard to be bad?" people will typically respond that bad homilies are bad because they don't deliver one simple message; ramble on and on; are either too abstract or too simple; are non-scriptural; don't relate to real life issues; emerge only out of the preacher's interests, ideologies, or life issues; have too many unrelated points; don't suggest a plan of action. Conversely, when pressed to identify those features which have made good preaching effective, people often reply that good homilies are good because they are to the point; address issues of critical importance to the lives of the hearers; are scriptural; suggest a mission or a plan of action as a result of the homily; feature a disciplined and reasonable use of time and end when they are finished. The successful preacher will want to lend a careful listening to these observations.

Three homiletic tools in particular, the Focus Statement, the Function Statement, and the Move "equip any preacher to negotiate these concerns successfully."

> **1. The Focus Statement.** It stands to reason that if a homily is going to be of value, its hearers must know what was said to them during the preaching. Further, it is ludicrous to imagine that a member of the congregation would be able to report the message of a homily if the preacher who delivered that homily cannot state its message succinctly. The truth is, however, that many homilies are poor precisely because the preacher cannot say, in one complete sentence, what his or her homily says. Therefore, it is important that the preacher's first step in beginning the construction of the homily is to write, in one clear and grammatically sound sentence, what the homily is to say. This statement is called the "focus statement." In his homiletic grammar, *The Witness of Preaching*, Thomas G. Long writes, "A focus statement is a concise description of the central, controlling, and unifying theme of the sermon. In short, this is what the whole sermon will be 'about.'"[31]
>
> To understand the focus statement better, imagine that after one has preached, each member of the congregation is asked to write, in one sentence, what the homily was about. If most of those statements sound alike, and if those parallel the preacher's own focus statement, one has succeeded. If they do not sound alike, why not?
>
> Recall the complaints of many congregants. ". . . [B]ad homilies are bad because they: don't deliver one simple message; ramble on and on; are either too abstract or too simple; . . . have too many unrelated points. . . ." The focus statement guarantees

---

[31] Thomas G. Long, *The Witness of Preaching* (Louisville: Westminster John Knox Press, 1989) 86.

that the homilist delivers one, cohesive homily. The technique I recommend is literally to write the focus statement down and place it in front of one—on the desk or wherever one works as one writes the homily. If segments of the homily construction occur to the homilist in bits and pieces as one is in motion throughout the day, keep the focus statement in one's pocket. Refer to it frequently, like a litmus test. As the homily builds, consult the focus statement repeatedly. If the homilist discovers that he or she is inserting ideas in the script that do not contribute to the elucidation of the focus statement, delete those ideas! If retained, those are the very ideas which people will later lament as "the second or third sermon that was delivered in this morning's never-ending homily." Any ideas which do not contribute to delivering the focus statement are to be eliminated.

It does sometimes happen that one realizes that one has constructed significant pieces of the homily that do not contribute to the focus statement, but that seem superior to the original intent of the focus statement. Then it is acceptable to replace the focus statement with a better one, but caution is necessary so that one's homily preparation does not become an endless procession of dismissing focus statements and replacing them with yet new and better ones. Generally, it is acceptable to replace the focus statement once or at the most twice; beyond that, it's better not to regard that technique as an option. Before experimenting with one's ability to create a focus statement, we will proceed to the next significant tool for preaching—a companion tool—and then we will experiment with both of them simultaneously.

2. The Function Statement. Thomas Long has also developed the "function statement," which he describes as "a description of what the preacher hopes the sermon will create or cause to happen for the hearers. Sermons make demands upon the hearers, which is another way of saying they provoke change in the hearers (even if the change is a deepening of something already present). The function statement names the hoped-for change."[32] The function statement is a statement of intent; it is an infinitive clause with the broader sentence which begins with these unchanging words "I am preaching this sermon to . . . ."

---

[32] Long, *The Witness of Preaching*, 86.

To conceptualize the function statement more clearly, perhaps it is helpful to imagine that after one has preached, each person in the church is asked to describe their "mission," or what it is that they are supposed "to do" as a result of having heard the sermon. That task is the function statement, and if most people could say the same thing and if what they say parallels the homilist's own intended function statement, the homilist has succeeded. Furthermore, the focus statement and the function statement must be in partnership with one another.

It will be useful to experiment with the construction of several focus and function statements as companion sets. Four texts have been selected below. Obviously, each preacher would arrive at a unique message each time he or she approaches a biblical text for preaching, but the preacher must try to enter into the thought behind these constructions.

EXAMPLE 1: ACTS 2:42-47 (a description of the evangelical power present in the community life of the primitive church). For this simulated preaching, imagine a particular congregation that is hoping to attract new members to the faith but that is somewhat weak in Christian service and attentiveness to the poor. Perhaps in their case, preaching on the second chapter of Acts could be valuable if it developed according to the following plan.

Focus Statement: When Christians tend to the needs of others, they are proclaiming the Gospel.

Function Statement: To incite hearers to witness to the Gospel by making a commitment to praxis.

In this case, the focus and function statements are in harmony with each other, they both suggest clear and concrete concepts, and they provide direction for the preacher to construct the homily.

EXAMPLE 2: LUKE 20:27-38 (the Lord's response to the question of the marital status in heaven of the widow of the seven brothers). In this pericope, the Lord's answer can be heard to promise believers that the values and wonders of the eternal realm are so far beyond present reality, that one will no longer care about present concerns and that the wise person would begin immediately to be attentive to the eternal verities. Perhaps a preacher has been trying to entice very pragmatic congregants to develop a greater appreciation for transcendent treasures of virtue. In that case, the following construction could be of value.

Focus Statement: The concerns of the eternal realm are so beyond present concerns, one can't even imagine correctly about such things.

Function Statement: To entice the congregants into re-examining how closely their own values parallel the values of the Gospel.

EXAMPLE 3: LUKE 9:10-17 (the miraculous feeding of the five thousand). A preacher whose congregation is weak in terms of service to the poor might appeal to the fact that Jesus certainly could have performed this miracle singly by causing a plate of food to appear in the lap of each member of the crowd, in fact he fed the crowd by using the contributions of others: the small boy's food items as well as the efforts of the apostles in distributing the meal.

Focus Statement: Jesus showed his care for the hungry by utilizing the loaves, fish, work, and organization of others.

Function Statement: To convince hearers that they are the distributors of Christ's active care for the hungry.

EXAMPLE 4: MATTHEW 22:34-40 (the greatest commandment). The same hypothetical parish we have had in mind could be very enthusiastic about liturgy and devotion, but less attentive to social outreach. In such a context, the preacher may wish to provide a prophetic voice calling for greater attention to love of neighbor as an obedient response to God. In that case, the following statements could represent valid preaching strategies for that text.

Focus Statement: One fulfills one's mandate to love God by loving one's neighbor.

Function Statement: To clarify for the congregation that the greatest commandment, to love God, is fulfilled by showing caring concern for other people.

3. The Move. The third essential tool in the preacher's toolbox is the "move." A move is the basic unit of measure in a homily. Developed by Professor David Buttrick and developed in his encyclopedia homiletic grammar, *Homiletic: Moves and Structures,* Buttrick offers this description: ". . . when we preach, we speak in formed modules of language arranged in some patterned sequence. These modules of language we will call 'moves.'"[33]

---

[33] David Buttrick, *Homiletic: Moves and Structures* (Philadelphia: Fortress Press, 1987) 23.

Buttrick demonstrated that the Western mind can only listen attentively for a specified amount of time. In 1987 Buttrick noted that it took about four minutes for a concept (a move) to become sufficiently established in the hearers' minds and that four minutes was about the maximum length of time a speaker would be able to maintain the listeners' attention for a single concept.[34] Hence, Buttrick proposed that a homily is comprised of a series of moves, with each move requiring about four minutes. Buttrick would be the first to note that the Western attention span is constantly becoming reduced in length so that nearly twenty years after his work has been published, he would probably admit that a move today could be even shorter. I propose that two and a half minutes is ideal for the Catholic congregation, which also awaits the eucharistic feast after the preaching.

What does a move do? What does it look like? The string of moves in a homily represents the sequence of ideas which comprise the homily. Each must connect logically to its neighbors, yet each must stand distinctly separate from its neighbors so that the limitations of the attention span of the listeners are respected. A well-formed and distinct move enables the hearers to recognize that they have grasped the idea the preacher is trying to establish at this particular point in the homily, an idea upon which subsequent ideas are built. Similarly, the well-formed move allows for the psychological pause a hearer needs to experience before commencing on the next leg of the journey. If a speaker talks on and on and no natural break is provided for a psychological pause, hearers will be overwhelmed by the content being presented and will be unable to grasp it.

By way of demonstration, read the following nonsense paragraph. I call it a "nonsense" paragraph because there is nothing cohesive or logical about the various ideas strung together. As one reads this paragraph, note how many different ideas are heard.

All of our faculty members received new computers this year. Every faculty office was recently equipped with a new laptop. All of us professors have new ones this year. Computers had been getting old and, of course, it's desirable for all of us to use complementary systems, so the school splurged on a new set of computers. We all have them now. Every

---

[34] Cf. Ibid., 26.

faculty member in our school has a new computer this year. Nowhere is the climate more beautiful than in the Midwest. The midwestern weather is ideal. If you want to enjoy a beautiful climate, go to the Midwest. The Midwest's four seasons are all distinct; each with its strong variation in temperature with its attendant sensations. The changeable scenery, of course, is magnificent, from the delicate pastels of spring, to the rich verdant fields of summer, through the rainbow explosion of colors in the fall, to the purifying white of winter. The Midwest has the ideal climate. Recently I found a new dentist. I have a new dentist to care for my teeth. I just recently became a patient of Dr. Devine, an excellent dentist. I needed a new dentist because I had moved to another state. I know it's always important to have a dentist nearby, and so I began a careful search for dentists in my area. It took a long time but I finally found one I like. I finally have a new dentist in my area. My grandparents taught me lifelong lessons about the value of hospitality. They were the most hospitable people I've ever known and they passed that value on to me. I enjoy extending hospitality and when I do, I feel connected to my grandparents. I recall that at my grandparents' home, if Grandma was opening the front door to admit company, Grandpa was in the kitchen simultaneously opening another door: the refrigerator, from which he was taking refreshments to serve the arriving guests. Company was always cherished and well received under my grandparents' roof and they passed their spirit of hospitality on to me.

Hopefully the reader identified four ideas: (1) our faculty members have new computers this year; (2) the midwestern weather is the best; (3) I have a new dentist; (4) I learned to be hospitable from my grandparents. Each idea constitutes a move. Each idea stands separately from the others; there is no overlapping. Had we been listening to an oral presentation of this paragraph, we could have taken a psychological pause once we grasped my intent and we would have done that before the speaker would have delivered every sentence in the script. Once I began a new idea, we would have had a subconscious signal to return to a more careful listening attitude as I commenced with a new idea.

Of course, it is easy to see the divisions of subject in a nonsensical paragraph containing completely unrelated ideas. Obviously greater care is required for the necessary but subtle signal of a division when the material consists of the various components of one unified message. Nonetheless, it can be done easily. The following paragraph treats one unified subject consisting of several "moves." Once again, try to count how many separate ideas are present in this paragraph and also try to locate the points at which new ideas begin.

Recently I received an annual appeal letter for money from the congregation of Sisters who taught me in school. Like many congregations, their funds are low today and so they send an annual appeal to their former students for financial assistance. Just lately in my mail I found that annual appeal from my former teaching Sisters for financial help. The Sisters ask for these donations to help maintain the convent and its ministries and perhaps most especially to care for their elderly and infirm Sisters. Understandably, their expenses must be quite steep. Collections like this help to ease the financial burdens of these graying and diminishing communities of Sisters. And so the other day I received the annual appeal for financial help from the congregation that provided my early education. We Catholic school kids of past generations loved our teaching nuns. Our school nuns held our total affection. We Catholic school kids loved our teachers! For us, we ranked our nuns among the many other women who cared for us lovingly and whom we loved in return: our mothers, grandmothers, aunts, friends' moms, godmothers, and the like. We knew we were in good hands with the Sisters and we liked being with them. Yes, we Catholic school kids of the past loved our nuns! In particular, my first grade teacher, Sister Mary Immaculate, won my heart. I loved Sister Mary Immaculate most of all. My first grade nun was my favorite. She had an enormously large class of seventy-two children and yet influenced me individually in such a way that earned her my particular affection, an affection which has endured for a lifetime. I loved them all, but Sister Mary Immaculate from the first grade is the one I loved most of all. For North American Catholics, in a unique way the nuns are the mothers of our faith. Unlike many other lands, we North American Catholics owe much of the establishment of Catholicism in our country to the nuns. Uniquely for Catholics in the U.S. and Canada, the nuns mothered us in our faith. Catholics throughout the world received the faith in various ways: the ancient churches from the apostles themselves; the great Christian nations from various well-known evangelizers like Saint Patrick and the Irish, SS. Cyril and Methodius and the Slavs, Saint Boniface and the Germans, and so forth. When European Catholics first arrived in North America, however, it was quite often the nuns whose pioneer schools, health care centers, orphanages, and catechetical efforts planted the faith or sustained it in the hearts of early North American Catholics. In a way that is unique in the Catholic world; for North American Catholics, the nuns are the mothers of the faith. So the other day I called my sister, Judy, who takes care of things like this in our family, and I said,

"Judy, write that check! Our nuns have asked for our help again and we need to be good to them, so send them a donation. Write that check, Judy, and send it on to the convent."

How many individual ideas are located in this lengthy body of sentences? (One might ask how many paragraphs are really contained in this material; homiletically, we would begin to ask how many "moves" are contained herein.) Although people unfamiliar to this manner of division often suggest some slight variation of the author's intent, hopefully most readers recognize the following ordering in the sample text: (1) Lately I received the annual appeal letter for funds from the Sisters who taught me in school; (2) we old-time Catholic school kids loved our nuns; (3) in particular, I loved my first grade teacher, Sister Mary Immaculate, most of all; (4) uniquely, nuns were the mothers of the faith for North American Catholics; (5) so (big sister) Judy, write that check!

In justice, a quick observation: here we are using some license in employing a variation on Buttrick's method of moves. He would expect a move to be much more fully developed than are any of those in this example, as would we; yet, this brief sample illustrates enough of Professor Buttrick's method for one to gain a sense of it here. Furthermore, we are using here a written text to demonstrate features of oral expression; written and oral communication is so different that one must make allowances for this demonstration. Back to our example.

Each of the five moves stands separate from its neighbors because it addresses a completely different idea; at the same time, each idea holds an important place in the logical movement of the entire document. The breaks between moves occur at the beginning or within lines 12, 19, 25 and 39. What safeguards the subtle division between each move for Buttrick, so that the hearer does not weave two moves together into a longer, unmanageable unit, is that no key word in the last sentence of a move reappears in the first sentence of the following move. Even more importantly, note that the message of each move can be communicated in one simple sentence; let us call that sentence a "focus statement" with a small "f" (as opposed to the Focus Statement with a capital "F" that governs the entire homily). Whereas the "Focus Statement," which guides the development of the entire homily, literally does not appear anywhere in the homily, the "focus statement" of each move does appear within its respective move. Not only does the "focus statement" for each move appear within its respective move, but, in fact, it appears several times. It is the first sentence of the move and then, using slightly altered words, it is repeated two more times; finally, it reappears as the final sentence in the move after the move has been more fully developed. Check it out. The first move is repeated below, with the "focus statement" underlined.

> Recently I received an annual appeal letter for money from the congregation of Sisters who taught me in school. Like many congregations, their funds are low today and so they send an annual appeal to their former students for financial assistance. Just lately in my mail I found that annual appeal from my former teaching Sisters for financial help. The Sisters ask for these donations to help maintain the convent and its ministries and perhaps most especially to care for their elderly and infirm Sisters. Understandably, their expenses must be quite steep. Collections like this help to ease the financial burdens of these graying and diminishing communities of Sisters. And so the other day I received the annual appeal for financial help from the congregation that provided my early education.

If we refer to the rest of the moves above, we will observe the same pattern. This repetition is essential for the move to form in the consciousness of the hearers and to signal the necessary subtle pause.

Furthermore, the use of the "focus statement" for each move provides an excellent memory aide for delivery; notes become unnecessary. Try this out. Without rereading the above sample paragraph (presuming one has read it at least once), it is likely that with a certain accuracy one can deliver that paragraph orally if one were equipped merely with the following notes (which is simply the collection of the "focus statements" for the whole address). Try it out.

1. Lately I received the annual appeal letter for funds from the Sisters who taught me in school;

2. We old-time Catholic school kids loved our nuns;

3. in particular, I loved my first grade teacher, Sister Mary Immaculate, most of all;

4. uniquely, nuns were the mothers of the faith for North American Catholics;

5. so (older sister) Judy, write that check!

It is important to observe the correlation between Long's focus and function statements and Buttrick's moves. Keep in mind that those guiding statements are kept before the preacher who is writing the homily and from time to time those statements will cause the preacher to delete some of the work which has unfolded, to rearrange moves or to rewrite the statements themselves.

If my Focus Statement for the above paragraph was "It is good for everyone to donate money to needy convents today" and the accompanying Function Statement was "To encourage the hearers to donate money to needy communities of Sisters," then the five moves might well remain as they are, except perhaps I would change Move 3 from being about my own favorite teacher to using her simply as an example by reforming the move to draw my listeners personally into the experience by adding "Didn't you have a teacher, a nurse, a catechist or someone who was Sister Mary Immaculate for you?" and Move 4, since it explains how all Americans—even those who are not Catholic school alumni of the convent years—are the beneficiaries of the Sisters and, therefore should feel drawn to donate funds to them.

But if my Focus Statement actually was "I loved my teachers, and in particular, I loved my first grade teacher, Sister Mary Immaculate, and I want everyone to know it" with a corresponding Function Statement of "To alert everyone to how much I loved my teachers, and in particular, my first grade teacher, Sister Mary Immaculate," then I would not need the last two moves, because they do nothing to help communicate my love for my childhood teachers.

Alternately, if my Focus Statement were simply "I loved my teachers and I want everyone to know it" with its corresponding Function Statement, similarly omitting Sister Mary Immaculate in particular, then Move 3 could either suffice as an example attached to Move 2 or it could be omitted altogether. The key concept here is that the moves correspond to the Focus and Function Statements.

One final feature which helps each move to invite fresh attentiveness and maintain it is the presence of variety in the structure or genre of each move. Each move must be built differently. If one move contains a narrative story, then another narrative story move should not appear in the same homily. A move can take many different shapes. It can feature a narrative, a series of examples, an illustration, a contrapuntal, a dramatic characterization, an explanation, exegesis, provision for hermeneutic or historical information from the world of the text, a series of questions and answers for the congregation to consider, a guided reflection, a sampling from literature, a bit of dialogue, the assignment of a task, and anything else that works. The key concept is that in an average Sunday homily, each move must be created by a different genre to avoid monotony. If, in some circumstances (especially if the homily is not too short), it is possible to repeat a move genre in the same homily, the two moves built the same way should never appear consecutively.

The combined use of these tools (Long's Focus and Function Statements and Buttrick's Move structure) comprise an excellent structure to ensure that a clear and succinct preaching event forms in the minds of the members of the congregation.

C. The Delivery of the Homily:
The Communicative Quality of the Preaching Event

1. Relationality: preaching as a two-way conversation. No two homilies can be identical in their delivery. Even if the preacher is preaching at two consecutive liturgies and plans no variation between the two preaching events, they will differ in subtle ways because the receiving congregation consists of different individuals. Preaching is a conversation between human persons and no two conversations are precisely the same. Note the word used intentionally in the previous sentence: preaching is not described merely as communication, but as that particular type of communication called "conversation." A conversation is not a monologue, which is probably the most typical way people view a homily; a conversation is mutual expression between two or more people. In the African-American call and response preaching style, it is easy to see the conversationality of the preaching event; pastor and congregants call back and forth with one another. Here I am not advocating that churches outside of that tradition assume the call and response method for their preaching. What I am advocating is that preachers understand that when they are preaching, they are engaged in a two way conversation between themselves and their hearers; the only distinction is that the communication of the hearers is made wordlessly. But it is made throughout the preaching event.

The preacher wants to stand in constant attentiveness to the congregants' input into the conversation, as they provide that input through physical responses, facial expressions, attentiveness or lack thereof, enthusiasm, visible expressions of agreement, assent, disagreement, encouragement, and the like. The members of the congregations are constantly communicating with the preacher during the preaching, and since their messages are rich with information about their abilities to hear, understand, and respond to the homily, the preacher very much needs not to miss those messages. A furrowed brow can be communicating that some have had difficulty hearing the last few words, understanding the last concept provided, or agreeing with what is being said. Within context, the preacher should be able to interpret that message, so that the last few words can be repeated more clearly, rephrased more simply, or communicated again with an acknowledgment that this is a hard teaching, but one which deserves careful attention.

The ability to read the congregants' wordless contributions to the conversation of the homily is called "calibration" of the congregation. Interestingly enough, it is difficult, if not impossible, actively to calibrate the congregation if one is reciting memorized material. One needs to be free of the dynamics involved in memorization in order to read an audience's various responses and respond to them. Accordingly, it is highly desirable for the preacher to be thoroughly acquainted with the material at hand.

Remember our earlier experiment with the presentation about my reception of the annual appeal letter from my teachers. Solely equipped with the brief, five-point notes which were provided, it would have been rather easy for anyone to have repeated that presentation. This reflects the value in notes. One should not read a homily from a script, for that impairs the relationality between the preacher and the congregation. One needs to know what it is that one plans to say about a particular concept. The purpose of notes is not to be able to read aloud what one plans to say; the purpose of notes is that the note reminds the preacher which piece of the homily (or which move) it is now time to present. In other words, in our presentation being instanced here, I should not need a script so that I can know what it is in Move 3 that I want to say about Sister Mary Immaculate. Rather, the short note "Move 3: Sister Mary Immaculate" is there simply to remind me that this is the point at which I am to talk about how very especially I loved my favorite teacher, Sister Mary Immaculate. Consider the absurdity of the contrary: if I, as the preacher, need to read those notes in order to learn which Sister was my favorite teacher, or why Sister Mary Immaculate was my favorite, then I am entirely too unacquainted with the material to be able to convey it to my listeners in any convincing way at all; in fact, a personal lack of conviction and authenticity will probably be communicated instead.

Furthermore, if the homilist feels that, indeed, he or she knows the material, but the move is too complex to remember it without using a script, then the homilist can be certain that the material is too complex for one move to form in the minds of the congregants, who will have neither notepads nor the ability to raise their hands to ask the homilist to repeat or clarify points they have not grasped. A move must be simple enough for the preacher to deliver without a script, or it is too complex for the hearers to grasp. This principle is not calling for a "dumbing down" of the homily; rather, it is calling for sophisticated concepts to be broken down into digestible parts so that everyone in the congregation can relate to the homily.

2. Sound Anthropology: good preaching evidences respect for the humanity of the members of the congregation. The theologian Sister Pamela Smith, ss.c.m., Ph.D., helps preachers who are strategizing toward an effective homiletic to understand the necessity of taking the human person into account. Many of the comments below reflect concerns she has raised in presentations. Many preachers acknowledge that their method of delivery is far from excellent. Sometimes they will admit things like this: "I know I'm long winded" or "I just can't figure out how to speak in an exciting manner" or "I've never been a public speaker and I'm just doing my best." We live in a world filled with brokenness, yearning for the healing lessons of the Gospel of Jesus Christ. We also live in a world where no one seems to have enough time. Marital relationships crumble in many instances because spouses have been unable to carve out enough time to keep their relationships loving and vibrant. Far too often, youngsters enter adulthood ill suited to take their place in society and sometimes with overwhelming problems because their parents could not find enough time to form them wholesomely. The world is far too broken to proceed without effective promulgation of the life-giving Gospel. No one has enough time. But at worship, members of this broken world, who are bereft of enough time, are willing to give the preacher eight to twelve minutes of their precious time. To fail in our task is to betray the broken world; it is to waste precious time. These are sins the preacher dare not commit. Using preaching time poorly is just a variation on that same theme. Therefore, a mediocre preaching style is a betrayal of the Gospel requiring remedy.

Perhaps an effective way to apply the necessary remedy is to understand that poor preaching technique manifests disrespect for the persons of the hearers. Preaching which is too simplistic insults their intelligence.

Preaching which is too complex shows disrespect for the various levels of catechesis they have achieved. Preaching which is too long shows disrespect for children who need to move often, and for senior citizens whose bodies often can't endure long sessions. If preaching communicates joy and a message of "God-loves-you-so-get-over-it" in the face of peoples' tragedies, it shows a lack of respect for their suffering as well as the integrity of the processes needed for authentic healing.

Many people, when asked to identify their criticisms of bad preaching, report the following: the homily had too many ideas; it was too long and painful; the preaching was not connected to the Scriptures; the material was inappropriate to this community; it contained a lack of clarity; it contained no challenge or mission; the preaching reflected the preacher's own preoccupations; it was too simplistic; and the like. The responsible preacher acknowledges that a careful response to such typical complaints constitutes a gesture of respect for the dignity of the persons in the congregation and a validation of the members' own experiences.

Therefore, the preacher must keep in mind that the members of the congregation are people who possess human dignity. They are people who yearn to celebrate their happy experiences. They are people who know the mystery of suffering and yearn for understanding, companionship, acknowledgment, and support in their sufferings. They won't value quick solutions, however, or suggestions which short circuit the healing process which an immature pastoral agent might suggest. They are people who are surrounded by joy, but also by suffering, crime, and evil and are hoping to find in the church and in the mystery of the Cross that the church conveys a recognition of the mystery of redemption which does not fail to respect their experiences. The person in the congregation expects and thrives in freedom and each needs the freedom to ask genuine human questions in the midst of life's vicissitudes. The members are subject to fear and limitation and they understand themselves and others as a people called to hope (even though they sometimes experience the death of a hope), and they find the systems from others in restoring that hope.

Therefore, the preacher would want to bear in mind three basic principles which underlie good preaching:

1. Grace builds on nature. The mind can only absorb what the body can endure. The preacher must always be attentive to the congregants' physical needs.

2. God is present in human experience and in this world. The preacher is certainly aware of the transcendence of God, but is also

aware of the immanence of God and the preaching reflects that awareness.

3. The good writer's principle: the universal is most effectively expressed in the particular. Examples: witness, lessons, and so forth often need to be concrete, imagery is important, and the local situation is often the best source for homiletic imagery.

Perhaps the best questions a preacher can ask as homily preparation begins are: Who are the human persons who are going to be touched by my preaching? What makes them tick? What makes them happy? What makes them hurt? How can I respect all of these issues as I preach?

3. Personality-type information can help the preacher communicate better. Investigations surrounding psychological typology have aided practitioners in many areas of human and pastoral care for decades. A variety of methodologies and tools exist; particularly helpful data has been presented by Chester P. Michael and Marie C. Norrisey in their work *Prayer and Temperament: Different Prayer Forms for Different Personality Types*.[35] This work can be successfully applied to preaching. The grounding for this work is found in Carl Jung's work with personality types.

Jung's work was subsequently developed by Katharine C. Briggs and Isabel Briggs Myers who produced the Myers-Briggs personality type indicator in 1962. Michael and Norrisey also incorporate the work on the four basic temperaments of David Kersey. In all of this, they help the liturgical minister to understand the liturgical appetites found typically within a worshiping congregation. Michael and Norrisey suggest that access can be gained to understandings of the dynamics operative within the congregants at worship by focusing on the four primary functions identified by the Myers-Briggs type indicators. The four functions are: "Feeling" (F), "Intuiting" (N), "Sensing" (S), and "Thinking" (T). Michael and Norrisey make a remarkable contribution by synchronizing these functions with significant spiritual teachers in Christian tradition. In doing so, they have identified the Feelers (Sensate-Perceivers; hereafter referred to as SP) with the Franciscan spirituality; the Intuiters (Intuiter-Feelers: NF) with the Augustinian tradition; the Sensors (Sensate-Judgers: SJ) with Ignatian spirituality; and the Thinkers (Intuitive-Thinkers: NT) with the Thomistic school.[36]

[35] Chester P. Michael and Marie C. Norrisey, *Prayer and Temperament: Different Prayer Forms for Different Personality Types* (Charlottesville, VA: Open Door, 1984).
[36] Ibid.

Michael and Norrisey show that each personality type has a primary symbol and a primary dynamic when attending liturgy. The primary symbol means that among the many symbolic realities one encounters at liturgy, most often one particular symbol tends to influence a participant most profoundly resulting from one's inner makeup (i.e., psychological type). Similarly, according to psychological type, it seems among all of the dynamics operative at a dynamic liturgy, each participant tends to be most attentive to one particular dynamic. All of the usual cautions surrounding the use of these kinds of materials remain operative in this case: it is incorrect to assume that one responds exclusively to one's category to the exclusion of all of the others; rather, quite often, these are matters of emphasis or nuance.

In this system, it is observed that the Feelers (Franciscan, SP) experience themselves to be gathering primarily around the symbol of the community and they are there to celebrate that community. The Intuiters (Augustinian, NF) would recognize themselves to be gathered primarily around the symbol of the meal with the operative dynamic of anticipation: looking ahead to that eschatological banquet that has been promised. The Sensates (Ignatian, SJ) gather primarily around the symbol of the Cross and find themselves basically commemorating that symbol. The Thinkers (Thomistic, NT) are gathered primarily to contemplate, with the focus of their contemplation being the word-event: the Scriptures and the preacher.

How can this information inform the preacher? Perhaps it is sufficient simply for the preacher to acknowledge the presence of these various types in the typical worshiping assembly. However, this information can undoubtedly help the preacher be mindful of the variety of congregants, for even greater effectiveness. For instance, the preacher who is mindful of the Feelers with their inclination to celebrate and their attentiveness to the community, might want often to lead the community toward praxis and toward responsible relationships to other people—to the world and to its environment through the preaching. Care to include delight when occasions of obedience are identified within the community and the world will also respond to this group's need for celebration.

The preacher can attend to the inclinations of the Intuiters by remembering, at least from time to time, to engage the meal symbolism of the Eucharist in order to contextualize the preaching within the eschatological dynamic and to muse upon the consequences of Gospel efforts in the world. The preacher can attend to the needs of the Sensates and their inclination to commemorate the Cross by taking care to situate the contemporary congregation within the timeline of salvation history. Mention of the events from the life of Christ, the sanctoral cycle, the lives of the Saints, and traditions from Catholic piety can draw the members of this group radically into the heart of the preaching. Perhaps the preacher can most attend to the needs of the Thinkers by treating their concerns outside of the literal preaching event itself. With their attentiveness to the word, such people often appreciate being drawn into Scripture study groups, ideally occurring early in the week and including the preacher to reflect upon the texts which will be preached the following weekend. Care given to the appropriate choice of hymnody containing lyrics which correlate to the scriptural texts and, of course, references to that synchronicity in the homily when appropriate, can also enhance the preaching experience for these people.

It must be understood that no single preaching event can cater to the preferences of every person or every group in a congregation. The value in acknowledging the differences which exist within a typical congregation is that it alerts the preacher to the types of constituencies requiring occasional specific attention in the course of one's ongoing preaching ministry. It is never recommended that any single preaching event be constructed with every personality type in mind. But in the course of three months, if the sensitivities of any particular personality type (or other acknowledged group) were never addressed, one would wonder why the preacher has chosen to exclude a segment of the congregation from the address of the Gospel.

4. Preacher as theologian. Preaching requires an accomplished relationship with the various theological disciplines because preaching is the primary location for the dispensation of theological information. It might seem pointless to suggest that a preacher, almost always a person with graduate level theological education, needs to be informed theologically, but the fact is we communicate as much by silence as we do by word. We communicate sometimes unintentionally, and even undeveloped concepts lurking in our consciousness seem to find expression often enough.

An example might serve. Some years ago, a parish priest confided in me that an angry woman approached him after Mass one day with the charge: "Father, I am scandalized that you are pro-abortion." The priest, whose support for all of the church's pro-life positions has been without exception, was horrified at the charge. He asked the woman why she felt so. She responded, "In the entire year you have been here, you have never mentioned *once* the struggle over the abortion controversy. When a Catholic priest refuses to speak up when this evil is so rampant, it suggests support for the abortion cause." The priest reflected and made a startling realization. Whereas his position had never wavered from the church's, he did have to admit to himself privately that he had been disgusted by what he had considered to be the vulgar and hysterical methodologies of the anti-abortion group in that parish and was, therefore, determined not to be linked with them. It was this determination which had held him silent week after week on the abortion issues and that had convinced his critic that he was pro-abortion. Whereas she had figured him out imprecisely, she had indeed figured him out. This stands as a lesson to every preacher. One's attitudes, even undeveloped ones, find expression in one way or another. Therefore, the preacher has a responsibility to have a developed understanding of the pertinent studies of theological investigations: moral theology, ecclesiology, Christology, eschatology, biblical exegesis, liturgy, Christian anthropology, theology of grace, mariology, pneumatology and sacraments. Questions about Eucharist including eucharistic adoration, Sunday worship in the absence of a priest, proper placement of the tabernacle, and the like are quite pressing today. What is the homilist's understanding of the principles underlying these issues? How does that understanding get communicated intentionally or otherwise?

That's really the issue with each of these theological areas: Is Christ a judge? Is he the King of mercy? Did his birth occur in the pastoral scene represented in our Christmas scenes every year, or did it more closely resemble a cardboard lean-to in the alley behind the bus station in any of our major cities today? What is the preacher's attitude about these things? It will emerge in one's preaching and that preaching is forming faith. One wants to be intentional about what one preaches and teaches. Therefore, the preacher of the Gospel, in a church which proclaims *lex orandi, lex credendi,* bears the responsibility to maintain a high level of theological literacy. Especially as those issues impinge upon the issues of the day.

D. The Sequel to the Homily: Analysis

The sequel to all of this is the analysis of one's preaching and imperative in this step is knowing that the key to better preaching involves better listening. Much of what has been discussed in this chapter addresses the preoccupation of the New Homiletic: the needs of the hearers. The

Focus Statement is designed so that the hearers can grasp the message. The Moves are employed so that the message is more easily accessible to the hearers. The Function Statement is designed so that the hearers have a clear sense of mission following each sermon. One is conscious of the intellectual and psychical needs and comforts of the congregants so that they can ingest the message more readily. One recognizes the importance of theology in preaching because the faithful have the right and the need to be formed by sound theology. Preaching tends to the needs of the faithful. Therefore, an ongoing program for improving preaching is an indispensably pastoral responsibility for any preacher, and an effective way to accomplish that task is to set about listening. What has one's preaching events communicated?

In a seminary homiletics class employing the methodology of this chapter, a successful way of checking the effectiveness of a classroom homily is for every student in the class to write down in one sentence immediately after the student preacher has finished delivering the homily: 1. What did this homily say? (Focus Statement); 2. What is the hearer supposed to do as a result of this homily? (Function Statement). The student-preacher is proven successful or unsuccessful depending upon how many members of the class heard the same Focus and Function Statements as well as how closely those responses paralleled the student-preacher's own Focus and Function Statements.

In the parish, something similar can occur to assist the preacher in understanding how effective his or her preaching is. In his 1967 volume, *Partners in Preaching: Clergy in Laity and Dialogue,* Reuel L. Howe proposes a program bearing the same title in which he suggests that several parishioners commit themselves to a period of several weeks on a rotating basis to evaluate the preaching in their parish.[37] Dominicans in the midwestern United States enthusiastically employed Howe's structure much to the enhancement of their liturgical preaching. A valuable variation on Howe's project could be to gather six to ten parishioners for one-half hour after a certain specified number of preaching events by a particular preacher (EG 6–8). Simply discuss before a tape recorder what the Focus Statement and the Function Statement of the homily was that day. An immediate benefit is that those parishioners involved will become better listeners of liturgical preaching. A secondary benefit is that the preacher would have valuable feedback for homily evaluation. And,

---

[37] Reuel L. Howe, *Partners in Preaching: Clergy in Laity and Dialogue* (New York: Seabury Press, 1967).

of course, when a preacher learns to preach better and the congregants learn to hear better, the Gospel is more effectively proclaimed within the world and the victory of the reign of God is more closely at hand.

WORKS CITED

Aland, Kurt, *et al.*, eds. *The Greek New Testament.* Third edition. Stuttgart: United Bible Societies, 1983.

Augustine, Bishop of Hippo. *Homilies on the Gospel According to St. John, and His First Epistle.* Volume II, Homily LXXX. Oxford: John Henry Parker, 1849.

Bauer, Walter. *A Greek-English Lexicon of the New Testament and Other Christian Literature.* Second edition, revised and augmented by F. Wilbur Gingrich and Frederick W. Danker. Chicago: University of Chicago Press, 1979.

Cooke, Bernard. *Ministry to Word and Sacraments.* Philadelphia: Fortress Press, 1976.

Dargan, Edwin Charles. *A History of Preaching.* Volume 1. Grand Rapids: Baker Book House, 1954.

Deiss, Lucien. *God's Word and God's People.* Translated by M. J. Connell. Collegeville, MN: Liturgical Press, 1976.

Dix, Gregory. *The Shape of the Liturgy.* New York: Seabury Press Edition, 1982.

Egeria: Diary of a Pilgrimage. In *Ancient Christian Writers.* No. 38. Translated by George E. Gingras. New York: Paulist Press, 1970.

Grasso, Domenico. *Proclaiming God's Message.* Notre Dame: University of Notre Dame Press, 1965.

Grisbrooke, Jardine, W., ed., trans. *The Liturgical Portions of the Apostolic Constitutions: A Text for Students.* Bramcote, Eng.: Grove Books Ltd., 1990.

Howe, Reuel L. *Partners in Preaching: Clergy in Laity and Dialogue.* New York: Seabury Press, 1967.

Justin Martyr. "The Works Now Extant of St. Justin the Martyr." In *A Library of Fathers of the Holy Catholic Church Anterior to the Division of the East and West.* Oxford: J. H. and Jas. Parker, 1861.

Klauser, Theodor. *A Short History of the Western Liturgy.* Oxford: Oxford University Press, 1969.

Michael, Chester P., and Marie C. Norrisey. *Prayer and Temperament: Different Prayer Forms for Different Personality Types.* Charlottesville, VA: Open Door, 1984.

O. Procksch, "λεγω." In the *Theological Dictionary of the New Testament.* Edited by Gerhard Kittel. Translated and edited by Geoffrey W. Bromiley. Volume IV. Grand Rapids: William B. Eerdmans Publishing Co., 1965.

Origen. *Homilies on Genesis and Exodus. The Fathers of the Church.* Edited by Hermigild Dressler, *et al.* Translated by Ronald F. Heine. Washington, DC: Catholic University of America Press, 1981.

Schanz, John P. *Introduction to the Sacraments.* New York: Pueblo Publishing Co., 1983.

Schroeder, H. J., ed. *Canons and Decrees of the Council of Trent.* New York: Herder and Herder, 1941.

Tambasco, Anthony J. "Word of God." In *The New Dictionary of Theology.* Edited by Joseph A. Komonchak, Mary Collins, and Dermot A. Lane. Wilmington, DE: Michael Glazier, Inc., 1987.

Wegman, Herman. *Christian Worship in East and West: A Study Guide to Liturgical History.* Collegeville, MN: Liturgical Press, 1990.

White, James F. *Roman Catholic Worship: Trent to Today.* New York: Paulist Press, 1995.

Mary Alice Mulligan

TEACHING DISCIPLES TO PREACH IN THE SERVICE OF WORD AND TABLE

1. HISTORICAL/THEOLOGICAL DESCRIPTION OF ROLE OF PREACHING AND RELATION OF WORD AND TABLE WITHIN THE CHRISTIAN CHURCH (DISCIPLES OF CHRIST)

The Christian Church (Disciples of Christ) began in frontier revivals and fellowships which claimed an essential unity among all Christians. Leaders attempted to recover or "restore"[1] a simple Christian faith, based on what could be learned about the early church from the Bible. In addition to denying the validity of separations between groups of Christians, Disciples valued the weekly observance of the Lord's Supper and practiced believers' immersion baptism. The longing for Christian unity and respecting other traditions and practices has placed Disciples at the ground floor of ecumenical conversations around the globe. One of our founders, Barton Stone, claimed "Unity is our polar star." One of our other founders, Thomas Campbell, claimed "In faith unity, in opinion liberty, and in all things charity." The foundational belief that divisions in the universal Body of Christ are sinful and work against our witness to the faith allows for tremendous diversity within this single denomination. In addition to allowing significant differences in faith and practice, Disciples have little hierarchical structure to make determinative claims upon congregational and pastoral life. Within our diversity, however, there is a central place for hearing the Word and for Breaking the Bread on a weekly basis. The standard Disciples' identity joke is: Whenever two

---

[1] Hence, the reference to these groups as "The Restoration Movement."

Disciples meet, they will have three opinions and the Lord's Supper. Our Commission on Theology discussed the historic significance of Communion within the Disciples tradition, noting: "In light of apostolic precedent, they regarded its celebration to be the one essential act of Sunday worship; congregations gathered at the Table even when they had no one available to preach a sermon. Insistence upon weekly communion made the Disciples a peculiar household among nineteenth-century Christians."[2] The emphasis on weekly Communion made Disciples peculiar not among all Christians, but certainly among the majority of Protestants, especially those on the frontier. That gathering at the Table[3] could happen even when no Word was proclaimed does not mean proclamation was not important. In fact, because of the desire to restore the Church to its earliest shape, the reading and interpreting of Scripture were crucial parts of worship. However many early Disciple congregations were regularly without educated clergy, yet the congregations still recognized that Bible reading and Breaking Bread together were essential to weekly worship. That many early Disciples preachers were not formally educated just made them seem closer to the preachers of the early church. After all, one Disciples scholar reminds us: "Christian preaching began not as a system of thought, but as a spontaneous and enthusiastic proclamation on the part of the followers of Jesus . . . ."[4] Similarly, early Disciples congregations shared the stories of Jesus from the Bible and broke bread together with prayers at the Table week by week. Perhaps our best known early leader, Alexander Campbell (Thomas' son), used the Bible to determine the faith and practices of these early nineteenth-century Disciples. However, there were obviously instances where Bible direction alone was not sufficient guidance. Because of the underlying principle

---

[2] "A Word to the Church on the Lord's Supper (1991): A Report of the Committee on Theology" in *The Church for Disciples of Christ: Seeking to Be Truly Church Today,* ed. Paul A. Crow, Jr., and James O. Duke (St. Louis: Christian Board of Publication, 1998) 142.

[3] Most Disciples refrain from using the term "altar" because of the belief that such language refers to the place where a sacrifice occurs. The sacrifice of Christ is a once-for-all, non-repeatable event. His followers devote their lives to him, but we do not interpret what we do at the Table as a sacrifice. Instead, we believe that, as the Bible indicates the early church did, we are invited to the Table of Jesus Christ to share in his meal and to experience his presence in a way different from all other experiences of him. Like the disciples of Emmaus, Jesus is known to us at the Table in the Breaking of the Bread.

[4] William West, "Toward a Theology of Preaching" in *The Reconstruction of Theology,* ed. Ralph G. Wilburn, *The Renewal of Church, The Panel [of Scholars] Report,* vol. 2 (St. Louis: Bethany Press, 1963) 259. This three-volume work was constructed for the church as the Christian Church (Disciples of Christ) moved from thinking of itself as a movement or "Brotherhood" and began to see itself as a denomination.

that Christ has already made the Church one, significant variation in theology and practice was allowed from congregation to congregation. This became troublesome as the diversity led to significant theological differences, which led to questions of what is "essential" to the faith and what are allowable "opinions." Some of this difficulty came as a result of the unique situation of the early frontier fellowships, often isolated groups of Christians who were under the care of a traveling "evangelist," who kept in contact and visited them as often as possible (much like our ideas of St. Paul's first-century connection to various communities of faith). Fellowships would be established by traveling evangelists, but the ministerial leadership was soon expected to be raised up from the congregation itself. As spiritual leaders became obvious to the group, certain persons were "set apart" for eldership. Hands were laid on them; thus they were locally "ordained" by the congregation, and no longer considered laity. A Disciples church historian notes: "Those who were thus set apart, dependent upon their gifts, were entrusted with the care of preaching (ministry of the word) and the administration over matters pertaining to both baptism and the table (ministry of sacrament). . . . For Campbell, the elders (occasionally referred to as bishops) were the ordained ministers of the church."[5] So, there was a distinct form or office of ministry, although locally ordained. Another distinction in this group was that Campbell refused to use the word "sacrament," opting instead for the term "ordinance" when referring to those behaviors and rituals necessary for ordering the life of the community of faith. Toulouse adds: "And, in Campbell's view, there were more than merely two ordinances. Christ ordained preaching, fasting, prayer, and the confession of sins as much as he ordained baptism and the Lord's supper."[6] However, in true Reformed tradition, Campbell understood the ordinances as a "means of grace." "Campbell never intended, in his refusal to use the word *sacrament,* to deny that God acts through the ordinances to communicate the divine grace of God's forgiveness."[7]

The other contributors to this volume come from Christian groups well known for being in the Double Feast tradition, those in the practice of celebrating Word and Table each week. Yet, this is not the situation for most Protestant groups, although their founders and even contemporary scholars firmly contend that preaching and Communion rightly belong

[5] Mark G. Toulouse, *Joined in Discipleship: The Shaping of Contemporary Disciples Identity* (St. Louis: Chalice Press, 1997) 169.

[6] Ibid., 138.

[7] Ibid.

in each weekly worship service. Obviously, sermon and Supper explain and reinforce each other. The message should be the same, although we might say the "language" is different. One act speaks in oral terms, the other in enacted ritual. The sermon assists in proper interpretation of the ritual actions. Although Protestant scholars, denominational leaders, and various ecumenical documents assert the importance of sermon and Supper in worship, there is still mere monthly Eucharist in many local settings. Thus, my denomination, the Christian Church (Disciples of Christ), an unfamiliar, small, frontier Protestant group, might be expected to follow the pattern of both conservative and mainstream denominations where preaching takes priority and Communion is celebrated just once a month or even less frequently. (Curiously enough, one notices that on the monthly Communion Sundays in those congregations, frequently proclamation of the Word is curtailed, thus serving to separate the connection between Word and Table even on the Sundays both are observed.) But worshipers in congregations of the Christian Church (Disciples of Christ) expect to have a full sermon and the sacrament ("ordinance" language is now rarely used) each Sunday. For this reason, it seems important for me to spend a bit more time describing this hybrid group, the Christian Church (Disciples of Christ), and the importance we place on both preaching and Breaking Bread.

Individual Disciples congregations all over the United States and parts of Canada live out what the scholars and denominational leaders claim—that communal worship requires the Lord's Supper. A typical Disciples scholar states: "The most general continuity with apostolic worship is achieved for the majority of Christians by a practice which ensures that worship can never be understood apart from the Lord's Supper."[8] However, the expectation that worship has both sermon and Supper does not mean they necessarily make sense together, not even in the twenty-first century, when seminary education and congregational training has increased, assisting an understanding of the meaning and link between sermon and Supper. Disciples scholar Susan Bond warns of the failure of consistency between pulpit and Table, using as an example the use of liberation language in the pulpit and sacrificial language at the Table.[9] The inconsistency of christological references may not be

---

[8] W. B. Blakemore, "Worship and the Lord's Supper" in *The Revival of the Churches,* ed. Wm. Barnett Blakemore, *The Renewal of Church: The Panel [of Scholars] Reports,* vol. 3 (St. Louis: Bethany Press, 1963) 231.

[9] L. Susan Bond, *Trouble with Jesus: Women, Christology, and Preaching* (St. Louis: Chalice Press, 1999) 11.

noticed by parishioners in the typical congregation, but that only means they have not been taught to attend closely enough to the content of the theology and Christology implied in worship liturgy. Although such inconsistency of Christology is not unique to Disciples, it is disturbing in the Double Feast tradition, where Word and Table should be expected to be connected parts of a unified worship liturgy.

It is a universal claim in Disciples congregations that partaking of the Lord's Supper is an essential part of Sunday worship. Alexander Campbell was clear: "The breaking of the one loaf, and the joint participation of the cup of the Lord, in commemoration of the Lord's death, usually called 'the Lord's Supper,' is an instituted part of the worship and edification of all Christian congregations in all their stated meetings."[10] From the beginning, Communion was a necessary part of Disciple worship, yet scholars agree that what the ritual means may still not be clear in most congregations. Notice: "But among Disciples, there has been no real agreement on what the centrality of the supper really meant theologically. Everyone agreed on its central role in worship, but through Disciples history, not many congregations have contemplated the supper's theological centrality . . . ."[11] Thus it became easy, when other Protestant groups focused on the primacy of preaching, for Disciples to rearrange their order of worship to celebrate Communion before the sermon. Although no Disciples seemed willing to switch to the practice of monthly Communion, putting the Sacrament first meant that the theological understanding of the sermon as preparing the hearer to receive the Sacrament was lost. The lack of seminary training for many local ministers (and even those who were seminary trained were often educated in seminaries of other denominations) allowed popular trends and practices from other groups and denominations to be adopted into Disciples congregational worship. However, there is a recent trend to make sure new ministers are seminary educated and trained in Disciples history and polity; the practice of local, congregational ordination is becoming a rarity.[12] As a result, congregational leadership should be

---

[10] Alexander Campbell, *The Christian System in Reference to the Union of Christians, and a Restoration of Primitive Christianity, as Plead in the Current Reformation* (Cincinnati, OH: Standard Publishing Company, 1901 [1835]) "Breaking the Loaf," Proposition VII, 274.

[11] Toulouse, *Joined in Discipleship,* 157.

[12] There is still the common practice of having congregational "elders" (in addition to ordained clergy) participate in worship leadership, especially offering prayers at the Communion Table. It is less frequent now that these spiritual leaders are locally "ordained," although a commissioning (usually without laying on of hands) is still frequently performed when they assume their office.

remembering the centrality of the Supper and the rightful practice of allowing the sermon to serve as preparation for the Table.

Disciples homileticians often address the relationship of sermon and Supper, encouraging other Protestants to recognize the necessary connection and rightful practice of observing both in every worship.[13] Unlike homiletics professors at Catholic or Episcopal seminaries, those of us at ecumenical institutions, especially those enrolling students from many traditional Protestant groups (Presbyterian, various Methodist denominations, Mennonite, U.C.C.), must spend time explaining the important link between Word and Sacrament. In introductory preaching classes, I devote an entire lecture to this link, meanwhile encouraging students of all Christian traditions to be more intentional about working toward more frequent Communion as they move into parishes.

Ask any Christian about Communion and we will hear the belief that there persons are able to encounter Jesus Christ in a way different from any other meeting. Disciples of Christ would agree that Christ is present at the Table, but would claim that presence is not in the elements. Rather, we discover Jesus Christ present among us. Although there has been some anti-Catholic sentiment in our history, it arose mostly from a lack of understanding what is believed to happen during the Mass. Our inability to admit that the Sacrament is beyond comprehension, and a tendency in the Disciples movement to shun trinitarian language, especially regarding the Holy Spirit, led to an eagerness to be different from Catholicism, without always knowing what that meant. However, what may be said is that Disciples would not have intended to disrespect the presence of Jesus Christ in Body and Blood. Rather, the experience of Christ at the Table was believed to be Personal, other than and more than a change of substance. Blakemore claims the troublesome aspect of accepting the doctrine of transubstantiation is "the failure of this theory to account for the way in which the Christian knows his Lord to be present at the Lord's table . . . [For] the presence of flesh and blood is not personal presence . . . [I]n Christian worship Christ the Lord is a living Presence, a living and personal Presence."[14] We believe Christ is fully present, among us, at the Table. However, most Disciples of Christ are quick to add their own disclaimer that the Breaking of the Loaf is rightly beyond our comprehension. Our Commission on Theology agrees

---

[13] Some of the better known homileticians of the Christian Church (Disciples of Christ) include Ronald Allen, L. Susan Bond, Delores Carpenter, Fred Craddock, Joey Jeter, and Frank Thomas.

[14] Blakemore, "Worship and the Lord's Supper," 244.

that ritual provides more than we could ever articulate: "The Lord's Supper means more than the church is ever quite able to say about it." It is "an act of inexhaustible spiritual richness . . . ."[15] Thus it is appropriate to attempt to articulate the Gospel as best we can in our preaching, then allow that to lead to the ritual of the Table, admitting that in the end, our words are inadequate.

2. PREPARATORY STEPS BEFORE BEGINNING TO COMPOSE THE HOMILY

Although the first section of this chapter was more informative about my denomination, these next sections attempt to set out a brief homiletic instruction manual. The reader is invited to read the material I refer to and to take time to do the exercises suggested.

A Disciple preacher once told me her ecumenical seminary homiletics professor gave them twenty-seven steps for preparing a sermon, twenty of which were "pray." Surely she exaggerated, but it is an important reminder that we expect and need God to be a participant in each step of the sermon, from first reading of the texts, to studying and writing, to delivery, and to hearing and digesting.

Before one can even decide what to preach or what texts to use, one needs to be aware of the congregation. In one of my classes, I have students turn in a brief paper describing the congregation. Who are these people filling Sunday morning pews? Where do they come from? How long have they been members? What stages of life are represented? How do things get decided and accomplished in the life of this congregation? Who gets the ten closest parking places on Sunday morning?[16] Then they turn in a paper from a similar analysis of the neighborhood. Do businesses, apartments, single family dwellings, empty lots, dead-end streets, cornfields, or what surround the church building? Who are the people who live closest to the building? What are they doing on Sunday mornings? Has anyone ever invited someone from the neighborhood to join in worship? Has anyone ever been into any other building in the neighborhood? Who else was in there? Did they speak? Did the individual speak? Are there people on the street? What are they doing? Are people employed

---

[15] "A Word to the Church on the Lord's Supper," 139.

[16] The issue of parking spaces is one of congregational analyst Lyle Schaller's questions, which reveals whose needs are considered most important (senior pastor, visitors, the senior Sunday school class, persons with disabilities). See Lyle E. Schaller, *44 Ways to Increase Church Attendance* (Nashville: Abingdon Press, 1988).

in the neighborhood? How? How could one enter into conversation with them to discover what are the greatest needs in the neighborhood? What does one think they would say their greatest needs are?

I believe if a minister is going to preach a meaningful word week after week, she or he[17] must be aware of the congregation and its setting. The particular neighborhood of the church building is an important key to understanding what mission and ministry priorities the congregation may first need to undertake.

After thinking through the setting of the preaching event, we need to give a few thoughts to what preaching is about. Preaching is different from any other form of speech. One can do Bible studies in the church building (Sunday school or Wednesday evening); one can lecture on the Christian faith; one can write books about God. These are important, but they are not preaching. In preaching one does not merely talk about God or even the Good News of Jesus Christ, although a lot of people stand in pulpits and do just that, as if any talking about God is preaching. However, I contend that in our proclamation, God is at work, too. Preaching proclaims the Good News of Jesus Christ, and in the proclamation, preaching mediates an experience of the divine. What does that mean? Preaching creates a place for the congregation to encounter God in the Spirit of Jesus Christ. Quite an awesome task. No other speaking in the entire world is like preaching. Week after week, our preaching can be *life* to the people of our congregation. The encounter with God should never be boring. Sermons can bring worshipers into the presence of the most Holy God: How could we dare let that get old?

St. Paul knew the "performative" power of spoken words. He tells us, "So faith comes from what is heard . . . " (Rom 10:17a).[18] The words we speak from the pulpit help shape how Christians experience God and the world. Our preaching words show the hearers where God is at work; we help them envision the Realm which God is even now bringing into being among us. Pulpit words construct a "faith world" in the consciousness of the congregation.[19] Yet, our spoken words are vulnerable

---

[17] Throughout much of the history of the church, only males have been in ordained leadership, so the male pronouns have always served. With the limited expansion of ordination to include women, we could use both pronouns or alternate them. However, for the sake of brevity and in an effort to offset some of the continuing gender bias in church practice, I use just feminine pronouns to refer to seminarians and ordained persons, acknowledging that females and males can be in pastoral leadership.

[18] In this chapter, biblical quotations will come from the New Revised Standard Version.

[19] For a fuller discussion, see David Buttrick, *Homiletic: Moves and Structures* (Philadelphia: Fortress Press, 1987) 11.

in a way written words are not. Even as we speak, the sounds pass out of existence. Listeners cannot stop to go back over that last sentence (as one can in writing). The sentence evaporated as it was spoken, and now is gone. Replaced by another. So when we preach, the people better "get it" the first time, because once our words hit their ears, they cease to exist—unless the people *remember* what we say.

The modern world we live in bears a striking resemblance to the fleeting quality of words. We live lives on the move. We may dutifully show up for a class or committee meeting, and give the evening our close attention, but on the way home we still need to stop for milk and cereal for breakfast, and we cannot forget that one child needs $2 in quarters and the other one needs poster board and a single dollar for lunch, because the lunch lady cannot give change. Even in the midst of a day off (if we ever were to get one), we keep track of time. Every day we have one eye on the long-term projects of our parish ministry: one eye on the day-to-day operations and one eye on the ultimate plan of God for the final coming of the Divine Realm. The folks to whom we preach share these qualities of life in the fast lane.

Some North American anthropologists claim that our congregations are people who think "movement" in ways no previous generations have. They estimate that in any given year, 25% of the U.S. population changes residence. One out of four people is on the move, every year. And they are sitting in our pews. So, our preaching must be geared for their thinking, because how they think determines whether they hear us. If the people are thinking in movement, and our sermons do not have movement, they will have difficulty hearing us. The meaning and style of our speech has to fit their reality. The term we are going to use for the phenomenon of the meaning of the sermon "getting in" to the understanding of the congregation is "forming in consciousness."[20] The meaning of the sermon must *form* in the consciousness of the congregation, or the words will not be heard.

Consider the different realities of city kids and rural kids identifying wildlife to clarify the idea of whether and how things form in consciousness.[21] On a stroll through the woods, some rural kids actually "see" bachelor buttons, phlox, nightshade, daisies, clover, mayapples, poison ivy, and jack-in-the-pulpit. On the same path, most city kids see "plants,"

---

[20] The concept of the sermon's meaning "forming in consciousness" is detailed through the entire text of Buttrick, *Homiletic,* but see especially xii.

[21] David Buttrick uses a brief form of this example. It appears as two sentences in *Homiletic,* 8.

maybe recognizing some have flowers. The realities they *see* are different. Bachelor buttons, mayapples, clover, never *form* in city kids' consciousness, unless someone stops to point out and identify the various plants. Obviously, naming the plants one time will not be enough. So, we might think of ourselves in the pulpit identifying the world, week after week, according to the Christian understanding. The ability to identify one experience as something else gives us the communication ability we call "evangelism," by the way. For example, "The moment you found your father's surgery was successful, you called it relief. We Christians call it grace." Faith comes from hearing! Shifting a congregation's way of comprehending the world and helping the faith world take shape within its consciousness are not easy tasks. In addition, such tasks are rightly daunting, because people's faith is shaped through our preaching. Susan Bond puts it this way: "And to the extent that the average congregation learns any historical, systematic, or constructive theology, they learn it primarily from preachers."[22]

Once we have some sense of what preaching is doing, we need to decide what we will preach. Although I believe preaching prepares the congregation for the Table, it is not always necessary for the sermon to make direct reference to that preparation. In choosing biblical texts from which to preach, the freedom within the leadership of the Christian Church (Disciples of Christ) means, of course, that some preachers use the lectionary and some intentionally avoid it. I encourage lectionary preaching for the practical reason that beginning ministers should not have to spend time hunting for a "suitable" Scripture. The more serious reason is, however, that I encourage students to follow the liturgical year for the education of their congregants and for helping the congregation become a community of faith together. Advent should mean something in the life of the Church. The Advent lections help us learn what that "something" is, especially in the life of who we are as a congregation. My father, ordained in the Methodist Protestant Church in 1939, advised me early on to see the lectionary as a tool and not a prison, however. And so, I allow students to choose other readings, realizing that sermon series and special occasion sermons are also meaningful in the life of a congregation.

When I first taught preaching, I spent quite a bit of time on exegesis. Although this is still important, I am finding time spent considering hermeneutics is becoming more central. As I become more convinced that

---

[22] Bond, *Trouble with Jesus,* 3.

there are no uninterpreted events, the possibility of doing exegesis without hermeneutics becomes fainter. I usually have students read Thomas Long's twenty-page chapter on "Biblical Exegesis for Preaching" in *The Witness of Preaching*.[23] He presents clear and helpful material about dealing with a passage of Scripture and the process for opening the text to modern understanding. In doing exegesis, we are invited to watch over scholars' shoulders as they dig into Scripture and attempt to bring out the meaning from a text's original setting. Scholars are attempting to uncover what a biblical book or passage meant to the people who first heard it, but of course scholars can never be free from their own interpretive lenses.

I teach four steps for exegesis, keeping in mind that each of us is socially located. The readers of this chapter might do well to participate in the steps outlined here. After choosing a lection text, remember the social and cultural perspectives will always be influencing how one reads and understands biblical texts and the material written about those texts. The first step is to delve into the passage unassisted. Pray over it, then read it from several different translations. We need to hear it out loud, for that probably was how it was originally encountered. Jot down initial reactions to the passage. What do we remember hearing or thinking about this passage before? What questions arise now? Be especially attentive to what God seems to be doing in the passage.

The second step is to read some brief, general information about the entire book (to help set the stage). An article from *The Interpreter's Dictionary of the Bible*[24] would provide such an introduction. So would the introductory chapter from a good commentary.

Third, we need to engage the scholarship on the particular passage we will be preaching from. Remind ourselves of our earlier questions. Find several commentaries, preferably including some written by women and people of color, produced by different publishers. How do these scholars explain what God is doing? Pay special attention to how the minor/voiceless characters are considered (or ignored). If the last, the lost, the socially unimportant, the sinners, hookers, and bums were Jesus' most frequent companions, we need to be especially attentive to them as well. If the scholars are not attentive to these folks who live in the shadows, gutters, and margins, something is wrong with their work. Read someone else.

---

[23] Thomas G. Long, *The Witness of Preaching* (Louisville: Westminster John Knox Press, 1989) 60–79.

[24] *The Interpreter's Dictionary of the Bible*, ed. George Arthur Buttrick (Nashville: Abingdon Press, 1962).

In this third step, we also need to pay attention to key words and phrases which are echoed elsewhere in the Bible. They may be keys to helping us figure out how this little passage fits into God's big story.

The fourth step is actually the beginning of hermeneutic preparation. Admit our own vantage point. Where are we used to standing in reading this text? Many of us need to let the passage address us as persons of privilege, and hear what it says to the oppressed. Then, in light of this message, reflect on how it may proclaim the Good News of Jesus Christ to the particular listening congregation we face on Sunday. Is there a particular word as we approach the Table? Before we proceed in sermon construction, we need to delve a little more deeply into hermeneutics.

There are places for straight Bible lessons, but the pulpit is not one of them. What it meant to converse with a woman at a well or how far an ancient character might have walked in a single day are interesting pieces of information, but they do not make a sermon. Texts are preached because they call us to be engaged beyond the historic facts and original ideas. They invite us to use the meanings to cast light into our own lives and the world we live in. Marjorie Suchocki comments about the power biblical texts exert: "It is as if the text always reaches beyond itself into the lives of its hearers. . . . In that encounter, the text is read from a context that enters into the reading of the text itself. Between text and context, a timely word emerges that speaks directly to the hearer. The paradox obtains that every age reads a 'different' text, even while reading the same words."[25]

Biblical interpreters who seem to claim an objective platform from which they do their interpretation are actually revealing that they believe their standard Western European (usually) male viewpoint is objective, when it is merely what has been dominant in Western Christendom for much too long. Exposing the impossibility of objective scholarship is hampered, as biblical scholar Elsa Tamez points out, because even the "biblical tools, such as dictionaries, commentaries, and concordances, tools that are regarded as objective because they are scientific, . . . are undoubtedly susceptible to being biased by sexism."[26] Of course, we can easily see that not only sexism, but classism, heterosexism, ableism, and racism bias scholarship. Authors of exegetical resources have their own social location. So, as we read what they say, we must already be doing hermeneutics.

---

[25] Marjorie Hewitt Suchocki, *The Whispered Word: A Theology of Preaching* (St. Louis: Chalice Press, 1999) 55f.

[26] Elsa Tamez, "Women's Rereading of the Bible" in *Feminist Theology from the Third World: A Reader*, ed. Ursula King (Maryknoll: Orbis Books, 1994) 199.

The term comes from Hermes, whom we remember from our study of Greek mythology was the messenger of the gods. But he was also the god of boundaries, luck, successful herds, and eloquence. This wing-footed Greek may be a good logotype for preachers trying to bring some meaning from texts written millennia ago into the twenty-first century. What we want to avoid is the mistaken notion that even a Greek god would be able to deliver an uninterpreted message.

Various scholars invite us to remember the pretext, text, and context as we attempt to interpret the Bible.[27] Since much of what many of us have been taught through the years has come from a position of privilege, most of us tend to interpret the biblical word for today from a position of dominance. Thus, even the marginalized often identify with the powerful characters in pericopes. This can lead to the shameful experience of women and other less powerful persons viewing oppressed persons in the text as appropriately set aside or treated as unimportant. In effect, we have come to read the injustices in biblical passages as justifiable. Renita Weems claims that the marginalized, the oppressed, and the powerless may come to interpret those like themselves in the text as appropriately marginalized, oppressed, and without power. When they internalize the dominant viewpoint, she concludes, they are "forced to side against the marginalized in the Bible."[28]

For those of us working to bring a word from God out of the Bible and into the life of our congregations, then, we must work to listen to the voiceless characters in Scripture. We must attend to the minor characters, for Jesus seemed quite insistent that the least, the infirm, the powerless, and children would be first citizens in the Realm of God. But listening to those characters is not enough; we must help their voices be heard by others. Weems concurs: "It has proved the task and responsibility of marginalized readers today, both female and male, to restore the voices of the oppressed in the kingdom of God."[29] We must hear the silenced voices of non-dominant readers. For those of us who are in privileged positions in society (privileged by class, gender, and/or race), we must find resources to help us interpret Scripture from the

---

[27] See, for example, Renita J. Weems, "Reading *Her* Way through the Struggle: African American Women and the Bible" in *Sisters Struggling in the Spirit: A Women of Color Theological Anthology,* ed. Nantawan Boonprasat Lewis, Lydia Hernandez, Helen Locklear, Robina Marie Winbush (Louisville: Women's Ministries Program Area, National Ministries Division, Presbyterian Church [U.S.A.], 1994).

[28] Weems, "Reading *Her* Way Through the Struggle," 70.

[29] Ibid., 74.

viewpoint of those special friends of Jesus, the poor and oppressed (the non-privileged). One way to do that is to utilize resources by women and persons of color, especially persons from Third World communities. We must learn to listen through the ears of the oppressed.

Bond calls for a christology-from-below, which is grounded in the experiences of human living. Such experiences provide a starting place for thinking through biblical passages. She refers to Asian theologian C. S. Song, who urges beginning to interpret with a "'people hermeneutic,' grounded in the experiences of the poor, the marginalized, and the suffering."[30] Tamez supports this position, claiming the poor actually have the correct vantage point. "The poor . . . are in a privileged place, hermeneutically speaking, because we conceive of the God of life as one who has a preferential option for the poor."[31] The hermeneutic vantage point of the least is essential to finding a fuller understanding of Scripture.

Catherine and Justo González, writing about preaching, encourage the work "being done from the perspective of the traditionally powerless as they experience the empowerment of the gospel, not only in an inner sense, but also in the sense that it compels and enables them to strive for justice . . . [T]hey refuse to leave the gospel in the hands of the powerful, to be used for their purposes, and insist that a proper interpretation of Scripture is freeing rather than oppressive."[32] To back up their claim, the authors show how many of the biblical stories are about or addressed to those without power or position (miniscule Israel, herdsmen, exiles, occupied people, hillbillies from nowhere Galilee, minor religious band following a dead man). Apparently those who believed they had a message from God centuries ago believed also that frequently the most crucial voices were on the margins. Those excluded from society's power centers have God's special attention. If we are to find persons analogous to the subjects of Scripture, we best look not to the CEOs in the high-rise office buildings, but to those facing hypothermia every night, as they bed down under the overpasses.

So, how can our preaching come from a hermeneutical perspective of the poor and oppressed? We need to spend time where they are.[33] Tamez

---

[30] Bond, *Trouble with Jesus*, 115.

[31] Tamez, "Women's Rereading of the Bible," 198.

[32] Justo L. González and Catherine G. González, *The Liberating Pulpit* (Nashville: Abingdon Press, 1994) 15.

[33] For suggestions for getting where the poor are, see Mary Alice Mulligan and Rufus Burrow, Jr., *Daring to Speak in God's Name: Ethical Prophecy in Ministry* (Cleveland: Pilgrim Press, 2002).

reminds us that common people are interested in biblical study. They want to join the scholars to assist the work. Traditional biblical scholarship alone cannot provide valid interpretations for Scripture. The academy must invite trained church leaders, as well as the least educated layperson into the effort to hear God's message for today. Tamez adds: "Most of the professional biblical scholars I know work with grassroots communities." Why do they consider this necessary? She reminds us, "because the final goal of biblical research is to give meaning and dignity to the lives of persons and communities."[34]

We have heard from a womanist, an Asian, a white North American woman, and Latin Americans, but these are not the only ones emphasizing the importance of listening to the marginalized and crossing between groups of persons to bring out Scripture's meaning. The Nigerian, Justin Ukpong adds his voice:

> In inculturation hermeneutics the primacy of the reading activity is located not among individual theologians working in isolation but among theologians working within communities of ordinary people—it is the ordinary people that are accorded the epistemological privilege. The Bible is seen as a collection of the ordinary people's experience of God in their lives and communities reflected upon and expressed in stories, prayers, and so on.[35]

Reflecting back to the work the preacher has done in analyzing her congregation and neighborhood, she should be able to discover where some of the voiceless and neglected are, so entering into conversation first about life in general and eventually about the Bible, with those who have a hermeneutical privilege, may be quite possible. I encourage every minister who intends to present her congregation with a meaningful word from God to get with the poor to listen.

3. PROCESS AND STAGES OF SERMON CONSTRUCTION

There are preaching classes which teach several different systems of sermon preparation, to give the students some choice as they move into their parishes. However, I contend one system is plenty to learn in

---

[34] Elsa Tamez, "Reading the Bible Under a Sky without Stars" in *The Bible in a World Context: An Experiment in Contextual Hermeneutics,* ed. Walter Dietrich and Ulrich Luz (Grand Rapids and Cambridge, Eng.: Wm. B. Eerdmans Publishing, 2002) 13.

[35] Justin Ukpong, "Inculturation Hermeneutics: An African Approach to Biblical Interpretation" in *The Bible in a World Context,* 20f.

a single semester. So, the system I teach is modified from the work of homiletician David Buttrick.[36]

Just as there are broad strokes and details in many tasks, there are two major components to constructing the sermon according to our system: the structure and the individual moves. The structure serves much as a skeletal system does to undergird the presentation; the moves correspond to the various types of tissue which give the parts of the structure shape and depth. We begin with the broad strokes of determining the basic skeletal structure of the sermon, which serve as the joists or supports for the second part of our work, developing the details of individual moves.

Many preachers attempt to bridge the gap from ancient texts to the present by drawing analogies in their sermons. We have all heard the "Who are today's lepers?" sermons. There is merit in trying to figure out how "now" is like "then" in an attempt to hear God's voice in analogous situations. However, I am interested in teaching something slightly different. After doing the exegesis and hermeneutical investigations, we try to figure out what the text was doing in the consciousness of the original hearers. What was their field of meaning or understanding? Once we figure that out, the sermon we write will be an effort to reproduce that consciousness in the consciousness or listening experience of our own congregations.

Students learning to preach need to give up the "three points and a poem" idea. We need sermons which speak to the way people think and live day to day which, as was previously claimed, are described by "movement." Our behaviors and even our thinking seem always "in process." People live "orchestrated" lives, so they get to the end of the day with all their tasks accomplished. If people's lives are structured movements, it makes sense that the sermons we prepare would be structured movements as well. We need to communicate the Gospel in the same way that people think and live their lives. Sermons need structured, purposeful movement.

Accordingly, we are going to preach in steps which move the congregation intentionally from one place, through several steps, to land in

---

[36] The original system is explained in detail in David Buttrick, *Homiletic*. Although I supply footnotes for direct quotations and important parts of the process from this text, there will be phrases and whole ideas which come from Buttrick that I have modified and incorporated into my own work and lectures so that the exact places to footnote escape me. This is not intended to take any credit away from Professor Buttrick, who is the creator of the original system, and to whom I owe a great debt.

a new place. Like traveling across a stream using stepping stones, our sermons invite the congregation to move from one idea to the next in a planned structure and conclude with the congregation's safe arrival at a new location or space. The skeletal plan for the trip is called the "basic structure." The developed steps are called "moves."

Meaningful sermons must not merely tell people where they should be in the faith. They must assist people's trip from where they are, through the necessary steps of growth, to end up in a new place or with a new idea in the faith. If we share the journey in language the people can hear, understand, and remember, then when they reread the Scripture, they should be able to recollect the ideas which got them to the other side. This is the goal of the system I teach. The congregation should be able to remember the steps where the sermon took them.

Plot and Intention

Before moving to create a structure according to this modified Buttrickian system, we need to consider the plot and intention of the sermon. Let me use an example from church life (not from Scripture or a sermon, but from a board meeting). Anyone who has been involved in congregational leadership has probably survived numerous board meetings. Consider this particularly baffling style: After being called to order, there is twenty minutes of meaningless chitchat; then every department report is fifteen minutes of chatter and two minutes of substance. The last twenty minutes before adjourning is drivel disguised as new business. Board meetings following this plot last almost two hours for about twenty minutes of business. One could see this as a tremendous waste of time (an hour and a half for each of the thirty people present). Bruce Roberts, professor of Christian ministries and director of the Indiana Peer Group Study Program at Christian Theological Seminary, explained the intention of such a meeting. The chitchat establishes relationship; it is a process of trust development which has to be reinforced each month. Churches cannot exist without relationship processes. Such board meetings are not wasting time. The leaders are just trying to do two things at once—business and relation building. Their stated *intention* is to do the business of the church. That business included developing and reconfirming relationship, although that was an unspoken agenda item. It almost made a double intention—business and relationship. Now consider another plot for an evening meeting. Board members gather an hour before the meeting begins and have dinner together. In this way, they get the chit-chat out of their systems; the meeting begins on time, reports are briefer, and they keep to their designated end time. The stated *intention* (business meeting) and the more personal relational *intention* (trust and community building) are still met. The intentions remain the same, but the *plot* of the evening is quite different from the first congregation. The revised plot makes the entire evening more pleasant for everyone, even those who are chit-chat inclined, because the not-so-important part of the evening for them (the actual board meeting) is briefer. The board meeting example reveals two plots (distinct dinner and meeting or combined relationship building and meeting), each of which met the stated intentions (church business and relationship building). One plot was, however, clearly superior.

In the structures we devise for preaching, we are creating such plots. Think of storytelling. Any time we tell a story, we make plot decisions. Does it tell better if we begin with the crisis? If we delete all the stuff about what else is happening, does the meaning become clearer? What needs to be highlighted to make the motivation make sense? Just as we are making decisions about what to emphasize, what to delete, what to skim over every time we tell the simplest narrative, so are we making choices as we write sermon structures. Every time we plot a sermon, set up an outline, write a sketch, we are making choices. We are creating plots which serve the intention or purpose of our sermon. "So in a sense," Buttrick says in *Homiletic*, "every plot is a confession of faith."[37] We choose to convey these thoughts about God and life (and not other thoughts) in this particular way. Our choices are witnesses to our faith. Our theology is at work interpreting, deciding intention, and creating plot, to pass on to the congregation a consciousness of the meaning of a particular Scripture.

It is easy to tell the intentions going on in the board meeting example (at least it was once Professor Roberts pointed them out to me). But what are our intentions in preaching? We are going to attempt to draw out from a Scripture a particular structure of meaning. Our intention in preaching is to project or construct a particular understanding within the congregation. But we also must take the specific congregation into account. The intention must be to construct a meaning structured from the text and for the congregation before us. Plus, we intend for our sermons to do something. Comfort, confront, rally to praise? We are not only forming congregational consciousness, but *re*-forming and *trans*-forming it as well. Our sermons are preached to do something. The plot serves the intention.

[37] Buttrick, *Homiletic*, 290.

Structures

The first part of the system is to determine the basic structure for the sermon. This is a simple logical progression through the basic ideas of the sermon, which forms a very simple conversation. Here is a basic example.

1. Our faith gets charged up on Sunday morning.
2. But look out! By Wednesday we are running on empty.
3. Working together can keep us energized.

Here is another example.

1. Society teaches us to think "Me first."
2. But, Christians are invited to think of others first.
3. Then, oddly enough, we find joy.

These are very basic structures, beginning with an idea the congregation can identify with easily, then inviting them to look at a different, yet logically related idea, and finally moving to what may be a new place or an important resulting idea. A sermon built from either of these examples would develop the three ideas, one after the next. The basic structure sets the strategy.

Notice the difference between these structures and the outline of "points" from our son's report on autism.

What We Can Learn about Autism:

1. Who is likely to get it?
2. Symptoms
3. Educational possibilities
4. Medical interventions

In the autism outline, the "points" are isolated; one does not flow to the next with a conversational logic. The points could be listed in any order, and we would still get the same information. Merely giving information like this is not preaching. In our preaching system, the structure forms a simple conversation, which provides the steps or ideas to take the congregation logically from one place to another.

Yet, most of us are not interested in pulling a sermon structure out of our imaginations. We want the basic meaning and purpose of the sermon to come from the Bible, so we look to the lectionary passages to help us shape the structure of the sermon. The preacher attempts to interpret a particular message from God for this congregation from a particular passage of Scripture. She is trying to help the people experience the consciousness, sense the movement, of the passage.

Before turning to the passage on which we have done our exegetical work, let us look at a particular passage, Exodus 1:8-22.[38] Of course, first we would read it and follow the steps of exegesis and give some thought to the hermeneutical vantage point. Shiphrah and Puah have been almost invisible biblical characters on the landscape of Western male scholarship, yet women scholars and people of color, especially those from oppressed or traditionally excluded groups, hear in this passage a remarkable story of courage and comprehending God. If we set out the passage, step by step or moment by moment, it might look like this:

vv. 8–10	New king set on oppressing Israelites.
v. 11	King tells taskmasters to oppress Israelites.
v. 12	Oppressed prosper.
vv. 13–14	Oppressors become ruthless.
vv. 15–16	King to midwives: "Kill the Hebrew boys."
v. 17	Midwives fear God; disobey king.
v. 18	King questions midwives.
v. 19	Midwives lie.
vv. 20–21	God blesses midwives; Israelites prosper.
v. 22	Pharaoh tells everyone: "Kill the Hebrew boys."

Setting out the story step by step allows the structure of the passage to come clear. There are three moments when the pharaoh exerts power over the Israelites. We see easily that pharaoh is afraid (not an unusual reaction when one perceives a threat to one's power or privilege). Since pharaoh is the worldly power center, he exerts power over the taskmasters who also respond in fear. That is, they do what pharaoh wants. They oppress the Israelites, eventually ruthlessly. We can hear them say they are just doing their job, following directions. We might call them "collaborators."

Then pharaoh exerts power over the midwives, Shiphrah and Puah, but their reactions are different. In an ironic parallel, these powerless women seek to do the right thing, according to what they understand of God's direction, which is in direct defiance of the royal command to kill off the Israelites. The midwives refuse to be collaborators. The story seems intentionally constructed to show us an ironic contrast between how collaborators and powerless midwives respond to the power plays

---

[38] Buttrick gives a fine example of his steps of analysis and structure creating in *Homiletic*, 306–17.

of the social order. Setting out the moments of the passage enables us to see this construction easily.

After completing this simple plot analysis, we want to push the meaning deeper into a theological analysis. What in the story has to do with God? We see that the Israelites, people who are precious to God (because each person is precious to God, filled with the divine breath and stamped with the divine image), are being treated in two very different ways. The command to oppress them has two distinct reactions. Some of those commanded by pharaoh are loyal to God; the others are loyal to pharaoh.

When we think of such a plot in the life of our congregation, we might remember another Hebrew male child, whose life was threatened at birth by the ruling powers. He did not have the midwives' protection years later when the collaborators cried, "Crucify him." Although we do not want to "preach Christ" into every text from Hebrew Scripture, all Christian preaching is done in light of the Cross and Resurrection, even when our sermons do not mention Christ. The coming of God's Messiah means nothing to those whose allegiance is already pledged to pharaoh; but to those whose allegiance is pledged to God, it is a stunning birth of divine promise. If the birth of Hebrew boys means God's divine intentions for the earth are being moved along, if it means God's story is broadening to become more and more inclusive, eventually to include even the unclean Gentiles which we are, then this scene of devious midwifery heralds a coming new age. Those who benefit from the old age are naturally going to do all in their power to squash it (or throw its bearers into the river).

We can already sense some similarities between the passage and modern life, which is what we need for meaningful preaching. The congregation needs to hear a word from the preacher which makes a difference in where they are now, or else the time in the pulpit becomes mere Bible study.

We want to establish what we might call a "field of meaning" for this passage from Exodus. We do not get it word by word; we move to a sense of the passage, a flow of the meaning, which helps us choose how to construct the sermon structure. Remember, we want the congregation to share an experience of the consciousness of the text, get the "meaning" which is much more than learning pieces of exegetical information. Situations in the contemporary world can help us "get" this passage of Scripture. By investigating the two reactions to the ruling power, we begin to understand not just the taskmasters and the midwives, but the entire field of meaning and the consciousness of those different reactions. We know there are human power sources in the world (political, social, familial, economic, even congregational) which are nonchalant about crushing those who are precious to God. Entrenched systems of power are always ready to kill off any threat to their power, privilege, and comfort. And God's precious ones are smashed. Look around. Oppression is rampant; the taskmasters are already ruthless. And the church of Jesus Christ is lured, seduced, into joining step with the taskmasters. We know the church well enough to know we can often be counted among the collaborators. Nevertheless, those who would follow God are called to a different response. Christians are to offer themselves to God as buffers, midwives, who protect the most vulnerable. After all, we know Jesus himself was crucified by entrenched powers; but we also know he has risen victorious. Thus, he is still calling us to be more than *advocates* for the powerless; we are to be *physical protection* to the powerless, poor, and neglected, the easy targets of society. We are called to physical deeds, not mere words. Here is the theological reality. God is expecting certain behaviors from the church. Unfortunately the church more often looks like taskmasters than midwives. This distinction between reactions to how society treats the most vulnerable provides our theological field of meaning for the passage.

To summarize what we did here: We could call it plot analysis or exegetical analysis of the theology, which we did in three pieces. We set out the basic steps (or scenes or moments) from reading and researching the passage itself. We next analyzed what those steps meant. This was basic plot analysis. Then we thought through the theological meaning, the theological analysis. What is God doing? What is God expecting? As a final piece, we began to draw some contemporary ideas about what God may be expecting of us. Now we are ready to move to creating the basic structure, the skeleton of the sermon.

How do we decide what to preach from the theological work we have done? We need to prune the passage to a basic structure for preaching, which creates a particular understanding or meaning in the congregation. From what we have learned about this passage, what shall we preach at this time to this congregation? If we are going to attempt to re-create in the consciousness of the congregation the consciousness of the text, we need to remember that we are not preaching to individuals about individual faith, but rather to a congregation into whose communal consciousness we are attempting to construct a "faith world." So, as a first attempt, we can set out the ideas of the passage in a modified sequence:

1. The *pharaoh* (one in power) wants to kill off all challenges.
2. The *taskmasters* (average managers) were quick to comply.
3. But *powerless midwives* (certain nobodies) stayed faithful to God.
4. God is on the side of the oppressed *Hebrews* (whoever is power-less).
5. Of course, worldly power is calling us to collaborate.
6. But, we can refuse. We can side with God.

The key is to set out the ideas in simple sentences, which follow one after the other with an easy logic. Buttrick recommends "scribbling out our moves in conversational sentences," which helps us determine if they follow one another with the same kind of simple logic conversations use.[39] This sequence of sentences has a conversational logic to it, but as a sermon, it stays pretty much right in the field of the text. We want a message which enters the contemporary world of our consciousness. So, we need to give up the specificity of pharaohs and midwives, which keeps the meaning in the past. Here is another try at the same basic structure:

1. Power structures try to squash challenges.
2. Most groups comply with the power brokers.
3. But sometimes, little nobodies obey God instead.
4. After all, God is on the side of the oppressed.
5. Of course, worldly powers try to get us to collaborate.
6. But we can side with God.

So, here is our first attempt at a sermon structure. The structure seems faithful to the passage, although different from merely going verse by verse. We have drawn out a field of understanding by analyzing the plot and modifying the sequence of movement.

For a moment, let us compare this system to a verse-by-verse exposition sermon. Verse by verse exposition is, in effect, just biblical study with an occasional application section tacked on. In addition to being so predictable that people will drift away only to drift back in when our voice changes for the application section, that kind of exposition-application preaching treats Scripture as a past event. The congregation is invited to look back at Scripture, as if God were alive then, and then they are offered lessons for a modern era, as if we are now on our own to try and emulate it. Alternatively, the modified Buttrickian system claims

---

[39] Ibid., 71.

God is alive now. In addition to claiming that God is alive, we need to claim that Scripture is a living document. It is not some past tense Word of God, some 2500-year-old, dust-covered document from which we distill a lesson and try to breathe life into for the twenty-first century. Notice that in our own experiences of hearing Scripture read, we hear in the present tense. "I, Paul write these things to you," not "I, Paul, wrote to you." While the Easter Scripture is being read, we see Mary collapsing against the cold stone of the tomb, while behind her the One she thinks is the gardener approaches. We see her in our mind's eye, not our mind's *memory*. We do not think, "There she was." We think, "There she *is*, ready to collapse with grief." We feel her present grief. We might even share her consciousness (her awareness) as the text is being read. Christ's resurrection must be experienced as present to us and to our congregations, not as some ancient magical event. The preacher is called to present the faith as mattering to this world now. So, no exposition of Scripture hauled into current application does God or the congregation's faith justice. Instead, from reading, prayer, and study we determine a field of meaning from the text which transcends time. Then we establish a basic structure for communicating that into the consciousness of our people today. Our basic structure, made up of those six sentences, sounds like a simple conversation. Buttrick comments, "You will notice, the basic structure has been written out *as if talking to someone.*"[40] The statements follow each other with a simple logic. Although we have not followed the sequence of the pericope, the basic structure we have set up takes us through the meaning of the passage. And, when we read the Scripture again, the structure should easily come back to mind.

I am convinced that the sermon succeeds or fails on the strength of this portion—the basic structure. As we prepare to work through these steps of analysis to create the basic conversation or structure, read the basic structure aloud. It must sound natural. If it does not follow smoothly, we have to change it. The pieces must follow one another without confusion. The conversational logic, which is the basic structure of the sermon, keeps the congregation from getting lost. These simple sentences are the move starts for the developed sermon. They need to be as simple as we can make them. We cannot have frills in these statements. We want clear, short, simple sentences. For example, instead of "Most middle management types find the easiest thing to do is follow society's lead in oppressing those who are weaker than they are," we want "Collaborators

---

[40] Ibid., 311.

squash the weak." Don't get me wrong, there will be places for sophisticated language development and intricate word use, but not in the basic structure. The sentences of the basic structure must be simple.

After reading the entire basic structure aloud, ask ourselves, does it make sense? Is it believable? Do the sentences follow one another with a basic conversational logic? If not, we have to change the basic structure. If, at this stage, we feel like the sermon structure is not great, but will serve our purpose, stop and make the structure better. The basic structure supports the rest of the sermon. If it is faulty, the sermon is doomed. People may remember an illustration, or even one idea, but the *meaning* of the sermon will not form in the consciousness of the congregation.

Listen to people discuss someone else's sermon over coffee. What do they remember? People will tell about the pastor's dog's nervous tick, or about some child who was pulled out of a ditch and saved, or about some prank the pastor pulled in college, or about the minister's daughter performing in a ballet recital. Why are *these* items the things worth remembering? What do we want people to remember from *our* sermon?

One of my favorite pastimes is to ask people what the sermon was about. And so someone might say: "The rich man was told to sell all he possessed." Then, I might ask: "Who could do that?" "Not me," is the typical reply. Probably the preacher wanted the congregation to remember something else. What do people remember from sermons? They rarely seem to remember anything about God, or anything theological. Another painful effect: most sermons seem to have been about the past. "Jesus told a rich man to sell everything." Nothing there relates to the lives of the people in the pew. They may remember an illustration, but when asked, they cannot tell you what it illustrated.

But the truth is, we preachers want our sermons to matter. When our people are stranded in life's circumstances, we want the theological, faith-meaning we have communicated in our preaching to make a difference. We want the faith we helped form through our preaching to help them get to a safe shore. So, if the basic structure of the sermon is not quite right, we need to keep working on it.

Let's take another text, Numbers 27:1-11, and go through the steps again. We begin the basic plot analysis by setting out the moments of the pericope and then thinking through the actions.

1. Mahlah, Noah, Hoglah, Milcah, Tirzah are orphan daughters of the Manassite clan (making them invisible nobodies, without men to make them visible).

2. They come before Moses, Eleazar the priest, the leaders, and, in fact, all the congregation.

3. They say, "Give us our father's portion."

4. Moses goes to Yahweh.

5. Yahweh says, "Give them their inheritance."

These are invisible female nobodies, who have been orphaned while still unwed. In addition, they have no brothers to take them in. They pluck up their courage to go before all the power people and ask for their unborn brother's inheritance. Instead of being laughed out of court, the human powers inquire of the divine power about the request of these invisible ones. And the divine power says, "See them. Give them the inheritance."

So, we can push a little deeper into a theological analysis. We see two groups of people interact. These five orphan daughters of the Manassite clan pluck up enough courage to ask for what would have been seen as an outrageous request. They want their brother's land, even though they do not even have a brother. They are asking for something not theirs, yet they believe they have a right to it. And their very lives may depend on the answer.

The other group is Moses, the head priest, all the leaders, and as a matter of fact, everyone else in all twelve tribes. To their credit, they do not just stone these invisible females. Moses takes the request to Yahweh.

Yahweh is the third voice here. She says, "Give the females their inheritance."

Perhaps figuring out what is going on in the field of meaning here is not too difficult this time. These daughters, who are people without power, have the audacity to approach Moses, but they are not asking for *justice*. It was justice that had already determined that each family would receive a fair portion of land by the male descendents. Giving each family a fair piece is justice. These women ask for *mercy*, a step beyond the justice understanding of the day.

What may be most incredulous is the reaction of the powerful. Moses, Eleazar, the leaders, and everyone in the entire society agree to find out what God thinks. This is an amazing event. How often have leaders tried to find out what God thinks should happen? Before the United States imposes economic sanctions or drops bombs in the Middle East, do the powerful ask what God thinks about the resulting deaths?

When we stop to think about it, the only predictable voice here is God's. Of course the women deserve more than justice. They, who are beloved of God, deserve mercy. What else is possible for them? To be left to die by the road, because they are the wrong gender? They have no land, no father to care for them or get husbands for them, no brother to take care of them and protect them from the whims of society. Of course Yahweh says give them their inheritance.

From this point, we should be ready to form a basic structure. Here is a first try:

1. Defenseless women appeal to the top authority for mercy/justice.
2. Top authority follows God's direction.
3. So, the women receive mercy/justice.

Such a structure makes sense, but it has no pizzazz or punch. It is not a very interesting little conversation. We need to keep working on it:

1. Even the powerless have power to ask for mercy.
2. The powerful authorities may be uncertain.
3. But God wants mercy for the powerless.

This structure is really only a little better. So, I have one more suggestion. We could think of the field of meaning again. There are the powerless, asking for what appears to be more than a family's fair share. They ask for mercy; and they receive it. But how would the population of the twelve tribes react to Yahweh's generous mercy? I think they would be shocked. The leaders, the rest of the Manassite clan, and the people of the other tribal families would not expect invisible women to receive a man's inheritance.

From this side of the women's liberation movement, we might easily see the justice of God's *mercy*, but that is not what these ancient people would have experienced. So, I have an idea to try out. We could lay a situation in the contemporary United States—that of poor, single mothers—right on top of the whole field of meaning from the passage. How does the meaning of this passage relate to the situation of young women of all colors, who are making every effort to survive on mere table scraps from the welfare and always precarious food stamps? What about these women who have no chance for an "inheritance" from a system which claims to be just? Their children are wearing shoes with holes in the soles which are a half size too small; meals consist of macaroni from a box and peanut butter on white bread, with some out-of-date mint jelly which was given to them at the church food pantry. The children have raggedy underwear, except for the littler ones who do not have any underwear at all. When these women stand in line at the check-out with their food stamps, people stare in judgment at their choices. How dare they buy cookies? Our society has decided that only certain people deserve a free ride. Some widows, for example, receive Social Security benefits forever; their monthly payments are larger than welfare, and they are not required to search for work. Certain farmers receive welfare for not raising certain crops. Banks receive welfare in the form of financial assistance and tax breaks. Corporations receive welfare in the form of tax abatements if they locate in a certain town. The airline industry received *fourteen billion dollars* in welfare after September 11, 2001. Armament factories receive welfare in the form of over-inflated contracts. If a corporation goes belly-up, the executives are taken care of. These accommodations sound like welfare for the wealthy. But, if a young mother runs away from a man who beats her, sends her to the hospital, and threatens to kill her next time, we call her a freeloader if she asks for public assistance.[41] Perhaps we should ask Yahweh if poor single mothers should be paid for the important occupation they have of rearing our children. What do we think Yahweh would say?

Preaching a sermon about the requirements of justice and then mercy might reproduce in the experience or consciousness of the congregation the meaning field of the text. Such a sermon would also mean something theological for today. Do our congregants think Yahweh was more concerned about Hoglah than Yahweh is about Shirley, who lives across the street, is rearing her daughter alone, and could not afford to ride to the hospital in the ambulance her neighbor called when the daughter confided her mother had been sick for more than a week and was too weak to walk, because the driver said her Medicaid might not cover the trip?

So, what structure might we create from our analysis and this field of meaning? Here is a possibility:

1. History is over full with desperate women.
2. We know God loves each person.
3. So, we think justice is enough.
4. But, Yahweh demands we learn mercy.

From this structure we could look seriously at the difference between doing what society might easily call justice and what Yahweh calls mercy.

Perhaps this is a good place for the reader to pause and develop a structure for the passage from which one is preparing to preach.

---

[41] For additional information about the tenuous and unjust situation many poor mothers face, see Theresa Funiciello, *Tyranny of Kindness: Dismantling the Welfare System to End Poverty in America* (New York: Atlantic Monthly Press, 1993).

Moves

Once we develop a basic structure for the sermon, we need to think about fleshing out those basic sentence ideas. We call each of the basic sentences a *move start*. The individual parts we are ready to develop are called the *moves*. Each move consists of only one main idea, the idea expressed by the basic sentence. For example, Move Start 2 above, "We know God loves each person," is the singular idea of the second move. All material in that section of the sermon supports that idea's forming firmly in the consciousness of the congregation. One of the most painful and common complaints about sermons is, "She wandered all over the place. I'm sure she had worked hard, had good ideas and all, but I didn't really grasp it." Like most preachers, we want the congregation to grasp the meaning of the sermon. Keeping the content of each section or move limited to the single idea of the move start will help the idea to form in the consciousness of the congregation. All material which is not about that one idea needs to be eliminated. Once formed firmly, it will allow the congregation to follow us to the idea of the next move.

Before looking at the development of a specific move, here are some general guidelines. Experts believe it takes about three and a half minutes for an idea to form in the consciousness of a group. Then after about four minutes on the same idea, the consciousness of the congregation begins to wander. So, the single-idea sections of the sermon that we are calling moves need to be between three and a half and four minutes in length.

Another important guideline is that the preacher needs to paint the images for the congregation or they will not see what we want them to. Images are crucial to our thinking. Some folks even argue we think in images. We may have abstract ideas and label them with imageless terms, but the images are there in our thinking and remembering. The preacher needs to be clear what she means with the images she constructs for the congregation. For example, "She leaned slowly into the door to close it, hating the squeak that always preceded the click." We picture a person at the door; we hear the squeak and the click. The preacher has created the image for us, images of sight and sound; and the image, as brief as it was, had meaning—some sense of secrecy perhaps, or just frustration at the old noises she always heard. We want the meaning of our preaching to stick in the minds of our people; images help us do that.

Some additional helpful notes: keep thinking to limit the range. We want depth and power. Our moves are drilling for understanding. Those who drill for water do not use a shovel truck or land mover; they use a specialized drill bit. We want depth, not breadth in the individual moves. One way to keep the focus limited is to keep mindful of the single idea of the move. Seminarians and other academics have a unique tendency when they write for reading; they frequently use doublets. However, in spoken communication, asking people to consider "this" and "that" splits their focus. Dividing the attention of listeners makes it too complicated for them to follow the progression of the sermon. Even more than individuals, group consciousness cannot see two things at once. As we write for hearing, we want to eliminate as many doublets as possible.

This inability to visualize two things at once is a key reason I oppose the use of first-person story in preaching.[42] When we begin talking about our own experience, even the most mundane event, the congregation leaves off thinking about the sermon ideas and begins thinking about us.[43] As with the use of doublets, the consciousness of the congregation cannot hold two ideas at once. As a result, both may drop from consciousness, or the congregation's attention may be only on us. The most significant problem with the use of personal story in the pulpit, whether we are trying to illustrate a point or establish our authority or connect with the congregation, is that it makes *us* the focus of attention. Preaching is not primarily about us. It is inappropriate to have the response to the sermon be "He's like us" or "She has a real call" (which translates, "She has authority"). The sermon needs to have God as the focus, not the preacher's healing, not my right to preach, not my legitimate demand for authority in the congregation. Preaching is about *God*. It is about proclaiming the absolute unconditional grace of God poured out with divine abundance on every living thing.

Let me make sure I have expressed this idea correctly. The sermon needs to be about God, but if it is to be meaningful, we need to understand how humanity fits into God's vision and plan, so obviously people need to have a place in the sermon. However, what I am claiming is that we need to keep the sermon from being about the preacher, so although

[42] Bond argues, additionally, that personal story allows the congregation to see experience as "a valid norm by which to adjudicate theological claims" (Bond, *Trouble with Jesus,* 26).

[43] This is why so many people can report little pieces of information about their pastor's upbringing, family vacations, pets, and so forth. Listen as people leave worship. They share back similar incidents ("I had a dog that ran away, too. Boy I loved that dog. We think he got hit by a car.") completely separate from what the aim of the sermon was. When these items are used as sermon illustrations, their meaning separates from the idea they are supposed to be "illustrating." The anecdote of the pastor's life sticks, but the meaning of the story in supporting the idea of the movement of the sermon is lost.

first-person plural stories are acceptable, first-person singular stories are not. Appropriately, we can speak of the painful rejection some women have received from the church, but not the specific painful experience the preacher had. In shorthand, our system has no place for "I statements" in the sermons.

One final guideline: the rule of three is a real rule. The communal consciousness of the congregation is not able to hold a list of four words or four images in a move. If your move has four parts, or if any part has four examples, pieces invariably drop out. This is not to say each move needs to have three parts. Especially for the most important or most powerful moves, the fewer pieces the better. That is, two examples are more effective than three; one is more effective than two. The sermon is stronger if we keep the rule of no more than three parts in each move.

Some additional guidance may assist our writing. Certain words tend to blank out in speech, for example, "one," "this," "that." In written language, we can write a whole paragraph, then refer to it as "this idea." If the reader needs to refresh her understanding, she can re-read it. But she cannot re-hear something. Oral language works differently. Try to omit uses of the words "this" and "that." They do not form. Also, sentences that begin with "it" usually fail to form. Sentences need firm starts. Then, get rid of any extra wordiness. Change "It never seems to fail that people need God in the end" to something direct, with a firm start: "People end up needing God"—same idea, much stronger sentence. Get rid of the "it" start; cut out the mush; keep the words that mean something. We must work on making our language interesting, use turns of phrase, expand our use of verbs. Especially at the beginning and end of the move, we need short, strong sentences. Of course, we do not want to preach the whole move in short sentences; it will sound choppy (and the resulting breathiness is especially deadly for women), but we need to keep from starting with weak words like "it." Work to make the sentences convey strong ideas. An exercise we might try when our rough draft of the sermon is finished is this: Go through our moves circling all the "its," "thats," "theres," and "thises." Then, try to get rid of them all. We will be amazed at how tight the move can become. Paring down the junk makes the meaning clearer, which is, after all, the goal.

Another helpful practice is to remember that spoken word sounds convey meaning. Listen to good poetry read out loud. The sounds mean; how the words meet the ear assists the creation of meaning. So, if we want to talk about the fierce love of God, we must use words which sound fierce—"God's love would take on a tiger in the densest thicket."

One needs to slow down to speak it. The densest thicket is impenetrable, after all. Hear the difference when we say instead, "God's love would face a she-bear in the shadowy woodlands." The *sounds* mean something different, even though the words mean very much the same. So, check the moves; determine what sounds would be most helpful: abrupt, hard sounds? lots of round vowels and lush diphthongs? sounds which ripple and roll along faster than regular speech? or distinct tones to slow separate sounds for the ear?

It might feel odd to try to follow such firm rules in writing the individual moves of the sermon, but we want to do everything we can to communicate the Gospel to our people. I invite the reader not to reject the guidelines just because they feel strange. Recognize they feel odd, but be willing to give them a try. Buttrick notes: "Being natural is not the purpose of homiletics; serving the neighbors in the gospel is."[44] Preaching has different rules to follow from when we write for someone to read. Writing for hearing has to follow the rules for hearing.[45] Our preaching also has different rules to follow because we are speaking to a group. We are used to one-to-one conversations, in which we can jump from topic to topic, leave sentences unfinished, stop each other, and even talk at the same time. Yet, still the meaning gets across. Even when talking to a small group, say, giving directions to a group of four, we can be pretty free. But once the group we are speaking to grows to more than a dozen, something happens. A group consciousness comes into existence. Then, whether we are preaching to forty or 250 or 3,000, certain listening traits become predictable in the group. Since we want our preaching to be effective, we pay attention to the traits which affect a group's listening.

Now, on to the construction of the actual move itself. We take one sentence of the basic structure. That sentence is the move start. It expresses the one idea of the whole move we are working on. One way to begin to concoct a move is to make a chart. In the first column, we need to give some serious thought to the single idea we want to communicate. Write down the move start. Is it straightforward, simple? Can we say it another way to communicate more clearly? Is it general enough to make sense? Does it have a theological component or implication? We might try writing the idea in several different ways, especially noting if there are theological pieces to consider. In the second column envision concrete

---

[44] Buttrick, *Homiletic,* 39.

[45] See H. Grady Davis, *Design for Preaching* (Philadelphia: Muhlenberg Press, 1958), especially "The Hearing Situation" in Chapter 10, 164–68, and "Writing for the Ear" in Chapter 15, 265–94.

images of the move idea. People yearn to see theological truth. Jot down illustrations. Perhaps stories or quotes we remember or quick images which seem to show the idea. This is the place to let our imagination have its way. List anything we can that explains or demonstrates the idea of the move start: old bumper stickers, Sunday school lessons, television advertisements, a statistic we learned in eighth grade, an experience from an urban vacation, that witty comment our niece made, something we read in seminary.[46] The third column is for noting roadblocks. What will keep our congregation from accepting this claim? There is an opposing idea out there. Is the barrier theological? something cultural? Only after we have worked on this chart are we ready to figure out a strategy for the move. That is, after the charting we are ready to plot the move.

Now we are ready to construct a chart for an actual move.[47] We can use the move start "We love to worship God together." The idea of the whole move is limited to the meaning of the sentence "We love to worship God together." Nothing else gets in the move. This means that we have to eliminate ideas like claims of the value of daily private devotional time or reminders of an earlier move about God's faithfulness.

So, in column one, can we say the idea in another way? Of course. We could say: "Our corporate worship is special," or "Gathering on Sunday morning is the highlight of the week," or "Our congregation loves to have church." We need to be aware that gathering in a particular building on a particular morning of the week does not mean we are actually giving the Creator the honor and glory and reverence the divinity deserves. We want to make sure the move focuses on worship of God, not fellowship with other members. In the second column we fill in concrete images, illustrations, examples, and quotes which show the idea. We might use kids around the campfire at summer camp, the bumper sticker "Follow me to First Christian Church," the candlelight Christmas Eve service, how the older members shuffle arm-in-arm through the snow to get here. There are many of these images and illustrations. Then we move to the third column asking, what are the roadblocks? We cannot pretend there is no counter-evidence to the idea that corporate worship is precious to people. Mrs. Marvel had a stroke two years ago and she still refuses to give up playing the piano for worship, so worship is torture. The Jeffersons fight every Sunday morning over getting to

---

[46] Any of these personal examples can be turned into anonymous stories in the actual writing of the sermon, to keep the congregation from focusing on the preacher's book reading habits, her vacation, her niece.

[47] Buttrick leads us through designing a move in *Homiletic*, 43–53.

worship on time. They arrive in worship, late, with battle fatigue. Hector sits in the choir loft and plans his weekly menu; Marlene sketches out the closing for her trial on Monday; Curtis naps about halfway back; the sermon once again wanders around beating people up for twenty-five minutes or so. Unfortunately, roadblocks can often present a longer list than the illustrations. However, if this is the case, it may indicate that the move start is not something we really believe. We cannot preach something we do not believe ourselves.

After working on the chart of our move idea, we are ready to set up a plot. We note two or three ways to make clear statements of the single idea. Then, we might use two or three examples of meaningful worship. However, we have to admit the existence of barriers to this idea. People have experiences where worship services are less than meaningful. To deny the barriers would only make people hesitant to accept the move idea. So, we give voice to the opposition people feel to the idea: "Even when we have dragged the kids out of bed, argued all the way here, and fall into the pew already exhausted, somehow offering God our worship refreshes us, maybe not always, but usually." Or: "We've all known occasions where musicians have made more noise than music, yet somehow the joy of worship comes through."

Then we think through the plot and see if it needs reworking. We might start with the image of kids around the campfire, then address the barrier by admitting we might arrive at worship irritated yet finding peace, then describe the presence of God experienced corporately at someone's funeral—a particular one (remember we have to image for them): "Remember how we gathered at Elder Sanders' homegoing? How much pain we all felt at losing him when no one was ready. But didn't the preaching and the choir and the family comments and our singing and praying together make us recognize his memory will always be among us? And didn't we almost see him singing with us at the very gates of heaven? At times like Elder Sanders' homegoing, we know the joy of worshiping the Eternal One together." Or we might ask them to remember some baptism, perhaps the first one in several years, or just last Easter (which would insure that almost everyone present at the sermon today was present then, since almost no one misses Easter). Whether we use a big event or a small one, we have to draw the congregants into the experience, enough to allow them to share the consciousness of the idea. Their re-experiencing Elder Sanders' homegoing has to defeat the power of the Sunday morning arguments. The barrier has to be overcome, since that is what holds them back from accepting the idea of the move.

With that practice of charting and plotting, we are ready to construct moves for an actual sermon. To begin, we take one of the ideas from the basic structure of the Manassite sisters passage. The sermon will be moving people toward mercy, but we can look at the idea of an earlier move, which we noted in the basic structure as "So, we think justice is enough." The idea comes from the biblical passage's showing that the Israelites had learned from Yahweh the necessity of making sure each family received a just inheritance through the male children. The single idea we want to form in the consciousness of the congregation is, "So, we think justice is enough." How else might we state that idea? We might say, "We believe equal distribution is fair"; or, "Giving everyone the same amount seems right"; or, "Who wouldn't agree that dividing something equally is fair? Justice is giving the same amount to each person." These sentences fill in the first column of our chart, rephrasing and clarifying what we mean by the move start sentence.

In the second part of the chart, we fill in images and other support material. We learned in childhood that if there are six children, the cantaloupe is cut into six pieces; if eight children, eight pieces. Another item to note is the Israelite land distribution policy. Every family received land, which passed from father to son. In our modern world, we consider it just that each person pays the same sales tax on items. Most folks think it is appropriate for poorer families to receive aid for college education, because it makes the "playing field" a bit more level. Something within us is troubled when Bill Gates' "worth" is announced. It does not seem "fair" for one family to have such wealth. We remember the bumper sticker: "Live simply so others may simply live."

The third column contains the barriers to the idea. Even though something within us wants fair distribution, we really admire Bill Gates. We would like to be Oprah, recently announced to be a billionaire. In responding to the biblical tradition, we suspect giving all the land to the eldest son is not actually going to be just. In the modern world, many secretly (or publicly) resent the assistance given to the poor, especially able-bodied persons of another race. Our selfishness kicks in whenever we tussle with justice issues. And, besides, who can really say what is just?

Now, from this material on the chart, we pick and choose to plot a move on the one idea. See all the possibilities? We could concoct a number of totally different move plots from our brief time thinking about the one idea. Once the move is plotted, we would go on to make a chart for the next move. From that chart, we would be ready to sketch the plot of that move. Following this process, we chart and plot each move of the sermon.

Now would be the appropriate time to stop and make charts for each move start from our basic structure (the basic conversation). Then we must decide what pieces from the chart we will use to plot each move. Once the individual moves are plotted, we are ready to construct a full sketch of the sermon. For clarity, we might number our moves and write the move starts in bold. Under each move start, we would repeat the idea of the move in a second sentence (sometimes even a third). Then we would develop more fully the pieces chosen to fill in the move. At this stage we are constructing a sketch, which can still be changed if, for example, we decide one of the moves is too full, or images in different moves are too similar, or the material in a move does not actually support the move idea. We can easily fix these problems at this stage. But, before we finish the sketch and are ready to write the full sermon manuscript, we need to consider points of view and then work on the introduction and conclusion.

Point of View

In addition to the hermeneutical work with Scripture passages, there are other considerations in dealing with perspective in the sermon. We need to think through a "point of view" for each move, which assists in getting the moves to form in the consciousness of the congregation.

So, we need to remind ourselves what point of view is. We probably remember from college literature class that basically, point of view is merely deciding who is going to tell the story: first-person plural, third person, an omniscient source. In a move, point of view begins with determining whether it is from "our" first-person plural view, or "they" or "you." (And, of course, since we are writing our own sermon, we choose the point of view.) But point of view is more than source. Think of a camera shot. The camera can show the whole room or merely one little object, however the camera operator decides. The preacher must set the perspective, for even the point of view is able to serve the Gospel. We are passing on to the congregation what we hope they will see, think, and feel from the specific point of view we establish.

Some of us may find it disconcerting to realize we have all that responsibility. But every sermon—thus, every move—has a point of view. That is, each has a place from which the subject matter is projected. We can make the point of view work for the Gospel message by choosing it and crafting it, or we can just let whatever point of view happens to get written into the sermon be whatever it is and do whatever it wants. It makes sense to create a perspective which is in the service of the Gospel. Establishing point of view, after all, does not take away a person's right to disagree or reject our point of viewing, or even our interpretation of the Gospel.

Just as word-sounds convey meaning, so does point of view. Where we stand in relation to our subject conveys meaning. For example, we might consider preachers who attempt to convey an objective observation of the faith; that is, they talk *about*. They preach as though their looking at a topic can take place outside the arena. But we are all standing someplace, looking at one thing rather than another. In addition, attempting to be somehow objective is inappropriate when discussing the faith. God should not be treated as an object for our study during worship. Mary was not objective when she came flying down the hill yelling, "I have seen the Lord. He is risen!" Whenever we discuss the faith we do so from a particular perspective. Any speech, any consciousness, in fact, is oriented in time and space. We always have a point of view, although it can change in a moment. It is appropriate to use our language to shape what the congregation receives from the sermon. Buttrick claims that *"Perspectival language forms the consciousness of a congregation;* it shapes congregational point of view."[48]

As we maneuver on in our sermon construction, we think through the point of view we need according to the idea and strategy of the move. How can we do that? Sometimes we can send out cues and signals which obviously establish the perspective of our speaking, as in the case where we note, "Many of you may remember simple days of summer vacation spent at Grandma's." The words tell the position of the consciousness of the move. What we say directly establishes from where the story or material is told.

But we can use ingredients other than direct cues. Whenever we speak, perspective or point of view is there. We need to learn how to shape and control the points of view our speaking implies. To help think through the varieties of different categories for point of view, I use material from David Buttrick, who sets up a number of point of view categories and angles of perception.[49] His list includes stance (whence we speak), orientation (the direction of our intending, for example, we may move back in time, sweep around the room, or move inside our psyche), distance (visual, spatial, temporal, attitudinal, emotional, treating the past as ancient or recent, for example), focal field (parallels camera

[48] Ibid., 61.
[49] Buttrick discusses point of view categories in ibid., 57–65.

lens, but of space and time—all the starving people or folks lined up at an urban mission for Easter dinner), lens depth (degree of self engagement), focal depth (the distance of seeing into people and things).

In addition to these angles of perception, point of view can express attitude. We can choose to talk *about* a person's reaction to a situation, like "Martha was upset when her sister abandoned her kitchen duties to sit at their teacher's feet." Or we can "give voice" to the reaction: "Martha slammed the plates onto the table, glaring at Mary absorbing the fleeting words their teacher shared." Especially when we give voice to the congregation's questions or anger, when we speak their feelings and attitude, the sermon becomes theirs. Giving voice can also make the position clearer. The congregation feels and sees what we invite them to feel and see, so they know better what we mean.

Although point of view may vary in the sermon, each move of the sermon needs to have a single point of view. We need to establish the point of view early in the move, then keep it consistent throughout the one move, although the angle may shift (that is, we might move farther back in history, deeper into a psychological investigation, or more and more joyous).

We can use the story of the widow of Nain (Luke 7:11-17) to work on a sermon exercise for point of view. After we have figured out the basic structure, have charted each move and are working on sketches for each move, we are ready to add in considerations of point of view. If, in one move, we try to have a perspective of both the celebrating crowd of rowdy Jesus-people, carousing into town and also the funeral procession of the boy whose mother, a widow, has no hope of survival, the move easily splits into pieces. Each part is too brief to form. One solution would be to establish another vantage point first, which allows a look at each group. For example, we could invite the congregation to sweep the scene. "Look at the city of Nain, where two processions are about to cross paths. One is a rowdy, celebrating group, the other a funeral procession, where the worst thing that can happen to a widowed mother has happened." We need to control the point of view so the congregation does not have its consciousness scattered. We need to have only one point of view in a single move. Remember the angle of the point of view can move in or out or forward in time or place, but it cannot change. If we want the people to feel the crush of the world, we get right in their face with images which are crushing. But we cannot get them to feel the crush of the widow's loss and the merrymaking of the Jesus crowd in one move. So we ask: What do we want the people to feel—the joy or the crush of death? We can have only one point of view per move.

However, sermons appropriately vary perspective from move to move. If in the first move we give the broad overview, noting the celebrating disciples and the funeral, we do not want the congregation to feel too intensely one or the other. We are overviewing, after all, not just how Nain is, but how the world is, how life is. "Life is an ironic mix of people's experiences. Some folks seem to glide from one party to the next; other folks seem to experience one heart crushing event after another."

In the next move, we might use point of view to hone in on the experience of those who do get smacked down time after time. Those who feel the full weight of life's crushing circumstances which are too much to bear, and yet they bear them. The point of view could get as close as the face of the widow whose son is dead. She does not even cry. All of her energy is focused on putting one foot in front of the next, and then the other foot, and then the other again. The vantage point must stay on her, not backing up to see any of her relatives in the procession, because this woman, no matter how many people surround her with sympathy, is absolutely, crushingly, alone.

The third move, where we want to reproduce in the consciousness of the congregation the joy of having her son restored to her, must be huge. The pain of our close look at her absolute solitude must be overcome by this move. Our point of view in the second move took us right into the bloody hell of her life. Some of the congregation lives there, too. So, we cannot take the sermon there if we cannot bring them home safely. The third move must recover. If they are not going to end with joy, we cannot preach this passage. It is too painful. It would be unfaithful (and cruel) to indicate that Jesus cared enough about the widow of Nain to restore *her* son to life, unless there is also a hopeful, even glorious, word for the mothers in the congregation who have seen their sons' blood spilled out on the sidewalk and who know the walk to the grave. If we want to preach the passage, but find that we cannot reproduce the joy of the restored son, then we have to find an alternative structure. If we cannot reproduce a legitimate consciousness of victory over death, we have to preach a different idea in move three. One alternative would be to have the third move make a dramatic change in point of view. Have God's divine point of view correspond to the mother. Communicate how the excruciating pain of the mother is exactly what Jesus feels. How he wishes he could reach down to our sons, sprawled out on the bloody sidewalk and say "Get up." But Jesus knows it does not work that way. The pavement lynchings go on, and Jesus, too, is crushed by the ungodly loss of all those precious lives. We may or may not be able to make an allusion to the procession Jesus faces after Nain on his own trip to Golgotha. God knows the excruciating pain of the senseless deaths of sons and daughters throughout the world.

Then we need a fourth move, obviously. What will it do? It has to recover from both the second and third move. The final move now needs to be a challenge to the church to figure out how to stop the killing. The point of view needs to be straightforward, perhaps very little emotion—just determination that the holy thing to do is get the killing to stop, no matter what it takes.

Now we might take the sketch of our sermon moves and add notes of what point of view considerations we want in each move. What kind of perspective do we want? What sounds will help? How deep do we want to peer? What will we avoid?

Introductions and Conclusions

Introductions have two functions, according to the system we are using.[50] First, they establish the hermeneutical orientation of the sermon. That is, they let the congregation know how Scripture is being read and interpreted in this sermon. The introduction reveals what hermeneutical key is being used to open the passage for them. For most of us, we want our people to understand that our interpretation of Scripture is not necessarily a literal one, yet we believe the Bible contains divine truth. Marti Steussy[51] once put it this way: "Just because something didn't happen doesn't mean it isn't true." The Bible can be heard as God's truth without being considered a history book. So, the introduction first shows how we are opening Scripture. For example, if we begin with a story of the man who discovered what he believed to be the remains of Noah's ship, high in the Himalayas, and we show him kissing the decaying boards, explaining he was not worshiping them but rejoicing at being able to handle this ancient treasure of God's direction, we are setting up a hermeneutic of literal interpretation. According to this introduction, the Bible is a history book. If we begin with a Hindu myth about Vishnu's many incarnations and tell it as a meaningful folktale, the congregation can easily translate the interpretation to Christian Scripture. So, in introductions which use examples of great art, mysteriously containing yet revealing the great truths of the universe, we show

---

[50] Buttrick discusses introductions in ibid., 83–96.

[51] Steussy is the MacAllister-Petticrew Professor of Biblical Interpretation at Christian Theological Seminary in Indianapolis, Indiana.

reverence for the book without binding it to the role of a history book. The introduction provides the hermeneutic orientation for the sermon.

Second, the introduction gives focus to consciousness. We bring the congregation's consciousness onto a whole field of meaning, and then get them ready for the first move. I have an image of a team of horses. In the introduction, we take the reins of the individual thinking processes in the congregation and hitch everyone together into one consciousness, moving them together into one shared field of meaning, specifically pointing them toward the first move.

A preponderance of sermons begins with the mistaken notion that introductions must get attention. Preachers seem particularly fond of introductions which have nothing substantially to do with the meaning of the sermon. My experience is that our people are already paying attention. They are leaning forward eager for the sermon to teach them something important. They are looking to us for a word from God. We do not need some catchy, cutesy story about what our toddler did this week to get their attention. We have their attention. Some cutesy story may, in fact, serve to deflate their anticipation. They want God, not cutesy. It does take a sentence or two for them to get oriented to our presentation, but we already have their attention. So our first sentence does not have much essential content, but it still needs to be working toward the whole of the sermon meaning. We are pulling the congregation together into a single consciousness. The introduction helps them focus on the field and gets them ready for the first move.

Some details: an introduction should be between seven and twelve sentences long (yes, count them). As strange as it might seem, seven to twelve sentences are boundaries for a helpful introduction. The material in the introduction should be familiar to the congregation. Take into account who they are and whether we are speaking in a language they can understand. Following the last word of the introduction, we give the longest pause in the entire sermon, cuing the congregation that the body of the sermon is beginning. Studies show attention is most acute following a full pause. Preachers might as well use it.

Conclusions are not as easily defined, although they, too, must do two things.[52] The obvious thing they do is conclude the sermon. That is, conclusions must stop the sermon. Of course, this makes the last sentence of the conclusion especially important. We can use some form of repetition in the last two sentences, but I find a short, tight declarative sentence works best.[53]

[52] Buttrick, *Homiletic,* discusses conclusions, 97–109.
[53] "The last, brief sentence in a sermon should simply stop" (ibid., 103).

Conclusions also have a second task, but this is the less easily defined part. Conclusions must assist the intention of the sermon. They "fix" the meaning in consciousness. Buttrick says, "Conclusions are simple systems of language. They will fix consciousness, fulfill an intention, and quit."[54] If the basic structure of the sermon can be compared to crossing a brook stone by stone, then the conclusion can be compared to a stop-action photo of the crossing. It lays out a "stopped, reflective consciousness in a congregation."[55] Conclusions must not rehearse the walk across the stream. We do not merely repeat the move starts. Conclusions give a different perspective of the whole crossing. Canadian homiletician David Jacobsen[56] likens conclusions to a painting of the meaning of the sermon, as if the preacher were saying, "Here we are when we understand the sermon." Conclusions show the intention of the sermon fulfilled. If we want our congregation to be empowered to advocate for the poor, our conclusion needs to galvanize their energy. If the intention is to get the congregation on its feet in awe of the grace of God, we need a stop-action moment of "Wow." Conclusions "set" the meaning like a good custard.

Some folks have a habit of not writing out the conclusion, believing that the spirit of the moment will help them conclude most powerfully. However, experience argues the opposite. A well-written, tight conclusion ends the sermon with a powerful support for the entire meaning. We have all heard sermons that just dribbled off. What a shame! I once heard a person in the narthex say, "The preacher had three or four good endings for her sermon. I wish she had stopped after the first one of them."

One sure way to paralyze the outcome of a sermon is to use a conclusion which circles back to the introduction. Years ago, preachers loved this technique. Stand-up comedians still use it, closing with some joke which brings the consciousness of the audience back to their first joke. But preaching is not the same as stand-up. We want movement from where the congregation began. Our task is not merely to walk their consciousness around the park and send it home. We want to lead them someplace new. The circle-back conclusion leaves the congregation feeling contented, complete, and satisfied—right back where they started. Actually, one reason circle-back sermons are popular may be because the congregation feels so good at the end: no threat, no new territory to deal

---

[54] Ibid., 98.

[55] Ibid., 101.

[56] David Jacobsen used this phrase while still a Ph.D. candidate at Vanderbilt University.

with, no challenge, no growth. However, such a comfortable ending is not accurate to the Gospel.

A few details about conclusions: keep them in our own voice (no quotes); use simple, direct talk (the language of childhood may actually communicate best); utilize simple nouns and verbs; cut out the flowery adjectives and adverbs (we need to have picture language, that is, conclusions need to be concrete); let the congregation see what we mean (they need to grasp our intention; conclusions fulfill the intention and stop the sermon).

This is a good place to stop reading and write out a sketch of ideas for the introduction and conclusion. When this is added to the sketch of the moves, including the point of view notes, we have a full sketch of the sermon. Here we can rearrange, delete, change, and expand the various pieces before the final writing. Before turning to the task of writing out the manuscript, a brief look at imagistic language assists the process.

Imagistic Language

We turn now to images, metaphorical language, and illustrations which are used in sermons to clarify, to put flesh on, the theological content. We are giving people an image which they can pull back up at a later time. But we want to ensure that when they recall it, the image has the theological idea still connected. So part of our work is to look at strategies for proper use of imagery.

There is a rash of narrative preaching these days by ministers who believe a story carries its own theological freight. They believe the story provides theological content to the congregation's consciousness. I contend a story alone does not fully communicate the Gospel. Imagistic language is appropriately used to serve the theological purposes of the sermon. Stories do not *make* the theological purpose. Certainly, sermons cannot form without images, but we must not expect imagery to do more than it can do. Images need theological bone structures to give them meaning.

We admit that story has always been important to human beings, but the sermon cannot just be a story. Our lives make sense as a story. Events are seen as part of a continuing series of events which constitute what each person means by "my life." The Christian faith maintains that God has come to earth in human flesh (in-carna-tion), so the *story* of Jesus Christ is at the heart of our learning the faith. In fact, one of the goals of the preacher is to help people understand their little life's story within God's big story. The point is not to see how God fits into our life, but rather understand how our lives, which we hold so dearly, fit into the life story of God who, by the way, holds us dearly too. We want to use images and story because Jesus comes as flesh to earth—flesh carrying the divine. Story is a natural way for us to learn the faith. In fact, any imagery, any figurative language, communicates in an incarnational way. It is natural to the faith of "God-with-us." Theological ideas need to be communicated. The theology is the skeletal system to the faith. Ideas give the faith structure and strength. But to put flesh (image) on those theological bones is crucial. Because of the power of image, however, we need to be careful how we use them.

Illustrations, like all the language in the move, are there to serve the one idea of the move. Any extra stuff in the illustration works against us. All too often, illustrations (stories) in sermons take on lives of their own. The story becomes the main "thing." Once the story becomes the focus, the idea becomes secondary. So, we want to *use* the illustration, not have the illustration use the rest of the move for its purposes. The illustration must be of a piece with the rest of the move. If it separates from the move, the congregation drops the logic. They may remember the illustration, but they will not remember what it illustrated. We keep the move together by making sure we avoid doing anything which might split off the congregation's consciousness. For example, introducing an illustration usually works against us. We want the illustration to work like a flashlight on the idea, not circling the air before it lands on what we want the congregation to see. We want the light from the illustration to zap right on the idea, so the people can see the idea. Another clue for keeping the illustration connected to the idea is brevity. One way to keep it brief is to write out the illustration, then cut everything which is not essential for showing the idea, limiting the whole illustration to five or six sentences. All the extra sentences which make for a great story might be expendable because we are not telling a *story,* we are illustrating an idea. The story is not going to carry the theological freight. We use the story to illustrate the theological idea.

Let me reiterate the warning against use of first-person stories. Of course, it is acceptable to give voice to our experiences, but in a way which invites the listener to consider ideas or situations, but not to focus on the preacher. We do that by avoiding first-person telling, using instead plural, inclusive language: "Each of us knows the embarrassment of family, like when our grandmother picks us up from school with a tissue tucked in the sleeve of her blouse and she calls us 'Sweet Baby' in front of the most popular kids." The members of the congregation can identify with the feeling, even if their embarrassing story has slightly different details. They recall their own teenage embarrassment instead of thinking about the pastor's grandmother. After all, sermons need to help the congregation know God. Illustrations and stories need to help people see *their* place in God's universal story. They certainly do not need to be gathering more cute little information about the pastor and her family. Anytime we use a first-person story to communicate something about the faith, we run the risk of having the listeners split their focus. They are thinking simultaneously about the faith and wondering about the pastor's life.

Writing the Manuscript

Here are some rules as we progress from our sketch of the moves to writing the full sermon. As we begin to write the first move, we need to write the single idea of the move twice at the beginning of the move. That is, we need to state the idea in two different sentences which mean the same thing. One key sentence does not work. Let's take our example: "We love to worship God together." The second sentence of the move would reiterate the exact idea in different words: "Nothing beats our Sunday morning gathering." You could even add a third sentence meaning the same thing: "Communal worship at First Church is the best." Congregations need several sentences to hear the idea. The sentences need to be short, with very few or no adjectives or adverbs. The first sentence must not be compound or have more than one idea. The idea sentence is called the *move start*. The move start sets the boundary and begins the formation of the idea. Then we construct the content. Of course, we cannot just define our theological ideas in the move. The congregation needs us to help them experience the subject, the meaning of the idea of the move. We write out the content of the move which we plotted in our sketch, paying attention to our own suggestions for point of view.

Since in each sermon we will be piecing together three, four, or even five moves (depending on the timing of a typical sermon in one's congregation), we want to shape each move with a different internal structure. That is, we want the moves to have different plots. Notice what this means: in the "We love to worship God together" move, we cited one example, then addressed a barrier, then developed a little more fully the illustration of the homegoing service. There are many possibilities of internal structures for moves, for example, we could list three examples; or we could give a definition, statistics, and an example; or we could give some explanation of the idea and then a bigger illustration. Lots of possibilities exist for internal patterns, but we need to limit our internal structure for a *move* to no more than three parts.

At the end of the move, we restate the idea of the move start in order to stop the move. We need again a short, direct sentence (it may even quote the move start exactly) to be the last sentence of the move. Just as we wanted the people to go with us to the new idea when we began the move, we want them to step off again when the time comes. The last sentence of the move must set the idea again, like closing the gate. Remember the move needs to be between three and a half and four minutes, from the move start sentence to the last sentence of the move which reiterates the move start idea.

Now we should stop and write out our full sermon manuscript.

4. EMBODIMENT/DELIVERY

Christian Theological Seminary bookstore manager Charles Allen reports a singular request about women preachers. People call the bookstore asking, "Is there a book on protocol for women's pulpit garb?" As much as we might hate to admit it, "presentation" is still an important issue. For women especially, what is worn in the pulpit matters. Male and female preachers need to become comfortable in whatever clothing they are going to be wearing regularly in the pulpit. We probably remember hearing about the country preacher who was invited to preach in a big city church one Sunday, and the lay leader invited him to wear a black preaching robe, which he did. After worship, the lay leader asked how he felt preaching in the robe. The man replied, "I think I would have been more comfortable in my pants." We need to find that balance between wearing what we are comfortable wearing, and making ourselves become comfortable in what we are expected to wear. There are robes, stoles, and even albs which are so ornate that wearing them seems purposely to shine a spotlight on the person, thus eradicating what some might say was one of the original intentions of clerical garb, namely to make the person invisible or at least anonymous. When I began teaching, I did not comment at all about pulpit attire, but each semester the questions come. I encourage preachers to wear whatever allows them to move freely, to gesticulate fully, and to bend over and sit without worrying about revealing any body parts.[57] As we shake hands with people after worship, we do

---

[57] Many preachers stand in long traditions of specific robes they are expected to wear for preaching, but this is not universal. I am surprised at the number of women who

not want anyone to remark how stunning they think we look in our robe. Is not the point to help the congregation get to know God better? Would we not prefer a comment about some new experience of divine grace? If we find people frequently commenting about our earring(s), we might consider leaving such jewelry in our study. I always say a word to students about making sure their shoes are comfortable. Men and women deserve to preach in shoes which are not hurting their feet. I discourage wearing shoes with pointed toes or high heels. The preacher wants to stand firmly, without any sense of tentativeness coming from not being completely balanced or comfortable.

A firm stance in the pulpit makes for a more confident presence. I encourage beginning preachers to stand with their feet slightly apart (maybe eight inches). Pay attention that we are not favoring one foot, for that will make us appear slightly off balance, not firm. Behaviors from nervousness such as rocking back and forth or shifting from one foot to the other can be overcome, and eliminating them will give the preacher a more solid appearance of authority. On occasion, we might ask a trusted friend to pay special attention to such behaviors and give feedback.

For those who are inclined to abandon the pulpit and preach from the chancel or nave, I urge reconsideration. Staying in the pulpit puts us in line with the great tradition of preaching. Those who choose to speak their messages strolling around the nave intend to give an air of accessibility and connection with the congregation; however, such behavior may actually just serve to make the Gospel appear less important. Homiletician Charles Rice reminds us of the power and continuity with the tradition of all those who have preached from these very pulpits. We do not preach in isolation, but in communion with those who have mounted the pulpit through the centuries and those who sit in the pews before us as we mount the pulpit today.[58]

It makes sense for beginning preachers to step into the pulpit with a full manuscript of their sermon. Each semester I have at least one student who argues she cannot preach from a full manuscript. I respond that students do not need to follow the manuscript word for word, but they must

---

are opting out of wearing robes or albs, in favor of suits or dresses. Although completely acceptable in certain congregations, we need to remember that we will not be standing behind the pulpit throughout the entire service. Many worship spaces have chairs in raised chancel areas, facing the congregation, where the preacher of the day is expected to sit. Attention to the length of hemline makes these seated experiences much more relaxed.

[58] See especially the discussion in Charles L. Rice, *The Embodied Word: Preaching as Art and Liturgy* (Minneapolis: Augsburg Fortress, 1991) 46.

have the manuscript. None of us is able to find every word we want on a moment's notice, and beginning preachers do not need the added pressure of having to compose (even from a detailed outline) in the pulpit. Congregations should not have that pressure either. A full manuscript is especially helpful in keeping the preacher, no matter how seasoned, on track and reminding her when it is time to sit down. The Holy Spirit is able to inspire the sermon as it is being written in the minister's study as well as in the pulpit. Unfortunately, it seems that often those who enter the pulpit without a full manuscript have done so because they have not fully prepared the message. Too many pastors allow other demands of the week to push sermon preparation to the end of the list of tasks. However, if almost every congregation cites preaching as one of the most important responsibilities of the minister, we must make room for adequate study, meditation, and preparation time. Making ourselves have a full manuscript every time we step into the pulpit is one way of ensuring that we have spent significant (even if not enough) time preparing the sermon.

Once the sermon is written, there are concerns about delivery. One of the most common answers to questions of pulpit presence and delivery has to do with connection to the preacher. People want eye contact. They want authenticity from the preacher. This does not mean the preacher needs to leave the pulpit. Quite the contrary. If the preacher remains in the traditional place, people are well able to make eye contact (the pulpit is constructed with visibility as a key component), and sense connection and authenticity. Those with imperfect voices or even annoying delivery habits are often excused if people feel a link to the messenger.[59]

In the classes I teach, we videotape the first sermon. Each student (individually) and I sit down to watch the tape together. During this viewing I first ask the student to comment about delivery, any particular things she appreciates or might want to work on or change. I try to offer praise about such things as good instincts for delivery and when the use of voice has been particularly effective. Additionally, I share ideas about what might make for better communication. The practice is not to "fix" her delivery, but to make each student aware of her own pulpit presence and habits. Occasionally I have to point out something the student ignores, such as a particular repetitive gesture or licking of the lips. After that, I leave it to the student to make the decision about what she corrects

---

[59] For additional responses from laity about delivery and sermon listening, see Mary Alice Mulligan and Ronald J. Allen, *Make the Word Come Alive: Lessons from Laity* (St. Louis: Chalice Press, 2005).

or modifies. Only the first sermon is taped. After that the student must learn how to ask for feedback, which is excellent preparation for the actual parish.

5. METHODS FOR RECEIVING FEEDBACK

Many preachers rely on the momentary feedback they receive while delivering the sermon, and the few words spoken as they shake hands at the church door to determine whether their preaching is on target. Although in some congregations a call and response pattern to the sermon allows for quite a bit of information to be communicated to the preacher, even this practice has limits. Most parishioners would agree that sermon feedback during delivery or at the church door is insufficient, yet few congregations have in place any other method for communicating with the pastor specifically about preaching.

As intimidating as the idea might be, some additional form of feedback is highly desirable, both for allowing the congregation to articulate their experience in the pew and for making the minister better able to proclaim the Gospel message. I encourage pastors to work with their congregational boards or pastoral relations committees to determine a method. Each congregation may need to try several methods before striking one which serves them well. Some preachers merely open a time after worship once every other month or so for congregational feedback. Anyone who wants to give a comment is invited to share an opinion over a cup of coffee in the announced Sunday school classroom. At the opposite end from this occasional, informal method is a highly organized system of sharing sermon preparation and response, such as the technique set out by John McClure.[60]

A congregation may decide to try something between these extremes. For example, the board may invite twelve to fifteen people into a two-month process with the pastor. The group meets once (but not on Sunday) to clarify the structure, to pass out a list of the Scriptures for the next two months, to talk about the congregation and what sermons should do, and end with a commitment from each person to attend four additional sessions, every other Sunday after worship. During the Sunday sessions they give feedback to the preacher: they tell what they heard in the sermon, report how they believe the sermon served the congregation,

---

[60] See John S. McClure, *The Round-table Pulpit: Where Leadership and Preaching Meet* (Nashville: Abingdon Press, 1995).

and share what the preacher might want to do differently next time. After the four, every-other-week sessions, that group is finished. Skip two months and have the board invite twelve to fifteen new persons into the two-month process. Such a commitment is brief enough that people do not feel imprisoned, yet it is significant enough that they will be able to say important things. Such a system of feedback invites about forty laity a year to concentrate on preaching. It teaches them about sermons, so they listen differently, and the pastor receives feedback from forty people. Probably those involved in the process will discuss sermons more easily with other parishioners and the minister on other occasions as well.

6. HOMILETIC CONVERSATIONS

Theology of Preaching

Within the opening weeks of the semester, I give a lecture on theology of preaching. It corresponds to the time we are reading Susan Bond's book, *Trouble with Jesus*. I return to the topic during the final week of class, and the students' final assignment is to write their own theology of preaching paper. The reader may consider the value of stopping at the end of this section and outlining her own theology of preaching ideas.

A local parish may have many activities, but the one focal point week after week is Sunday morning worship. And in that service, the preaching event is the one time people expect to hear something about God, the Bible, and their lives. Because of this standard pattern, most homileticians agree that congregations receive whatever theological instruction and formation they do primarily from preaching.[61] Preaching is doing something theological. Bond claims that "Preaching is theological by virtue of its method, arguing for a particular vision of truth within a particular group of people, in order that that group will shape its common identity and projects around that particular vision of truth."[62] Preaching is where the people are taught theology, in two crucial ways. First, they receive theological concepts and ideas from the pastor's preaching. Her sermons make theological claims and the people receive them. Second, sermons model theological method. Our preaching shows appropriate ways to reason theologically. Our preaching must model how we *do* theology; it is not just making theological claims.

---

[61] See, for example, Bond, *Trouble with Jesus,* 3; Buttrick, *Homiletic,* 19.
[62] Bond, *Trouble with Jesus,* 17.

If we agree that something happens in the preaching event, then both our theological creativity and precision in the pulpit can be a tremendous benefit (assistance) for encouraging maturation in the faith of the congregation. Preaching renames or re-identifies reality within the consciousness of the congregation. Like the city children taken out into the woods, the preacher points to the world and says, in effect, not just "plants," but slippery elm, sassafras, nightshade, and poison ivy. Some of these "plants" are harmful, and some are very helpful. In the same way, the pastor might rename the board of a bankrupt corporation whose employee retirement plans are now worthless but whose board members' fortunes grew after bankruptcy, as not "displaying the very best side of capitalism," as one Bush administrator claimed. However, such renaming is theologically weak, even deceptive. It is more appropriate to rename these board members as deceitful, greedy, and deeply wrong. When those who have the least are hurt by those who have the power, the behavior of the rich and powerful must be renamed: sin.

Theology is the study of the divine. Who is God? What is God about? How are we related to the divine? What do we mean by holy? How do we judge what is good and what is sinful? These are the kinds of issues we need to be discussing from the pulpit, every week. But this is not a reason to panic. Every sermon does not have to be a formal theological argument for the existence of God, followed by a formal discussion of the ethical implications of that claim. But if our people are going to learn something about God, and learn how to think about what we are teaching them about God, we need to model it for them.

Our preaching names God's presence in the world. As we worship together in God's presence, we are forming a common identity, an alternative consciousness, which then extends beyond the Sunday service. Our preaching invites people into a sub-culture or into a place where we see the world from an alternative perspective. We begin to see the world through the lenses which sermons help grind. In time, we come to see the world day by day through that consciousness.

Of course, as important as the rhetorical considerations of sermon construction are, we must also understand the importance of theology for homiletics.[63] The practical aspects of oral communication theory are

---

[63] Teresa Lockhart Stricklen traces why homiletics is not seen as belonging with pure theology in theological education, much to the detriment of the local church. See her "An Early History of the Separation of Preaching and Theology" in *The Academy of Homiletics, Appendix to the Papers of the Annual Meeting "Teaching Preaching"* (St. Louis, 2001) 20. This paper presents parts of her dissertation work.

merely part of what must be considered if preaching is to matter. Sermons must be theologically grounded; they must have appropriate biblical study and hermeneutical interpretation; they must have reasoned ethical and moral implications; and they must be rhetorically sound. To separate theology, ethics, biblical study, and the rhetoric of preaching does a terrible disservice to the preacher, to the congregation, and to the faith.[64]

As we think about learning to preach, the theological piece is crucial. How we present the faith shapes the life of the congregation. Jesus promised life, abundant life, available now. Our people learn it from the pulpit. Also we need to catch the importance of keeping our sermons theologically informed. Sermons are not little Bible studies or pulpit therapy to help our congregants have stress-free lives, although that is what some congregations are getting week by week from the pulpit. Our sermons need to be doing theology, modeling theology, interpreting Scripture, and ethically challenging changes in behavior. In short, sermons need to be creating lenses to see the whole world according to the faith. Our sermons, week after week, will be utilizing every class taken in seminary and all the good reading we continue to do after graduation.

One of the first things we need to do as we contemplate our own theology of preaching is determine our basic theological claims and norms. Various theologians suggest establishing norms such as credibility, theological appropriateness, and moral plausibility.[65] In light of such norms, Bond sets up two essential theological claims which she considers normative for her theology of preaching. The first is the claim "that God is unconditionally compassionate toward all of creation," which includes each living thing, particularly every person. The second is the claim that "God is unconditionally and passionately engaged in luring the world toward justice."[66] These two foundational claims undergird all other theological claims, all interpretations of Scripture, all assertions about the faith, and all moral and ethical directives. It is important for preachers to articulate to themselves their basic claims and know what norms are at work. If we react negatively to the stated norms and/or

---

[64] There is an exciting reversal stirring in some seminaries, especially within some Roman Catholic circles, to reconnect the various fields of theological education again, often seeing homiletics as the centering focus for the entire process of seminary education. Homiletics may be viewed as the heart of theological education because it calls on all the other "fields" to accomplish its task. Thus, preaching may be seen in coming years as the engine driving the curriculum.

[65] See, for example, Clark Williamson, *A Guest in the House of Israel: Post-holocaust Church Theology* (Louisville: Westminster John Knox, 1993) 18–25, especially 21.

[66] Bond, *Trouble with Jesus,* 29.

claims, this is a good time to stop and write out our own norms and basic claims. What is most basic about being a Christian?

From the basic claims and theological norms, we can then make claims about who Jesus Christ is and what the appropriate Christian response is to God's compassion for all and passion for justice. These are the statements which will be undergirding our preaching. In light of God's compassion and passion, and then in light of understanding a particular theme or part of Scripture, what is the divine word for this congregation at this time? Of course, we must be aware that the word we preach is not only to satisfy those seated before us. We must assist their growth, acknowledging that Christianity has been an oppressive presence as well as a liberative one not only for women, but also for the poor, the dispossessed, the infirm, the alien, and the outcasts. So it also becomes important for us to be aware of the history of the faith. From our awareness of how Christianity has been ill used, we are able to assess, in light of our norming claims, what word needs to be proclaimed at this time. One area which is particularly important to think through carefully is Christology. We might look at the models Bond discusses. She emphasizes the preaching of Jesus as proclaiming the Realm of God. She rejects the traditional substitutionary atonement theory and embraces what she calls the "primitive *Christus victor*" model.[67] Following these ideas, we might claim that the theological norms of God's compassion for the world and passion for justice, which we learn throughout Scripture but especially through the life, death, and resurrection of Jesus Christ, mean that our preaching encourages those who claim to be Christian to have unparalleled compassion for all of creation, with a special passion for helping the world move toward justice. Chung Hyun Kyung describes her theological norm when she explains her mother's uneducated theology. "Maybe she did not know what was orthodoxy and what was heresy, but she *did* know which things offered life-giving power . . . . 'Life-giving power' is the final criterion by which the validity of any religion is judged."[68] She has put her basic claim in different words, but it is certainly in line with God's compassion for all and passion for justice. Is what is going on in the manifestations of our faith, life-giving or life-taking, increasing abundant life or restricting persons' ability to live fully?

[67] Ibid., 39–48.

[68] Chung Hyun Kyung, "Following Naked Dancing and Long Dreaming" in *Inheriting our Mothers' Gardens: Feminist Theology in Third World Perspective*, ed. Letty M. Russell, Kwok Pui-lan, Ada María Isasi-Díaz, Katie Geneva Cannon (Louisville: Westminster John Knox Press, 1988) 65, 67.

For our preaching, we move from these basic norming claims to determine what we need to do in the pulpit. Right in line with the basic claims, we are aware that our preaching continues the preaching of Jesus Christ. We have been commissioned by the risen Christ to go on our way (which is actually his "Way") preaching. Then, we need to know what was Jesus' preaching about?

One of the key Scriptures we might look to for guidance is 2 Corinthians 5:16-21. God was in Christ, reconciling the world back to Godself. Jesus' job was to reconcile the ones who could not possibly care less back to the One who loved them more than life itself. We stumble along our selfish paths, clinging to our possessions, making possessions of other people, sinning just because we want to, and Jesus comes crashing in. *We* are somehow suddenly square with God. Reconciliation is the term I most often use when I think of the Realm of God, the reigning of God.[69] God's will for the world is that *everything* is set right again, reconciled. Jesus' ministry inaugurated God's reigning. We who believe in Jesus Christ can already experience the Realm. Eventually God will have God's full way with the earth, and the reigning will be complete. Until then, we have been given a ministry, the ministry of reconciliation. We proclaim Jesus Christ, the One who reunites us with God. Of course, this does not mean we become divine. We are united, as squabbling family members may reconcile, become reunited, get square with one another. And we carry on the ministry.

So our people come limping into church, hoping against hope that they will hear a word of life from the Lord. We need to make sure they hear words of divine good news, which make a difference in their lives. However, I want to be very clear that because God is passionately luring the world toward justice, we need an understanding of the Gospel which is thoroughly communal. The Gospel has social implications. The *basileia* is a communal reality, not personal satisfaction or individualistic assurance, not making sure individuals accept Jesus into their individual lives so each one makes it to heaven.

I remember the joke about the hitchhiker who was picked up by a Texan in a huge Cadillac. On the front seat, the hitchhiker noticed a pair of very thick glasses. "Don't you think you should put on your glasses?" she asked. "No," the Texan replied, "The windshield is ground to my

---

[69] I appreciate Teresa Stricklen's clarification "that *basileia* connotes less a *place* than the term "kingdom" signifies to us and more of an activity—the *reigning* of God (Stricklen, "An Early History," 20).

prescription." We who call ourselves followers of the Way of Jesus Christ need to see the world through the prescription he grinds for us as we travel along together. We are not given individual prescriptions; the communal windshield is ground to the prescription of Jesus. It gives us a communal vision. Since none of us is able truly to see the world properly (that is, clearly), we all need to have our vision corrected. What keeps us from going off half-cocked into some dream-world vision? We must depend on the faith community. Christianity has a communal requirement. Christ calls us to be a reconciled community. We are *mutually* responsible for how we live out the faith.

The mutuality and community requirements of the faith are part of what should keep the faith theologically sound. It also keeps our preaching theologically sound. We need to keep in theological conversation with our congregation, with our denomination, with good books, especially those written by folks who hold the theological norms of God's compassion for all and passion for justice, which leads to a preferential option for the least.

What happens when people forget the reconciled community, to focus on their own individual salvation or personal therapeutic satisfaction, is a closed-off faith which centers on the self. In such a situation, the needs of the individual believer become the most important consideration. There are huge churches which focus on personal growth ministries and programs which aim at meeting the felt needs of individuals. They have afternoon sport teams with expensive outfits; parenting classes to help relieve stress; Saturday workshops on investments; Bible studies aimed at helping people feel happy in their lives. From programming aimed at the felt needs[70] of individuals in the congregation, it is only a short hop until the gospel of individual prosperity can take over. From there, we can have congregations of millionaires who congratulate each other on hostile takeovers of family businesses and huge stock market gains. Sound far-fetched? What do millionaires do on Sunday mornings? Lots of them go to church, and people hold them in high esteem and never challenge their fortunes. However, such self-serving faith bears striking resemblance to those who were condemned by Amos ("You sell the poor for a pair of shoes") in whose footsteps Jesus followed, saying, "Woe to you who are rich. You have your reward."

---

[70] For a helpful look at the history and implications of "felt needs" in the church, see John and Sylvia Ronsvalle, *Behind the Stained Glass Windows: Money Dynamics in the Church* (Grand Rapids: Baker Books, 1997 [© empty tomb, 1996]) 41–43.

Our basic theological claims have definite practical implications. That is, our theological claims make a difference (or should make a difference) in how we interpret both Scripture and events in the world. Part of the preacher's job is to interpret events for the congregation through the lens of our basic faith claims. Our faith must inform our moral understanding. Various theologians have reminded us that for the Gospel to be actual Good News, it must be good news to the powerless, the vulnerable, and the victimized. Those who are most precious to God must also be most precious to the Church. If we are involved in hurting people by supporting the fat cats at the expense of the least, the last, and the lowest, the church must speak against our behavior. God's *basileia* is tending toward justice. God has a preferential option for the least. So must the Church. Our preaching must make this theological and ethical connection. The unfair distribution of power and necessities means many people do not have enough to survive. They do not have enough water, food, warmth, medicine, safety—not enough even to live. How much would our average church people have to give up to get to the place where they did not have enough? Money (in the form of possessions) and power are crucial matters for the church, and thus for the pulpit. But before we go lambasting folks from the pulpit, we have to get our own thinking straightened out.

Distribution of power and resources is not the real problem. Misunderstanding resources and power is problematic. Through the years people have viewed power (and possessions) from a zero-sum perspective. That is, if this person gets one more thing, it means I get one less, because there is a limited number of things. If someone gets more, I get less, so I scrape and scramble for everything I can. This is particularly dangerous when the "possession" is power. The fear is that the more power one has, the more vulnerable the other is. If someone has more, I have less. This is zero-sum power perspective. Such a view is decidedly Western in its individualistic understanding of the world. But we see it displayed in many cultures now. We plan first strikes, so no one can hurt us. We stockpile power, so others know we are more powerful than they.

Some years ago Sally Purvis attempted to clarify two different ways of perceiving power. The traditional view was what we might call "power over." This is power as domination. A person would hesitate to hit another because that person may hit back harder. Purvis called it "Power as control."[71]

---

[71] Sally B. Purvis, *The Power of the Cross: Foundations for a Christian Feminist Ethic of Community* (Nashville: Abingdon Press, 1993) 19ff.

The Christian understanding of power is, of course, the power of love. Purvis calls it "power as life"[72] in her book, *The Power of the Cross: Foundations for a Christian Feminist Ethic of Community.* The power as life model is focused on the amazing phenomenon of mutuality. We can think of it in sharp contrast to the zero-sum power perspective. When we understand power as life affirming, the more we share it, the more there is. Just as real love, divine love learned through Jesus Christ expands infinitely; so does power, when we understand it properly. We have power through the Spirit of Jesus Christ. When we use that power for the upbuilding of others, for the movement toward justice, for life, we find there is abundant life, abundant power which enriches the congregation and the life of the world. The power which the Spirit of Christ sets loose in the church is amazingly able to do more than we can ask or imagine.

For our preaching, then, we have to help our people see that the zero-sum perspective about possessions, power, life, money, is wrong. The church, as servant to the world, gives the life of Christ through itself and finds it has more life, in abundance. But we need to have a caveat very clear in our minds. For centuries, women have been taught the appropriateness of their individually giving themselves for the life of others—a man, for example, or their children, the PTA, the women's society, the good of society, whatever. So women (and other vulnerable persons) have been sacrificed on various altars—the family, the church. It does not seem appropriate for us to advocate self-sacrifice of anyone. The Christian faith is a communal faith. The congregation is a faith community. If we get rid of the confusion of English translations of Scripture, we find a preponderance of biblical directives given in the plural "y'all" and very few in the singular. When Jesus gives directions how to live, his plural statements teach us not only that we are a community, but that as a community we work and live and suffer and rejoice together. We are who we are together. When one person is abused by another, we come together as a community to fix the abuse. Jesus says in paraphrase, "You (singular) have heard it said love your neighbor and hate your enemy" (one neighbor, one enemy). "But I say to y'all (all you who claim to be following my way), love y'all's enemies and pray for those who persecute y'all." We might say that those who abuse the faith group as a whole or individually are to be treated with love by the group. If a woman beats her partner, the church does not send that partner home to bear it all alone, to sacrifice herself, as Christ gave himself for us. I hardly think the

[72] Ibid., 37ff.

abundant life Christ promises that woman includes getting beaten up by her family. No, the church has a responsibility to both women, which begins with protecting the one getting hurt. The abuser may not technically be an "enemy," but she must not be treated as if her behavior is acceptable. This is a simple illustration, but the church has to be taught that self-giving is a communal affair, not an individual sacrifice. To help us keep our sermons realistic, we need to remember that we are all stinkers, undeservedly loved with the infinite compassion of God. And we, with all the other stinkers, are being lured by God toward justice. Keeping a communal focus in the pulpit strengthens our preaching.

Weddings and Funerals

There is still a disquieting phenomenon in many seminaries. Only one basic preaching course is required for the M.DIV. degree, yet in almost every parish profile of what people want in a minister, excellent preaching heads the list. So, homiletics instructors have the impossible task of preparing women and men to be excellent preachers, at the same time they must teach them other practical aspects of the preaching ministry. In one of the final sessions in the introductory class, I reserve time to lecture about weddings and funerals. These are special occasion homilies, the writing of which needs to be addressed. But there are necessary details which students are not likely to learn in any other class. For example, students need to think through decisions about premarital counseling and what to do after there is a death in the congregation.

When I discuss weddings, I pass out a handout which I use in premarital sessions. It is not a compatibility form, but rather a guide for keeping us on track and making sure various topics get covered. As the wedding day approaches, the couple is bound to be excited and happy. But they also need to know we are serious when we advise them. Marriage is not to be entered into lightly or unadvisedly. Our job is the advisory one.

Actually, before we sit down for the first time, I usually discuss with the couple why they want a Christian rather than a civil ceremony, but then we go over it again in the counseling session. I am curious to know why they want to get married now. Sometimes this is the place they tell me she is pregnant, but it also allows any hesitance to be explored, or any reasons they are rushing.

It usually takes two sessions to get through the sheet of information (I fill in names of all the major actors in the wedding, date and time of wedding, phone numbers for getting in touch with the couple, information about previous marriages, children, music, special arrangements) and questions (we discuss what models they have had for marriage, what it is about the other person that makes one want to marry him or her, what they have fought about and how they got past it, etc.). The third session we go over the ceremony, especially discussing what they believe they are doing when they repeat their vows. There are many beautiful ceremonies available from various Christian traditions. I allow some variation, but they may not start from scratch. Marriage is hard enough; we need to have some tradition behind us and the traditional language is a good support.

Weddings are intriguing. For some folks it is about the only time they get into the church building. We need to remember that, especially when outsiders want us to perform the wedding. Our response will be heard as both the response from the church and frequently as the response from God. "We went to the church for help when we wanted to get married, and they said, 'No!'" Perhaps we are able to see ourselves most clearly as servants when we are dealing with people from outside the church. I think it may be especially important for us to think through our pastoral and priestly roles when same-sex couples approach us, for these are persons whose relationships are not yet legally acknowledged and who are often ostracized by the church. Extending the love and services of the church for a wedding may be a significant step toward reconciliation. For all couples, however, I see the required counseling sessions as an opportunity to educate. I want them to receive a Christian understanding of marriage. I want them to remember God is the source of all our love. Also, I curb and shape their ideas about the ceremony. For example, I do not allow secular music in the wedding (which is, after all, worship). They may have whatever at the reception, but the ceremony is worship.

At the rehearsal it is important for the clergy person to be seen as the one in charge (no matter what the mother of the bride or the wedding planner arrived thinking). I begin with everyone in place at the chancel, instead of beginning with the processional, so they know where they are to end up, regardless of how the processional goes. Once the ceremony starts, this is where they need to be. I tell them to trust me and not to panic. If the flower girl runs back to her parents' pew, or the bride is on the wrong side, or the attendants are out of order, it does not matter. I will make sure they get married.

The homily needs to be about eight minutes (two moves), not much longer. But I encourage ministers not to skip the homily. The couple and the witnessing congregation need to have the day illumined by the Gospel.

The funeral is the other big event clergy persons are called upon to lead people through. For those who have not done funerals before, my best advice is, trust the funeral director. She or he will be doing their best to keep the minister from making any mistakes, because it makes them look bad. So, the minister can follow their lead. If there is something she is not sure about, the minister simply needs to ask the funeral director (for example, Should I meet with the family in a separate room, away from the body? [By the way, they would typically have a separate room for the meeting, but would let the minister decide whether to use it.]) The funeral director will be dependable to tell the minister when to go, where to stand, and when to leave. They will ask the minister to signal them when she is finished, then they will direct the family. Some funeral directors have bad reputations, which they probably earned, but most are helpful and more discreet than we could hope for. They see their job as a form of ministry. Trust the title: funeral directors are there to direct.

Here are a few suggestions and comments about the minister's tasks, before death, at the time of death, and at the funeral.[73]

Before Death

1. Preach about death regularly. Let people know this is a natural part of the Christian life.

2. Assure people that we are available in any crisis. (They are not to hesitate to call us at any time, although we must be ready to set appropriate boundaries when needed.)

3. Give people the opportunity to think ahead. Some churches have files for keeping information. If a church does not have a system, figure out one. Many people are comforted knowing their wishes will be attended to. One might make up a form which lists music the family likes, names of pallbearers, clothing, what minister they want, an emergency contact for children, things they definitely do not want.

4. Let people know what they may expect from the congregation (meals, rides).

5. Help congregants think through expenses and how to say "No."

---

[73] Some of this material comes from numerous conversations through the years with my father, The Rev. Dr. Robert A. Mulligan, who always made himself available when I had questions about my own pastoral ministry. Other parts of this material are adapted from lectures by Ronald Allen in his Introduction to Preaching class, Christian Theological Seminary, Indianapolis, Indiana.

6. Especially when a minister moves to a new parish, go to the local funeral home, meet the people, and ask them to talk through their system. One would want to know if there are unusual customs (Do they expect the minister to say or do a particular thing? Do they throw flowers into the grave? Does everyone stay until the casket is fully buried? Does the minister always take her own car to the graveside in order to go to the house afterward?).

7. Tell the congregants that the pastor wants to be notified first and would rather be notified five times than not at all.

8. Remind people that our important life events are celebrated in the church building, and funerals appropriately belong there, too.

At the Time of Death

1. If a family calls in the middle of the night, it is not merely to inform us. They are asking us to *come*. The line I use is, "Is it all right if I come over (to the house, to the hospital) now?"

2. As soon as we hear, get with the family. They will be looking to us for leadership and some ritual action. Pray with them. Read Scripture. Touch. Set the time for the funeral. Encourage them to have it at the church, but do not press the issue. (Know in advance whether the funeral director is church service friendly. Many funeral homes charge about the same to have the service in their chapel as they charge to transport the body to the church, so the cost is equivalent.)

3. Set the time to interview the family before the funeral (usually at least the day before). We must determine each time who are the key family members for this meeting (we do not want sixteen family members telling us what they want, but it usually needs to be more than one or two making all the decisions).

4. At the interview (which is often the hour before visitation begins), ask:

> What shall I call the deceased?
> What do *you* want to have said?
> Find out what they do not want the minister to say. They know.
> Get concrete life stories of the deceased. Take notes. We want to find something with some lightness or humor in it, too.
> Get a concrete image of the deceased in mind. Listening to family stories will help make the life of the person more real.

5. At the visitation, go see the body. Sign the guestbook.
6. Make sure the church gets there with its ministry.

7. Encourage the family to close the casket before the funeral begins. The minister needs to be standing with the casket as they close it.

About the Funeral

1. Make sure musicians and other participants have an order of worship to follow, so they know who is doing what and in what order. If the denomination does not have a worship book with an order for the funeral, borrow someone else's and adjust it.

2. Speak to the family briefly before the service.

3. The funeral director will probably signal when to go to one's seat and when to begin the funeral.

4. Following the blessing or benediction to complete the service, step up to the family and speak a personal word of comfort. Touch them with at least a handshake. The funeral director will probably come forward to give directions.

5. If there is a "viewing" after the service, stand near the head of the casket. Wait and relax (one's pastoral care "non-anxious presence").

6. Remain with the casket when everyone else (even family) is dismissed. Lead the casket to the hearse and remain near as it is loaded.

7. The minister can usually ride with the funeral director to the cemetery (which means we do not have to be thinking about directions or anything else).

8. We lead the procession of the casket and pallbearers to the grave. Stand aside as the casket is set on the apparatus.

9. Stand at the head to conduct the committal service (before we get out of the hearse, we can ask the funeral director where the head will be).

10. Speak again to the family at the conclusion.

11. Make several follow-up visits to the family. Always remember the first anniversary with a visit or at least a note/phone call.

Some additional thoughts about the funeral service:

1. The focus is on God, but the service is also about the person and what she or he meant to the mourners.

2. Try to use the Lord's Prayer or a hymn near the beginning of the service to allow people to give voice to their own thoughts. Corporate voice helps release some of the pressure of the demanding and sad events.

3. At the homily, they will expect us to begin by speaking about the person. Their grief needs to hear about the person. Then turn on the

light of the Gospel (without expecting the homily to make everything fine again).

4. Lead the funeral with dignity; point toward the hope we believe in; thank God for the life of the deceased (even the worst stinkers had their moments for which we can give God thanks).

There are occasions when everyone knows a secret about the deceased (it was a suicide/she beat her children/he cheated on both wives), but no one is willing to mention it. We need to bring to voice the *feelings* of the listeners. Of course, we do not spread someone's business around, but we cannot pretend some people are not aware of the painful secrets. So we might speak of our desire for our mothers to be perfect, yet remind us all that none is perfect. Or we might speak of the anger some of us feel (we do not have to say "because she beat us" or "because he cheated on us"). Give people permission to be angry. Sometimes the emotions are mixed; family members are at each other's throats because a parent liked one child best and ignored the other, so we bring to voice the complex person the deceased was, and how even among the children there are different emotions at play. The gentle hints at the secrets allow the persons in the know to feel that we are being genuine; not pretending the person was perfect when she was a horrible stinker. But we never want people to leave the funeral knowing anything negative that they did not know before they arrived.

The one exception may be teenage suicides, because there is some evidence that instances of suicides increase after the first one. Express the shock and guilt which everyone feels when there is a suicide, but make sure to speak against it. We do not want any copycats. This is a fine line, because we do not want to condemn the person who died. But we want others to feel the unfairness and pain they left behind for family and friends.[74]

People do not remember much from the funeral. They remember our presence and our tone. We are representing Jesus Christ, so they will sense the presence of Christ through us. We will be forgiven easily for not knowing exactly what to do; it will be difficult to forgive us for not being present when they needed us.

As time goes by, allow people to say the same things they said at the interview. They may not have really been conscious at the time. They

---

[74] For more information about the specific emotions people are coping with in different circumstances, see Robert Hughes, *A Trumpet in Darkness: Preaching to Mourners* (Philadelphia: Fortress Press, 1985).

need to say these things again and again. The guilt people express may be legitimate ("I made her life miserable"). They may need to feel the guilt, but then we need to fulfill the priestly role at the appropriate time and pronounce God's forgiveness on them.

ANNOTATED BIBLIOGRAPHY

Allen, Ronald J. *Interpreting the Gospel: An Introduction to Preaching.* St. Louis: Chalice Press, 1998. A helpful "how-to" book from a Disciples homiletician, especially useful are sections about the congregation and using diversity in preaching.

Bond, L. Susan. *Trouble with Jesus: Women, Christology, and Preaching.* St. Louis: Chalice Press, 1999. Students consistently remark that this is one of the most helpful and accessible theological texts they read in seminary. It looks seriously at historical strengths and blunders in the church and provides assistance for preaching theologically solid sermons.

Brock, Rita Nakashima, Claudia Camp, and Serene Jones, eds. *Setting the Table: Women in Theological Conversation.* St. Louis: Chalice Press, 1995. A collection of essays by women Disciple theological scholars, looking at Scripture, identity, the life of faith, women in the Church, theology, and Communion.

Buttrick, David G. *Homiletic: Moves and Structures.* Philadelphia: Fortress Press, 1987. The most important and basic book for learning how to preach.

Dietrich, Walter, and Ulrich Luz, eds. *The Bible in a World Context: An Experiment in Cultural Hermeneutics.* Grand Rapids and Cambridge, Eng.: William B. Eerdmans Publishing Co., 2002. As North Americans continue to try to read the Bible devoid of context, this book offers three essays by Third World scholars, showing students the importance of understanding in context. Essays are by Elsa Tamez, Justin Ukpong, and Seiichi Yagi.

Funiciello, Theresa. *Tyranny of Kindness: Dismantling the Welfare System to End Poverty in America.* New York; Atlantic Monthly Press, 1993. The most disturbing and blunt look at what the welfare system does to the poor.

Hughes, Robert. *A Trumpet in Darkness: Preaching to Mourners.* Philadelphia: Fortress Press, 1985. A most helpful book for understanding what is going on and what is needed from the pastor by those attending the funeral.

Newsom, Carol A., and Sharon H. Ringe, eds. *Women's Bible Commentary.* Expanded edition. Louisville: Westminster John Knox Press, 1992, 1998. Most helpful, single-volume commentary available from all female scholars. Although we may wish there were more scholars of color represented, this is a "must have" tool for male and female preachers.

Rice, Charles L. *The Embodied Word: Preaching as Art and Liturgy.* Minneapolis: Augsburg Fortress, 1991. Especially helpful is his connection of altar and pulpit. Because of his own journey from Southern Baptist to Episcopal priest, his language is accessible to various traditions. He appreciates commitment to Jesus Christ, the Bible, tradition, and liturgy.

Thomas, Frank A. *They Like to Never Quit Praisin' God: The Role of Celebration in Preaching.* Cleveland: Pilgrim Press, 1997. Demonstrates the method and importance of celebrative preaching within the African American Disciples tradition, but is easily applied beyond those limits to assist Anglo, Latino, and non-Disciples preachers and congregations.

Toulouse, Mark G. *Joined in Discipleship: The Shaping of Contemporary Disciples Identity.* St. Louis: Chalice Press, 1997. A fine resource for learning more about the Christian Church (Disciples of Christ), with significant original source quotes.

Watkins, Keith. *The Feast of Joy: The Lord's Supper in Free Churches.* St. Louis: Bethany Press, 1977. Somewhat dated, but still a good resource for understanding Disciples at the Table. Quite accessible for laity.

Weems, Renita J. *Just a Sister Away: A Womanist Vision of Women's Relationships in the Bible.* San Diego: LuraMedia, 1988. Looks at biblical women through the eyes of the marginalized. A good exercise for our Western mind-set.

J. Sergius Halvorsen

THE CONTEXT OF
THE EUCHARISTIC LITURGY

Near my parish church, there is a large Victorian house with turrets, arched windows, ornate trim, covered porches and balconies, and a slate-tile roof which will probably outlast the timbers which support it. This house, however, stands vacant. Graffiti-covered plywood shields the windows on the first floor, while the windows on the second floor and the attic dormers bear wounds which were inflicted by more energetic rock throwers. If the house stood at the end of a cobblestone driveway on a hilltop overlooking a wooded estate, it would surely be worth millions. However, this house had the misfortune of lying just beyond the boundary of the eminent domain claimed by the state when the new freeway was built through the city fifty years ago, effectively destroying the old neighborhood. Few people in the market for a three-story Victorian house want to live one hundred feet from a major freeway, at the foot of an off-ramp. So, the house slowly rots, waiting for someone to put it out of its misery.

While old Victorian houses don't do well next to freeways, the same piece of land might be an ideal place for a gas station and a fast-food restaurant. "In real estate there is an old adage, 'location, location, location.' In communication the maxim is context, context, context."[1] The value of a home or a piece of property varies dramatically as a function of its

---

[1] Robin L. Meyers, "Worship Amplifies the Voice of the Preacher" in *Preaching in the Context of Worship*, ed. David M. Greenhaw and Ronald J. Allen (St. Louis, MO: Chalice Press, 2000) 31.

surroundings. In the same way, the value and effectiveness of preaching is intimately tied to its surroundings: its context. This chapter examines preaching within the context of the Eastern Orthodox eucharistic liturgy.

At a meeting of the Academy of Homiletics, I once had the opportunity to experience a homily which was a team effort consisting of a lector who read passages of the biblical text, a mime who dramatically interpreted the text as it was read, and a preacher whose commentary was interspersed throughout the reading/performance of the biblical text. Throughout this highly creative homily, I kept asking myself, "What can I draw from this that would help me preach in my parish?" It was a difficult question to answer because as I was asking the question I also knew that a performance homily would be unimaginable within the context of the liturgy of the Orthodox Church. But why? Initially, I thought that a performance homily with multiple participants would be too radical for the conservative Orthodox Church. But, even when I imagined a performance homily which maintained the doctrine of the Orthodox Church, it was still clear that such a homily would be inappropriate, not for theological reasons, but rather due to aesthetic reasons. Quite simply, the form of the performance homily would clash with the Eastern Orthodox liturgical context. The performance homily was engaging precisely because it was successful in creating its own unique liturgical context. The mime never spoke, and he only moved while the lector was reading. Likewise, the preacher only spoke after the lector and the mime had finished reading and performing. If any of the participants deviated from this particular form, the homily would have lost its effectiveness. The performance homily was highly creative and it had the appeal of being "something new and exciting"; nevertheless, it possessed a very discrete set of "rules" which had to be followed. The three participants in the homily were not at liberty to do anything they wanted.

The eucharistic liturgy—particularly that of the Byzantine rite—is an extremely elaborate ceremony, with carefully timed processions, entrances, litanies, incensations, readings, singing of liturgical texts, prayers, and *preaching*, all of which take place within a highly stylized liturgical space which includes a number of accoutrements including icons of all sizes, candle stands, an iconostasis with multiple doorways, an altar, a chalice, a paten, and an ornately bound book of the four Gospels. For an impartial observer, the liturgical context of the eucharistic liturgy of the Eastern Orthodox Church is perhaps even more imaginative—and stunning—than the context of the performance homily with the lector, the preacher, and the mime. Unlike the performance homily, the Eastern

Orthodox eucharistic liturgy elaborately sets the stage, as it were, for the preacher whose task it is to craft a meaningful word which functions in harmony with the larger liturgical celebration. Thus, one of the first tasks for preaching within the eucharistic liturgy is to understand what that liturgy is and how the homily fits within this larger context.

In some liturgical contexts preaching creates the primary shape and context of the liturgy. For example, in some forms of Sunday morning worship the preacher selects the Scripture passages to be read, and, as the homily is crafted, the preacher works with other worship leaders to select hymns which enhance the form and message of the homily. In these situations, where the homily is the primary focus of Sunday worship, it could be argued that the liturgy functions to support and enhance the preaching. However, within the eucharistic liturgy, preaching is an integral and *necessary* facet of a richer sacramental experience.

For liturgy to work properly, it needs to be transparent. If liturgy is an opportunity for the community to worship and enter into communion with the life-giving God, then that liturgy cannot be constantly drawing attention to itself. If people are constantly thinking about "the liturgy," it is unlikely that they will have much opportunity to have a meaningful encounter with the God who is ostensibly being thanked and praised. Someone once said, "In your first year at a new parish don't change anything, don't even move a cobweb, because you never know who will be attached to what." This bit of pastoral wisdom reflects the importance of stability and regularity for the ongoing life of the community. This is particularly evident in families with small children where the routine of eating, sleeping, bathing, playing, and so on is so essential for the emotional and physical well-being of the children and the parents. Anyone who has ever taken small children on a vacation knows how difficult it can be when the "regular routine" is disrupted. The importance of stability and regularity is not limited to families with children, as it can also be seen in traditional monastic life where daily life is highly structured, with particular times for prayer, study, meals, work, and sleep. Stability and regularity are the matrix within which we are able to work, learn, and grow. This is why, from week to week, the liturgy possesses a familiar structure and is celebrated in a consistent style. As someone once said, "Liturgy should be like an old pair of shoes. You just put them on, they fit perfectly and you go on with your work without having to think about your feet." The preacher who preaches within the eucharistic liturgy faces the challenge of dynamically preaching the Gospel in a way that does not draw unnecessary attention to the act of preaching or to the preacher.

The eucharistic liturgy should nourish the faithful, strengthen them with the teachings of the Gospel, and fortify their faith in Jesus Christ. Imagine a dinner party with friends on a patio overlooking a New England harbor filled with sailboats and fishing trawlers on a warm evening in late summer. The meal begins with appetizers and ice-cold cocktails served in tall slender glasses, bedewed with condensation. As the sun begins to set, braised Atlantic salmon, from the morning's catch, is served with honey baked squash and a crisp salad; and glasses are generously filled, and re-filled, with a spicy dry Shiraz. As the sky turns from rust to cobalt blue and the plates are cleared away, torches are lit, hot coffee is poured, and sweet blueberry pie is served with fresh whipped cream. On the drive home one doesn't necessarily think about the excellent wine, or the view off the terrace, or the flavor of the fish, or even the delicate sweet-saltiness of the pastry, as much as one is filled with an overwhelming sense of satisfaction, and joy. The meal was excellent because it gave people the opportunity to share a special intimacy as they shared an expertly prepared meal. This is exactly the way the eucharistic liturgy is intended to function; it is a multifaceted celebration which gives the participants an opportunity to encounter Jesus Christ, the living Word of God. As such, all of the different elements of the liturgy must function together harmoniously to facilitate an intimate encounter between persons both human and divine.

Preaching within the context of the celebration of the Lord's Supper places particular demands upon the preaching: the scriptural readings are prescribed by the Lectionary, and the so-called variable hymns are governed by the rubrics and the church year. The liturgical "menu" has been set, and the preacher is required to craft a word which will both nourish the faithful and enhance the larger celebration of the Lamb's High Feast. Yet, with particular demands come unique opportunities. Preaching in the eucharistic liturgy, one does not have to re-invent the wheel every Sunday; the preacher does not have to stand upon a lonely soapbox hoping that some will take notice. Rather, preaching in the eucharistic liturgy is like being asked to deliver the eulogy at the funeral of a beloved professor. No matter how well one speaks, the preacher knows that the dear teacher will be laid to rest, and somehow life will go on, but one trembles at being given such an honor precisely because there is such a great *potential* for doing good. It could be argued that all preaching, whether it is done within the eucharistic liturgical context or not, is attempting to accomplish the same thing: to facilitate a saving encounter with Jesus Christ. However, the eucharistic liturgy is a sacramental celebration of the life, death, and resurrection of Jesus Christ, and the preaching which occurs within that liturgy is most effective when it functions in harmony with the larger eucharistic context.

ARE THERE TWO CELEBRATIONS?

In most treatments of preaching within the context of the eucharistic liturgy, there is some reference to "word and sacrament." Sometimes this is referred to as the "problem of word and sacrament," and the assumption is that "word" and "sacrament" are two distinct realities which need to be reconciled. One also finds discussions about the relationship between the "Liturgy of the Word," and the "Liturgy of the Eucharist," and particularly how the homily should relate to the Eucharist. Questions such as these have received a great deal of attention during the twentieth century, most notably within the context of the liturgical movement. This discussion is based on a bipartite understanding of the eucharistic liturgy which gained considerable prominence in the first half of the twentieth century, most notably through the work of Joseph Jungmann,[2] and particularly that of Gregory Dix.[3] This bipartite understanding of the eucharistic liturgy not only gained almost universal acceptance in the liturgical movement, but it was ultimately codified in the liturgical reforms of the late twentieth century.[4] However, at the close of the twentieth century, the historical validity of the bipartite structure came under fire.

Upon closer scrutiny of historical evidence which had emerged since Jungmann and Dix, Paul Bradshaw and Thomas Talley argued that there is no evidence to support the idea that the present structure of the eucharistic liturgy resulted from the combination of two originally distinct elements of Jewish liturgy.[5] More important, however, is what Bradshaw asserts regarding the "first half" of the eucharistic liturgy:

---

[2] Joseph A. Jungmann, *The Mass of the Roman Rite,* 2 vols., trans. Francis A. Brunner, from the German, *Missarum Solemnia* Herder Verlag, Vienna Austria 1949 (New York: Benziger Brothers, Inc., 1951, 1955).

[3] Gregory Dix, *The Shape of the Liturgy,* fifth ed., 1952 (Glasgow: Dacre Press, 1945).

[4] The Roman Missal, first authorized in 1973 following the Second Vatican Council, labels the Mass with the terms, "Liturgy of the Word" and "Liturgy of the Eucharist." A similar codification can be seen in the "services of word and table," language used in the 1992 United Methodist Book of Worship.

[5] Paul Bradshaw, *The Search for the Origins of Christian Worship: Sources and Methods for the Study of Early Liturgy* (New York: Oxford University Press, 1992) 158.

> [The] Jewish meal tradition itself seems to have included what might be called "an informal ministry of the word," the custom of surrounding the repast with religious discourse and the singing of hymns. Hence the first half of the later eucharistic rites may be as much an outgrowth from that tradition as a legacy from the synagogue.[6]

While Bradshaw is content to say that there is no concrete evidence to support the bipartite theory, Thomas Talley confronts the theory more directly. ". . . the still frequently encountered hypothesis that the word liturgy is derived from the liturgy of the synagogue is not particularly helpful. Indeed, it has encouraged us to think of word and sacrament as distinct concepts that need to be *brought* into relation to one another."[7] Once Bradshaw and Talley had refuted the theory that the structure of the eucharistic liturgy resulted from the combination of two distinct rites in the first century, further investigation has revealed that the bipartite liturgical model is actually a reflection of the nineteenth-century theology and liturgical practice of the Christian West.[8] While the bipartite theory appeared to be a logical way for Western Christian participants in the liturgical movement to overcome post-Reformation "word/sacrament" obstacles, it is nevertheless a very recent theological development, and it may have created as many challenges as it overcame. This is particularly true for Eastern Christians who do not necessarily share the post-Reformation theological heritage which gave birth to the bipartite theory.

A number of Orthodox theologians have wrestled with the so-called problem of "word and sacrament,"[9] each with varying results. Unlike their Western Christian counterparts, Orthodox Christian preachers do not come from a tradition which has made a sharp distinction between word and sacrament. Orthodox Christians have always celebrated the Lord's Supper and, throughout the history of the Eastern Church, preaching has occupied varying levels of prominence, sometimes occurring within the Divine Liturgy and sometimes occurring at other times. However, in the Orthodox Church there has never been a theological

---

[6] Ibid.

[7] Thomas J. Talley, "Word and Sacrament in the Primitive Eucharist" in *Studia Anselmiana*, vol. 110 (Rome, 1993) 510.

[8] For a more detailed discussion of this question see my dissertation, "Encountering the Word: From a Bipartite Understanding of Word and Sacrament Towards a Holistic Perspective on the Eucharistic Liturgy" (Ph.D. diss., Drew University, 2002).

[9] A notable example is Alexander Schmemann's discussion of this idea in *Sacraments and Orthodoxy* (New York: Herder and Herder, 1965) 38.

struggle which placed "word and sacrament" in opposition and, thus, there has never been a need to establish this kind of liturgical taxonomy or make this sort of theological distinction. Orthodox preachers in the West face a dilemma because, on the one hand, they are influenced by the theological discourse of Western Christians which tends to make a strong distinction between word and sacrament, yet, on the other hand, the bipartite distinction is not valid within the Orthodox tradition.

It is important to note that the adoption of "word and sacrament" categories is not theologically neutral. The moment one speaks of "word and sacrament" a theological distinction has already been made.

> Numerous attempts have been made to "solve the problem of word and sacrament," all of which focus on demonstrating how the two are integrally connected. Despite the fact that each of the solutions to this so-called problem makes a unique argument for why "word" and "sacrament" should be considered complementary, it can be argued that their cumulative effect has been to heighten the distinction which they sought to overcome.[10]

From an Eastern Orthodox perspective, human language is absolutely essential to every form of pastoral ministry, whether it be a formal liturgical rite of the Church (for example, baptism, chrismation, eucharistic liturgy, confession) or an informal encounter between the pastor and a member of the faithful (for example, hospital visit, house blessing, seniors' lunch). It is, as St. John Chrysostom says, the spoken word which is the sole means available to the pastor to effect a cure of the human soul.[11] While the spoken word takes on different forms—be it an inherited composition (for example, Scripture, liturgical prayer) or one that is composed by the speaker—it is nevertheless always a spoken word which the pastor uses when preaching, praying the anaphora, or distributing Holy Communion.[12] Whether it is preaching, the recitation of a liturgical prayer, or a pastoral discussion, the medium is always the same. It is the sacramental use of human language that shows bread and wine to be the Body and Blood of Jesus; it is through human language

---

[10] Halvorsen, "Encountering the Word," 136–37.

[11] IV.2, Saint John Chrysostom, *Six Books on the Priesthood,* trans. Graham Neville (Crestwood, NY: St. Vladimir's Seminary Press, 1984) 114.

[12] As the priest gives Holy Communion to each of the faithful, he says this prayer: "The servant of God (n.) partakes of the precious Body and Blood of our Lord and God and Savior Jesus Christ for the remission of sins and unto life everlasting" (*The Divine Liturgy According to St. John Chrysostom,* 1967, second ed. [South Canaan, PA: St. Tikhon's Seminary Press, 1977]) 81.

that a water bath becomes a means of dying and rising in Christ; and it is through human language that God can soften the heart and reconcile sinners through repentance.

While the bipartite liturgical understanding might offer a tidy paradigm for reconciling the eucharistic liturgy with modern Western theology, it is not particularly helpful for preachers in the Eastern Christian tradition. Celebrating any liturgy requires that one understand how the different liturgical units function; one must be aware of the order in which things are done. The basic pattern of the Lord's Supper found in Justin's First Apology is that the scriptural readings are followed by an exhortation, then the community prays together and gives thanks, the people say amen, and finally the gifts are distributed. However, this pattern does not imply a bipartite structure, but simply an ordered celebration in which reading and preaching precede the shared meal. Often the dismissal of the catechumens is cited as proof that the eucharistic liturgy possesses a bipartite structure. However, just because the catechumens were dismissed from the celebration does not imply that those who celebrated the entire liturgy and partook of the Holy Gifts perceived that they were celebrating two distinct liturgies. Consider a Thanksgiving Day feast where one family invites its neighbors to join in their celebration. The neighbors agree to come over for hors d'oeuvres, but cannot stay for the meal since they have made other plans. Thus, the day begins with two families celebrating, but at a certain point, one family leaves. Just because the neighbors had to leave early does not mean that those who remain perceive the day as having two halves, or two parts. For the catechumens who were dismissed from the eucharistic liturgy, there would have been two parts (the part we attend and the part we do not attend) but, for the faithful, there is still *one* eucharistic liturgy.

The alternative to the bipartite approach is to understand the eucharistic liturgy holistically, as one celebration, and this has important implications for the preacher. Approaching the eucharistic liturgy holistically means that the homily is not an opportunity for the celebrant to explain how the scriptural readings are related to the Eucharist; nor is the homily an opportunity for the preacher to offer a liturgical halftime pep talk: "OK, team, having heard this reading and come this far this morning, let us go on to celebrate the Eucharist . . . . " The liturgy is never self-reflective, there are no prayers or liturgical texts which say, "We have just finished the transfer of the gifts, and we are about to begin the anaphora." Liturgy simply does what it does without any introductions or apologies. Thus, if preaching within the eucharistic liturgy is to function properly within its context, then the homily should function like the rest of the liturgy. The homily does not need to introduce itself nor does it need to offer liturgical commentary. Yes, the preacher can include "liturgical operators," references to the day's celebration ("Today we make a procession around the church singing 'Christ is Risen!'"), or references to previous sacramental commitments to the Gospel (for example, baptism, marriage, ordination), but the goal of the homily is not to reflect upon the liturgy. Rather the homily should be a word of faith, an opportunity for the faithful to repent from their sins and, by conforming their lives more perfectly to the teachings of Jesus Christ, enter more fully into communion with him.

The entire liturgy is a sacramental use of human language, whether the words be that of Holy Scripture, a homily, a composed liturgical text (hymn), a litany, or a prayer. From the first proclamation of the celebrant, "Blessed is the Kingdom of the Father and of the Son and of the Holy Spirit!" to the final "Amen" sung by the faithful, the Divine Liturgy is one holistic "eucharist word": a sacramental celebration through human language in which the faithful offer thanks to God for salvation in Christ Jesus, and through which God, in turn, can speak and transform human beings. Therefore, the task for the preacher is not to connect separate parts or to reconcile disparate actions. Rather, the task of the preacher is to craft a homily which offers the faithful a path to salvation in Jesus Christ.

PREACHER AS LITURGICAL POET

If the goal is for preaching to function in the eucharistic liturgy as an integral element of a holistic encounter with Jesus Christ the incarnate Word of God, then the best way for the preacher to approach the art of preaching is as a liturgical poet. In effect, the preacher is commissioned to compose a new liturgical text every week that will be performed only once; or in other words, the homily is a "proper" for one single, unrepeatable day. What, then, are the parameters for this kind of liturgical composition? First of all, the preacher/poet should recall that the homily is "performed" in exactly the same liturgical space as the reading of the Gospel: at the center of the ambo facing the community.[13] Additionally, the homily is delivered immediately following the reading of the Gospel. The placement of the homily in the order of the liturgy along with its

---

[13] When an Orthodox priest serves alone, this is where he stands to read the Gospel.

placement in liturgical space indicates that preaching is closely tied to the scriptural readings and, like the liturgy itself, preaching should be biblical.

Another consideration concerning the liturgical performance of the homily is that within the Orthodox eucharistic liturgy, preaching is the only liturgical element which is delivered in a spoken voice. All the other prayers, litanies, psalms, scriptural texts, and hymns are chanted. The simple fact that the preacher is using a speaking voice sets preaching apart as "something different." Thus, great care should be taken to craft a homily which is as "musical" as possible, it should be an oration which is pleasing to the ear and, furthermore, it should as much as possible emulate the language of Scripture and liturgical poetry. One of the most serious mistakes which could be made by the preacher would be to approach preaching as a lecture or a mid-liturgy extension of Sunday school. It is true that one can "learn" from the liturgy, but it is a unique form of learning, less like that which occurs in the classroom or lecture hall, and more akin to the formation which can happen when people listen to their elders' stories, or when one reads a life-changing book. Thus, preachers should seek to emulate the language of the liturgy which is concrete, poetic, biblical, rich with imagery, and which touches the heart and soul of the hearer.

Preaching in the context of the eucharistic liturgy should offer the hearers an opportunity to repent from their sins and enter into communion with Jesus Christ. In order to accomplish this, the language of the liturgy must define the language of preaching. Liturgy does not lecture, it does not speak down to the faithful, or say "you must repent." Rather, liturgy provides the faithful with words which give them an opportunity to express and, thereby, actualize their faith. Liturgy enables the community to say, "I believe," "Lord have mercy," "forgive us our trespasses," and "Christ is risen!" with greater eloquence and power than any single person could accomplish on his or her own. On Holy Thursday the liturgy enables us to say, "Come you faithful, let us raise our minds on high and enjoy the Master's hospitality and the table of immortal life in the upper room; and let us hear the exalted teaching of the Word whom we magnify."[14] On Holy Friday the liturgy enables us to say,

> Today he who hung the earth upon the waters is hung upon the cross. He who is king of the Angels is arrayed in a crown of thorns. He who wraps the

[14] Irmos of the ninth ode from canon for the Matins of Holy Thursday. *The Lenten Triodion,* 1978, trans. Mother Mary and Kallistos Ware (London: Faber and Faber, 1984) 553.

heaven in clouds is wrapped in the purple of mockery. He who in Jordan set Adam free receives blows upon his face. The bridegroom of the church is transfixed with nails. The son of the virgin is pierced with a spear. We venerate your passion, O Christ. We venerate your passion, O Christ. We venerate your passion, O Christ! Show us also your glorious resurrection.[15]

On Pascha the liturgy enables us to say, "This is the day of resurrection. Let us be illumined by the feast. Let us embrace each other. Let us call 'brothers' even those that hate us, and forgive all by the resurrection, and so let us cry; Christ is risen from the dead trampling down death by death, and upon those in the tombs bestowing life."[16] When these texts are sung and heard by the faithful they become "our words." They are not a philosophical articulation of a particular dogmatic teaching, nor are they a demand for moral rectitude. They are words which bring about a new reality, words which transform the faithful through their singing and hearing. They are words to which we can respond, "Yes, this is what I believe! Amen." They are words which allow us to encounter Jesus Christ. The preacher, therefore, is called to be a liturgical poet, a composer and a choir of one, whose task is to craft homilies which accomplish exactly the same thing.

PREPARING TO PREACH

When an Orthodox bishop, priest, or deacon prepares to serve the Divine Liturgy, a number of private prayers are prescribed even before the liturgy begins.[17] The fact that such rubrical directives exist is testimony to the emphasis which the Orthodox liturgical tradition places upon spiritual preparation. Both laypeople and clergy, through formal rubrics as well as informal practice, are required to make some degree of preparation before celebrating the eucharistic liturgy. The theological arguments for such preparation are varied, but underlying them all is the idea that the eucharistic liturgy is not some sort of spiritual panacea; one should not expect to idly traipse into church on Sunday morning, receive Holy

---

[15] Antiphon fifteen from the service of the twelve gospels on Holy Friday. *The Lenten Triodion*, 587.

[16] From the "Paschal Verses" from the Matins of Pascha. *The Paschal Service*, 1986, ed. John Erickson and Paul Lazor (Department of Religious Education Orthodox Church in America, 1997) 45.

[17] "Entrance Prayers" are prescribed for entering into the altar area prior to the beginning of the service, as well as special prayers for vesting, and there is also an elaborate rite for the preparation of the bread and wine for the liturgy (*The Divine Liturgy*, 3–25).

Communion, and immediately be sanctified. Certainly, God can and does work miracles, but the Christian life is not possible without vigilance and some degree of ascetical effort. The Orthodox tradition places great responsibility upon each individual Christian to come to the Sunday morning service prepared, with some degree of awareness of one's own weakness and a desire to be reconciled to the Author and Source of Life. If so much is expected from each of the faithful, how much more is expected from the preacher! It has been said that Archbishop Kiprian of the Orthodox Church in America[18] would say to his clergy, "If you are not ready to preach, you are not ready to serve." Whether or not the quote is properly attributed, it is most certainly true.

Some Orthodox priests have argued that they do not like to prepare formally their homilies, preferring rather to "Allow the Holy Spirit to inspire them, and guide their words." It is ironic, however, that while such priests would have God "turn stones into bread,"[19] in terms of their preaching they would never assume that God will miraculously make bread and wine appear in the sacristy on Sunday morning. Effective preaching can only be accomplished by a preacher whose heart seeks to do the will of God, whose mind is disciplined and trained in the art of preaching, and who works to carefully prepare each homily. Within the Orthodox Christian tradition there is perhaps no better advocate for excellence in preaching than St. John Chrysostom who was the Patriarch of Constantinople from 398 until his death in 407. While Christians from many traditions are familiar with the numerous extant homilies and treatises of this remarkable preacher, his legacy is particularly prominent in the Byzantine Rite where the most frequently celebrated form of the eucharistic liturgy is attributed to St. John Chrysostom. In *Six Books on the Priesthood,* St. John Chrysostom says that the preacher must have two essential qualities—contempt of praise and force of eloquence—and he emphasizes that both are necessary: "If either is lacking the one left is made useless through divorce from the other."[20]

Contempt of Praise

"Contempt of praise" is a potent corrective because everyone, from preachers to plumbers, love to be complimented on a job well done. But when St. John says that the preacher must have "contempt of praise,"

---

[18] 1904–1980.

[19] Matt 4:3.

[20] V.2, Chrysostom, *On the Priesthood,* 128.

he stresses that the preacher is a servant of Christ charged with the spiritual well-being of the faithful. "The Church of Christ is Christ's own Body, according to St. Paul, and the [one] who is entrusted with it must train it to perfect health and incredible beauty, by unremitting vigilance to prevent the slightest spot or wrinkle or other blemish of that sort from marring its grace and loveliness."[21] The preacher, just like a physician who is treating a deadly disease or serious injury, cannot allow concern for the short-term comfort of a patient to jeopardize the ultimate effectiveness of the necessary treatment. A small degree of discomfort is involved in even the most basic form of preventative medicine like a vaccination. The ultimate goal of preaching is healing and salvation in Jesus Christ. But since people are imperfect, sinful, and wounded, the way of salvation necessarily begins with repentance, and true repentance always includes an element of discomfort. Preachers whose only concern is to make a good reputation and win the praise of the parish will avoid the "sensitive issues" which are guaranteed to elicit a strong response from the community. However, by cultivating a contempt of praise, the preacher is empowered to ask difficult questions, to probe the cancerous lumps lurking deep within the tissue of human nature, which threaten the Body of Christ with spiritual death. When a preacher has a contempt of praise, there are no questions which are off the table—the whole of human experience is under investigation, and particularly those aspects of life which touch most intimately upon our relationships with others.

Contempt of praise is not to be understood as being callous toward those whom one is called to serve, and it certainly is not license to stand in judgment over the community. Rather, it is a way to ensure that the preacher is continuously oriented toward the proper mission of the Gospel. However, the challenge facing the preacher is that the community does not necessarily come to the eucharistic liturgy with a conscious perception of the need to repent. Someone once said, "If you are saying your prayers on Saturday night and you think that you are completely prepared to receive Holy Communion on Sunday morning, then you should go out and commit a sin, so that when you approach the chalice you will do so with the knowledge that you are a sinful person, and that you only receive Christ's Body and Blood by the grace of the merciful God who forgives!" While this is certainly a hyperbolic statement, it rings true, particularly for preachers. Christ came not to call the righteous, but

---

[21] IV.2, Chrysostom, *On the Priesthood,* 114.

sinners to repentance[22] so, if we are to hear the Gospel, then we must first be reminded of our struggle with sin.

Eugene Lowry has made very clear the importance of "upsetting the equilibrium" in preaching.[23] To upset the equilibrium of the hearers means that the preacher reminds them that life is not a "bed of roses," and even though the faithful may not have come to church thinking about their own particular pain and suffering, the preacher must constantly look for opportunities to invite them to examine their own hearts, their own lives, and their relationships with other people and with God.

Oftentimes when a preacher thinks about the problems facing the community, external threats easily come to mind. Just think about all the godless, secular, bigoted, cruel, cutthroat people, organizations, governments, and nations "out there" that threaten us every day! It is easy to think about people whose ideology is in opposition to the Gospel or to identify groups who openly criticize or ridicule the church. These "big targets" are easy prey for preachers who want to score instant points with their communities; preachers who want to stir up their communities' sense of righteous indignation toward the evil in the world. "Brothers and sisters, today we are confronted by a powerful enemy which is absolutely godless and constantly tries to lure us away from the truth . . . and God, we thank you that we are not like other people, extortioners, the unjust, adulterers . . . or even like the I.R.S."[24] Preaching which points out the evil "out there" is likely to elicit praise from the community because we are eager to identify the flaws in others, to see their faults, and point out their shortcomings. Furthermore, as long as we only focus on the evil which is "out there" in our enemies, then not only do we remain safe "in here" but we can smugly congratulate ourselves on not being like those "bad guys out there." Those who preach in such a way, however, are only going to make their hearers twice as much children of hell as they are themselves,[25] eschewing repentance for pharisaical hypocrisy.

A healthy contempt of praise liberates the preacher from the tyranny of self-righteousness and frees one to examine the dark side of the insiders, asking the question, "How do *we* sin against God?" Moreover, the preacher should ask, "How do *I* sin against Christ and his Holy Church?" If the eucharistic liturgy is an opportunity for the faithful to

[22] See Matt 9:13; Mark 2:17; Luke 5:32.

[23] *The Homiletical Plot: The Homily as Narrative Art Form,* expanded ed. (Louisville: Westminster John Knox Press, 2001) 28.

[24] See Luke 18:11.

[25] See Matt 23:15.

encounter Jesus Christ, then the preacher must confront the misconceptions, wounds, and sins which separate the community from their Lord and Savior. To receive the broken Body and spilled Blood of Christ in the consecrated bread and wine of Holy Communion is a profoundly intimate encounter with God. There is an Orthodox prayer which the faithful often read quietly after receiving Holy Communion which speaks of this intimacy:

> Freely you have given me your Body for my food, O You who are a fire consuming the unworthy. Consume me not, O my Creator, but instead enter into my members, my veins, my heart. Consume the thorns of my transgressions. Cleanse my soul and sanctify my reasonings. Make firm my knees and body. Illumine my five senses. Nail me to the fear of You. Always protect, guard, and keep me from soul destroying words and deeds. Cleanse me, purify me, and adorn me. Give me understanding and illumination. Show me to be a temple of Your One Spirit, and not the home of many sins. May every evil thing, every carnal passion, flee from me as from a fire as I become Your tabernacle through communion.[26]

The preaching within the eucharistic liturgy should be just as penetrating and sanctifying as the Eucharist itself.

The eucharistic liturgy is a fearful encounter with God, inasmuch as any encounter with the Divine is always accompanied by the realization of one's own unworthiness and sinfulness. When the Word of God comes to the Prophet, the reaction is one of fear and a recognition of unworthiness.[27] Likewise, when one encounters Jesus Christ, there is a corresponding sense of life-changing *metanoia*.[28] The aim of preaching, particularly when it occurs within the eucharistic liturgy, is to give the faithful an opportunity for just such an encounter. Therefore, a fundamental task of this preaching is to bring the hearer to repentance, so that having recognized the sin—having faced the conflict—the person will desire the love, mercy, and salvation of Jesus Christ.

Preaching which "brings the hearer to repentance" does not only refer to members of the congregation. In fact, if the preaching is to be effective, then the preacher is the one, first and foremost, who is called to repentance and salvation in Christ Jesus. Using Robin Meyers' terminology, preaching should be understood as an intentional act of self-persuasion. Meyers' argument follows the approach of listener-centered theory which

---

[26] This prayer is attributed to St. Simeon Metaphrast (*The Divine Liturgy,* 106–07).

[27] See Isa 6:5; Jer 1:6; Ezek 1:28.

[28] Luke 5:8; Matt 17:6; Acts 9:3-9.

says that when people are persuaded, it is not because they have been manipulated by a message but, rather, the listener responds to a message by creating questions in his or her own mind, and the persuasion, the change of mind, occurs as a result of the listener's own answer to these questions. "If this sounds very much like talking to oneself, it is exactly that."[29] Furthermore, Meyers argues that for maximum effectiveness homiletic self-persuasion is not something that the preacher clinically administers to the hearer as an objective observer, but rather, the homily is first and foremost an event which penetrates the heart and mind of the preacher. "[I]f listeners are expected to self-persuade, why should the preacher be exempt from the same process? If it is self-persuasion the preacher wants, why shouldn't it be self-persuasion that the preacher models? In other words, what if preachers viewed their homilies as *intentional acts of self-persuasion?*"[30] Preaching of this sort transcends the limits of argumentation or moral exhortation and ascends to the lofty heights only possible for true *martyria;* authentic Christian witness.

When preaching is understood in this way, it places an entirely new perspective on the idea of spiritual preparation. Not only is prayer and ascetical effort essential to help the preacher be a "good Christian," but in fact the preacher's effectiveness is directly linked to the preacher's own spiritual self-awareness. "What causes me to stumble? Where am I weak? Why do I doubt? Who has hurt me and who have I hurt?" Questions like these help a preacher to recognize and articulate the concrete struggles which he or she faces from day to day. When homilies are prepared with such struggles in mind, the preacher can deliver a personal word of hope and salvation that touches the preacher's heart as well as the hearts of the hearers. For the preacher who seeks to preach self-persuasively, the sacrament of reconciliation, or confession, is an invaluable tool, precisely because it is a sacramental and liturgical act of self examination and a verbal expression of our own weakness and sin. In recent times, confession has certainly lost standing in the public consciousness with many people regarding it as an irrelevant relic of outdated clericalism, and at worst as a form of spiritual voyeurism. However, it is ironic that the modern downfall of sacramental confession has coincided with the upsurge of talk therapy, and even the "tell all" television interview. Clearly, when people fall into sinful behavior, when they are caught up in

---

[29] Robin R. Meyers, *With Ears to Hear: Preaching as Self Persuasion* (Cleveland, OH: The Pilgrim Press, 1993) 12.

[30] Ibid., 15; emphasis in original.

the self-destructive momentum of addiction or anger or despair, there is a heavy psychological and spiritual toll. The damage is only exacerbated when people refuse to speak about their struggle, and especially when they work to hide their internal struggle from others. As the twelve-step movement is fond of saying, "You are as sick as your secrets." Christian confession, whether it be according to the formal liturgical rite of reconciliation or a deep, heart-to-heart talk with a trusted spiritual father or mother, is a powerful and effective means of spiritual healing. Sacramental confession gives the preacher keen insight into the challenges in his own life, and spiritual self-knowledge is a pre-requisite for preachers who seek to preach as an intentional act of self-persuasion.

However, one should *never* use the homily as an occasion for public confession! (For example, "Let me tell you, brothers and sisters, I struggle with lust just as much as anyone.") To use the liturgical homily as an occasion to reveal one's personal struggles always has devastating consequences. When one speaks of one's personal sins, the hearers automatically focus on the person of the preacher, what the preacher does, what the preacher struggles with. Yet, the goal of preaching is not to have people focus on the preacher, or scrutinize the preacher's life. Rather, preaching should help people to examine their own lives so that they might repent and come into more perfect communion with Jesus Christ. Preachers who speak about their own lives and personal struggles are robbing the people of an opportunity to examine their own lives and repent from their sins. The focus of the eucharistic liturgy is always on Jesus Christ who is the author of our salvation. Thus, preachers should take great care to avoid saying anything that places any emphasis—either positive or negative—upon themselves.

Preaching in the eucharistic liturgy should always invite the hearers to repent from their sins and open their hearts to the love and mercy of Jesus Christ. Therefore, the preacher-celebrant, as a member of the faithful and the "foremost of sinners,"[31] is the first to be called to repentance by the liturgical homily which is crafted to be an intentional act of self-persuasion. The celebrant does not stand over the community in judgment, but rather stands before the community as the one ordained to lead the community in prayer. The homily should address concrete challenges and sins facing each member of the community, while carefully avoiding the temptation to focus on the unique sins of one particular individual. In other words, the homily should be personal,

[31] 1 Tim 1:15.

but not confessional. Preaching is "confessional" whenever the preacher speaks about himself, or about his own struggles (for example, "The other day at a party I ate far too much and drank more beer than I should have."), and this should always be avoided. However, the homily must be "personal" inasmuch as it invites the community, including the preacher, to examine their own lives, and repent from sin (for example, "Have you ever said to yourself, 'I have eaten too much'? or 'I really should not have had that last drink'?"). Crafting a homily which calls people to repentance directly and persuasively is not easy, and there is a very fine line between preaching which is personal but not confessional. Nevertheless, it is essential for effective preaching, and those preachers who are actively engaged in their own ongoing spiritual formation who regularly participate in the sacrament of confession will find it much easier to craft homilies which are powerful and meaningful not only for themselves, but also for the communities they are called to serve.

Having meditated on St. John Chrysostom's first essential quality for preachers, one can see that "contempt of praise" is a powerful corrective for preachers who are tempted to say only that which pleases and placates their hearers. Furthermore, it points to the necessity for repentance in preaching, and particularly the necessity for repentance on the part of the preacher. Contempt of praise is not a license to preach callously or harshly, and it should never be interpreted as an excuse for speaking down to one's hearers and blasting them for their hardness of heart. Contempt of praise is *not* to be confused with contempt of the community! Rather, the effective physician of souls, must be aware of the concrete challenges facing the community, beginning with himself, and address these challenges with skill in a spirit of Christian love. The preacher, as the physician of souls and "the foremost of sinners"[32] must wield the sharp knife of the Word with the utmost care in order to expose the cancerous tissue of sin, so that God might work authentic healing in the faithful.

Force of Eloquence

The second essential quality for the preacher, according to St. John Chrysostom, is "force of eloquence." Simply put, force of eloquence is the preacher's ability to capture the imagination of the hearers and bring them on a journey. To preach eloquently within the eucharistic lit-

---

[32] Ibid.

urgy, one must employ language which is shaped by both the language of the liturgy and the language of contemporary society, and here is where we touch upon an aspect of preaching that sets it apart from the rest of the liturgy. Apart from the Bible, the eucharistic liturgy, particularly that of the Eastern Orthodox tradition, is one of the most ancient works of sacred art still used by the church. While certain compositions and texts have more modern provenance, the anaphora attributed to St. John Chrysostom is a fourth-century prayer[33] which, even in translation, sounds distinctly un-modern. The homily, however, delivered within the context of that ancient liturgy, is the most recent of liturgical compositions. Therefore, the challenge is to make a modern composition sound like it belongs in an ancient rite. The language of the liturgy is biblical, it moves and breathes in the stories, songs (psalms), and images of Holy Scripture and, therefore, preachers should be fluent in this same biblical language and homilies should themselves be biblical so that they might offer people an opportunity to enter into communion with the biblical God whose Son died and rose from the dead.

The preacher needs to be fluent in both the ancient language of the liturgy as well as the contemporary idiom so that the homily can speak to contemporary hearers while simultaneously resonating within the eucharistic liturgy. Liturgical worship, and particularly the liturgy of the Orthodox Church, is biblical worship. The figures, stories, and images of the Bible are the matrix in which the liturgy lives. Psalms and biblical canticles are chanted and sung in the liturgy and the composed liturgical texts are rich with biblical imagery. In short, the language of the liturgy is drawn from the Bible, so the language of liturgical preaching should also be biblical. This cannot be overstressed. In order for preaching within the liturgy to function properly, it must bring the hearers into the saving reality to which the Bible is the primary witness. This is exactly what the liturgy does: it gives the faithful an opportunity to encounter the God of Abraham, Isaac, and Jacob, the God who brought the people of Israel out of bondage in Egypt, gave them the Law on Sinai, brought them into the promised land, and who through the prophets promised to send a messiah, a Christ. This is the God we see when we behold the face of Jesus Christ[34] who was born of the Virgin Mary, who was baptized in the

---

[33] ". . . it was introduced into Constantinople from Antioch, probably by St. John Chrysostom in 398" (Robert F. Taft, "St. John Chrysostom and the Byzantine Anaphora That Bears His Name" in *Essays on Early Eastern Eucharistic Prayers,* ed. Paul F. Bradshaw [Collegeville, MN: Liturgical Press, 1997] 195).

[34] John 14:9.

Jordan, who was transfigured on the mountain, who raised Lazarus from the dead, who entered into Jerusalem triumphantly on the colt of an ass, who suffered and died on the Cross, who was raised on the third day and ascended into heaven. This is the God whose Holy Spirit descended upon the Apostles, and whom we receive through baptism and chrismation. In the eucharistic liturgy there is only one way to define God, and that is to recount the biblical witness of God.

To become fluent in the language of biblical narrative, image, parable and metaphor, preachers should be students of the Bible and constantly read the Holy Scripture. Cultivating familiarity and intimacy with the biblical text is essential for the preacher because it is the Bible which provides both the content and form of the Gospel of Jesus Christ. By internalizing the Holy Scripture, the preacher is better prepared to study the Lectionary readings which will be proclaimed on a given day. Moreover, biblical fluency enables the preacher to instinctively draw upon biblical examples and images when crafting the homily.

While personal study of Holy Scripture is essential, it is not the extent of a preacher's preparation. The preacher must also become fluent in the language of the liturgy; the preacher should live and celebrate that liturgy as fully as possible, not only the eucharistic liturgy but the ongoing daily, weekly, and annual cycles of liturgical prayer. One could argue that immersion in the liturgical life of the church is essential for the preacher on the grounds of piety: some degree of piety and holiness is essential for preaching, and the prayer of the Church is the primary locus for encountering Christ. However, the concern here is far more practical. In order to gain fluency in any language, one must speak that language, and the only way to become fluent in the language of the liturgy is to immerse oneself in that language. Essentially, familiarity with the liturgy gives the preacher a concrete encounter with the life-giving celebration of Christ's death and resurrection. It allows the preacher to become increasingly fluent in the language of salvation, the imagery, metaphor, and holy story of Christ's life, ministry, passion, death, and resurrection as it is liturgically celebrated by the Church.

Liturgical immersion and biblical fluency provide a sound basis for the preacher. The Bible is the primary witness of God's mercy and the liturgy is the de facto means by which the church encounters that saving reality in Christ. The liturgy does not ask which sayings of Jesus are authentic, it doesn't attempt a deconstruction of the Bible nor does it ask the Bible to answer questions it was never intended to answer. Rather, the liturgy, through its ritual singing and chanting of Holy Scripture, and the prayers and hymns which constantly reflect upon the Scripture, approaches the Bible with reverence and humility. This approach to the Bible is not naive, nor is it given over to literalism. Rather, the liturgical approach to Holy Scripture is one which assumes that the Gospel of Jesus Christ is *the* life-giving message. The liturgical approach does not seek to reduce Holy Scripture to dogmatic affirmations or systematic articulations of faith, but rather the liturgy assumes that the biblical story is our story; and through our ongoing participation in that corporate scriptural prayer of the Church, the biblical story increasingly becomes "our story." This approach does not set the Bible at a distance, biblical figures are not "historical characters," rather they are immediately present. Moreover, when biblical figures are rebuked, we are rebuked: "O foolish Americans! Who has bewitched you?"[35] When the figures in the Bible are consoled and given hope, we are consoled and given hope. When the church celebrates the feast of the Annunciation we sing, "Today is the beginning of our salvation, the revelation of the eternal mystery. The Son of God becomes the Son of the Virgin as Gabriel announces the coming of Grace. Together with him let us cry to the Mother of God: Rejoice, O full of grace, the Lord is with you."[36] When the church celebrates Christ's resurrection we sing, "Christ is risen from the dead, trampling down death and upon those in the tombs bestowing life!"[37] In the liturgy Jesus is alive today, and the milestones of his earthly ministry—celebrated throughout the festal cycle of the Church—are made present now. When preaching within the liturgy, as much as possible preachers should speak of the biblical narrative in the present (for example, "today Christ gives Bartimaeus his sight") because this is the way the liturgy speaks. We who celebrate the feasts of the Church enter into the reality of Christ's ministry, passion, death, and resurrection so that we might become Christ-like. Preaching within the eucharistic liturgy should provide the faithful with an opportunity to enter into that saving reality. Fluency in the language of the liturgy enables the preacher to craft a homily which is native to the liturgy in which it is preached. Moreover, this language is the language of Christian intimacy; it offers the means by which human words can bring us into communion with the incarnate Word of God.

In addition to biblical and liturgical fluency, a preacher seeking "force of eloquence" must also possess fluency in the contemporary idiom. This

---

[35] See Gal 3:1.

[36] Troparion of the Annunciation (*The Divine Liturgy*, 234).

[37] The paschal troparion (*The Divine Liturgy*, 181).

was certainly the case for the great preachers of the first millennium. Their biographies all begin same way: "The saint was born to wealthy parents, he received the very best education that money could buy, and having studied under the master rhetoricians of his day, he was poised to begin a brilliant career in civil service. Then as a young man, he was overcome by a love for Christ and the Church and he forsook the things of this world to proclaim the Gospel." Great preachers like Saints Basil the Great, John Chrysostom, Gregory Nazianzen, Augustine, Ambrose, and numerous others all began their Christian ministries with sterling credentials in contemporary communication skills of their day. These were men who could have entered—and in the case of St. Ambrose did enter—into the public arena as magistrates, governors, or influential figures in the imperial court. They were masters of communication and possessed the skills to enlighten, persuade, and convince their hearers. However, instead of using their communication skills to elicit popular support for a military campaign or advocate the cause of a wealthy patron before the civil authorities, the great preachers used their force of eloquence to proclaim the Gospel of Jesus Christ. They brought all of the best rhetorical skills of their day to bear on the task of building up the Body of Christ, and this is the challenge for preachers today. Thus, it is essential to understand what constitutes force of eloquence today.

In the time of the great preachers of the first millennium, lawyers, politicians, and philosophers were the key figures in shaping public opinion and official policy. In this era, to be effective in public life one had to be fluent in the law and trained in the accepted norms of legal and philosophical discourse. Likewise, today we see a similar phenomenon in the large number of elected officials who have backgrounds in law. Certainly, politicians and lawyers still have a tremendous impact upon public opinion and official policy, but unlike the first millennium, they are no longer the undisputed rhetorical heavyweights. While trial lawyers still earn their money by influencing juries using the vernacular, the majority of legal discourse is conducted in "legalese" which evades the comprehension of many laypeople. Furthermore, while politics is still big business, popular interest in governmental policy, election campaigns, and exercising one's right to participate in the democratic process pales in comparison to the public's interest in, and devotion to, television, film, and popular literature. Consider the ongoing success of the legal drama as a literary and dramatic motif. Television programs, movies, and books which dramatize the legal world continue to capture the imagination of the public at the same time that the public holds lawyers in very low esteem. This means that what lawyers actually say is not nearly as interesting to people as are the stories about lawyers that are written by John Grisham or produced by Dick Wolf of TV's "Law and Order" fame. For most people, debates between candidates for public office and speeches delivered by elected officials are not nearly so captivating as popular television programs or blockbuster films which dramatize the lives of politicians. Given the amount of time that people spend watching television and reading newspapers compared with the amount of time they spend listening to speeches from elected officials, it is clear that lawyer/politicians do not necessarily set the standard for "force of eloquence." In fact, the primary locus for effective communication and persuasion today is found in the popular media, particularly the advertising media.

From the Christian perspective, people are constantly tempted to sin. We are tempted to make decisions based on greed, lust, envy, pride or hate, and traditionally the church has maintained that the faithful are constantly engaged in nothing less than spiritual warfare with powers and principalities.[38] Yet consider for a moment the human sources of this temptation. It is true that some figures in public life are advocates of sinful behavior, but more often than not messages of temptation come to us in the form of stories. Some are crafted merely to elicit immediate satisfaction from the audience. Take for example the action movie cliché where in the end the hero folds, spindles, and mutilates the villain and his or her henchmen. Such a story plays directly into the human tendency to seek punitive justice, to desire an eye for an eye and a tooth for a tooth. "You wronged me, so I'll wrong you even more!" Another example of human sources of temptation is commercials, the expertly crafted short stories whose patrons invest millions of dollars so that we can watch them repeatedly every night. In television advertisements such as these, a shirtless muscular young man shaves with a "revolutionary" new razor and suddenly a beautiful woman wraps her arms around him and nuzzles affectionately against his smooth masculine face. This story says that a particular razor brings love and affection. An automobile designed to survive the harsh violence of war, painted bright yellow, speeds effortlessly across trackless wastes. Inside all is peaceful and serene, the children happily watch a video on a built-in flat panel display, the mother dozes comfortably in her seat, while the handsome father drives on with a look of pristine satisfaction. This is a story which tacitly

---

[38] See Eph 6:12.

promises power and invulnerability to everyone willing to pay more than the average annual American salary for an automobile. Even more clever is the somewhat abstract story of a handsome middle-aged man who is clearly frustrated as he tries unsuccessfully to throw a football through a tire swing. But perhaps the drug with a tall red flame for a logo, is the key to his sudden success. Now the man throws the ball, it goes through the middle of the tire, and suddenly he is warmly embraced by a beautiful woman who looks at him with pride and approval. Here, a single pill is the key to renewed love and intimacy. These are not examples of *ars gratia artis*. Rather, these are ingenious stories told to elicit a very particular change in the lives of those who watch and hear them. They are stories which take us from conflict, whether implied or explicit, to a resolution which always includes the use—and implied purchase—of particular goods or services. These are the commercials and advertisements which stoke the fires of greed, lust, envy, and desire, all for the sake of increasing profit and market share. These are compelling stories which, in recent years, have attained a level of artistic brilliance which often exceeds that of the network programming they subsidize. Just consider the phenomenon of someone enduring a relatively uninteresting broadcast of the Super Bowl just so that they can see the amazing commercials. It is no exaggeration to say that popular media is at least as effective a rhetorical force in shaping public opinion as are the speeches of lawyers and elected officials. In fact, modern advertising is perhaps the most influential form of public discourse in the Western world today.

The reason these stories are so effective is that they convincingly depict a better reality; they promise some degree of deliverance from suffering for everyone who drinks a particular soda, drives a particular car, or dines at a particular restaurant. And the rhetoric is effective! People continue to buy, and spend, and borrow beyond their means so that they can have more and more of the goods and services which are supposed to increase their quality of life. Inasmuch as the overwhelming majority of twenty-first century advertising genius advocates a life contrary to charity, humility, chastity, honesty, love, and the Gospel of Jesus Christ, preachers face a daunting task. The majority of the faithful attend the eucharistic liturgy once a week on Sunday morning, with a smaller number attending Saturday night vespers, or perhaps a mid-week festal liturgy. A generous estimate would say that the average parishioner spends two hours a week participating in the liturgy of the church with perhaps fifteen minutes of that time spent listening to the homily. The same average parishioner hears close to fifteen minutes of professionally crafted commercials in the course of just *one hour* of commercial television programming. Most people spend more than ten hours a week watching television,[39] which means that in the course of a week, for every fifteen-minute message the preacher delivers encouraging the faithful to take up their cross and follow Christ, the faithful hear a minimum of one hundred and fifty minutes of other expertly crafted messages encouraging them to gratify their immediate physical and emotional desires. Facing a challenge like this, "force of eloquence" is more essential for preachers today than it has ever been. If preaching is to be effective, it cannot simply articulate the Christian faith in abstract terms which are unrelated to the concrete challenges and struggles facing the faithful. Rather, the preacher needs to show the faithful that a life in Christ is not only a better way, but it is the *best* way.

The eloquent appeals which are expertly crafted by the advertising industry, all tell stories. These stories always identify a particular challenge, a need, a weakness which ordinary people face every day. Then, we see these ordinary people satisfying their needs or triumphing over adversity through their use of a particular product or service. The message is quite simple and tremendously effective: "Your life is hard and painful but if you purchase this object your life will get better." And people are not stupid, or unreasonable; they do not do things for no reason. Rather, every act, even the most destructive, is ultimately done for particular reasons, reasons which, in the mind of the individual, are quite compelling. Nobody wakes up one morning and decides that he is going to have an adulterous affair out of the clear blue. Rather, the decision is based on particular reasons: "I feel insignificant; my wife doesn't really satisfy my needs; there is no excitement in my life anymore. But, when I am with my mistress I feel alive and powerful." Now, these might not be good reasons to betray one's spouse, but they are still reasons which exert great influence in the mind of the adulterer. Any decision we make is predicated on the idea that our situation ultimately improves as a result of our actions. Even the decision to take one's own life, as devastatingly horrible as this may be, is a decision made by the person who concludes, for whatever reason, that death is ultimately a better option than a life of seemingly unbearable pain and suffering. Marketers understand that people are often in pain, and that they desperately desire to be healthy, safe, and loved. This is why goods and

---

[39] Some recent polls claim that average television viewing among adults is as high as thirty-five hours per week.

services are presented as offering solutions to the fundamental human challenges. However, the Gospel plainly says that there is only one way to overcome the intractable dilemmas of life in this fallen world, and that is through faith in Jesus Christ, obedience to his commandments, and a willingness to take up one's cross and follow him. In the end, the preacher's task is to show that the Gospel of Jesus Christ, the way of the Cross, is not only the only road to salvation, but is in fact the very best course of life that we can possibly follow. If this is not the fundamental conviction of the preacher, then why preach at all?

Years ago I listened to a series of taped presentations by a motivational speaker for salespeople. In this talk, the speaker told a story about an experience he had, early in his career when he was selling expensive, high-quality cookware. He had been making sales calls for several weeks and was having little success, and he reported these disappointing results to his sales manager. The sales manager asked, "Do you own a set of our cookware?" and the salesman replied, "No, actually I don't. They are pretty expensive, you know, and I just don't have the money to buy a set." The manager said, "If you are going to sell these products, you need to buy a set and use them yourself. Because if you aren't willing to invest in our product, then how do you expect your clients to do the same?" So, much to the objection of his wife who did not think they could afford new cookware, the salesman bought a set and used it. He discovered that these pots and pans were truly outstanding, and that they made cooking much easier and enjoyable. Furthermore, he discovered that his newfound enthusiasm was "contagious" among his clients, and his sales skyrocketed.

So, does this mean that preachers are supposed to market or sell the Gospel? No, because building up the Body of Christ cannot be measured in terms of numbers and spreadsheets. The kingdom of God is not of this world and the Christian is not called to be a salesperson, but rather "a slave of Christ."[40] However, what the motivational speaker discovered is that to be truly credible he had to be an authentic witness of a better way. Likewise, the preacher should be a witness—a *martyr*—of Christ.[41] The task of the preacher is to create a desire in the hearts of the faithful—a desire to be with Christ and to live according to his teaching. And the best way for a preacher to accomplish this is to show the hearers how a life in Christ is the best life which anyone can possibly know.

---

[40] Rom 1:1 *doulos christou.*
[41] Acts 1:8.

However, one must beware of the temptation to "lower the bar" of the Christian life. In the short run, the preacher can create a momentary desire for Christ in the hearts of the faithful by minimizing the ascetical element of the Gospel. Such an approach can be easily found in some of the "churches" whose "sanctuaries" are devoid of any visual reference to the crucifixion and whose preaching regards suffering as devoid of any redemptive value. The preacher who claims that faith in Jesus, along with a considerable donation, guarantees healing and material prosperity makes a powerful argument. But paganism has always been an easy sell: "Bow down before this statue and your life will get better." It requires a relatively small investment with the promise of a large payoff. However, the Gospel of Jesus Christ makes no such material promises, and in fact, the only material guarantee is that those who follow Christ will face persecutions and suffering. The way of Christ is the way of the Cross, and the preacher should proclaim this unequivocally. It is not an easy message to proclaim because it is not a "prosperity gospel." Yet, as Jesus says, his yoke is easy and his burden is light,[42] and not only do we have hope for eternal life in the kingdom of God that is to come, but we live in the confidence that Christ is risen and wherever two or three are gathered in his name, he will be there in the midst of them.[43] The promise of the Gospel, of true reconciliation with our Father in heaven, touches upon a need which cannot be satisfied by any material blessing. The treasure which we have in the Gospel, perfectly manifested in the broken body and spilled blood of Jesus Christ, is an opportunity for real hope, to be able to place absolute confidence in a merciful, just, and loving Lord. It is a treasure which infinitely exceeds all human expectations. The preacher's task is to kindle the desire for Christ in every person, especially those who think they are beyond salvation, and boldly claim that with faith in the crucified Messiah we are given the strength to stand in the midst of the dark storm of pain and suffering with the same confidence that we will have when we stand at the right hand of the King of Glory.

Possessing even greater force of eloquence than those who would have us deny others and follow our passion enables the preacher to make a case for denying oneself and following Jesus Christ. Preaching should address the concrete, tangible suffering of the people—their loneliness, their isolation, their sorrow, their grief, their hunger for meaning, their unfulfilled quest for unconditional love—and also show them how,

[42] See Matt 11:30.
[43] See Matt 18:20.

through repentance, they can find Christ, and in Christ find not only a "solution" but, in fact, discover the knowledge of God's truth in this world and in the world to come, life everlasting.[44] For the contemporary preacher, force of eloquence is the ability to powerfully, beautifully, and passionately proclaim the word of the Cross in a world which views the Cross as the ultimate foolishness. Indeed it is far easier to sell high-end cookware than it is to preach the Gospel of Jesus Christ in a world which perceives the Cross as ultimate foolishness and weakness. However, it is our claim that Christ is risen, that we can taste and see and hear that the Lord is good, today, and that, as St. Paul says, "the foolishness of God is wiser than men, and the weakness of God is stronger than men."[45]

CRAFTING THE HOMILY

Addressing the particular aspects of homiletic preparation, it would be helpful to provide a quick overview of what a homily preached within the eucharistic liturgy should look like. First of all, the homily should be biblical—it should explicitly proclaim the Gospel of Jesus Christ and give the hearer an opportunity to encounter our Lord and Savior Jesus Christ. Preaching occurring within the liturgy should never shy away from the so-called "scandal of particularity," since the creed which we sing is meticulous in defining the God in whom we believe. The liturgy of the Orthodox Church is very particular in its trinitarian language, at various times addressing different persons of the Holy Trinity, or addressing God as Father, Son, and Holy Spirit. Therefore, the preaching occurring within that liturgy should be just as careful with its "God language." On a practical note, one should always avoid generic language about God. Phrases like, "In God we trust" or "I believe in God" have a theological implication, but are vague to the point of being meaningless. In which god do we trust, and in which god do we believe, for there are many "gods" and many "lords."[46] We do not preach the gospel of god, but the Gospel of our Lord and Savior Jesus Christ, and preachers must be explicit.

---

[44] This is a paraphrase of the collect of the small litany following the second antiphon in the Divine Liturgy: "O you who have given us grace with one accord to make our common supplications unto you, and promised that when two or three are gathered together in your name you would grant their requests: fulfill now, O Lord, the petitions of your servants as may be expedient for them: granting us in this world the knowledge of your truth and in the world to come, life everlasting. For you are a good God and love mankind, and unto you we ascribe glory: to the Father and to the Son, and to the Holy Spirit, now and ever and unto ages of age" (*The Divine Liturgy,* 35).

[45] 1 Cor 1:25.

[46] 1 Cor 8:5.

Since we aim to preach biblically, the homily should always have the Bible as its source and the best place to begin is with the Lectionary readings prescribed for the day. The preacher's first task is to become familiar with the Lectionary readings, and then choose *one* reading which serves as the source of the homily. There is a style of lectionary preaching whose primary aim, it seems, is to identify a particular theme or idea running throughout the Lectionary readings together. While this is clever, it is not helpful. Yes, the Lectionary readings are often thematically related, and as preachers read and study the Lectionary texts, common ideas or images often emerge. However, the ultimate goal of preaching is to give the hearer an opportunity to encounter Jesus Christ, which means that the preacher is called to preach the Word of God in a particular way for a particular group of people. It is far more important to establish a meaningful connection between Christ and the faithful than it is to weave together themes from the Lectionary readings. In order to better focus on the pastoral challenges facing the people, the preacher should choose *one* reading to serve as the biblical source for the homily. Now, while crafting the homily, the preacher might discover that an idea or image from one of the other Lectionary texts is pertinent, and choose to refer to it in the homily. This is perfectly fine, and for that matter the preacher might choose to include biblical images or examples from biblical texts which are not included in the Lectionary readings for the day. However, choosing *one* text as a starting point for the homily helps the preacher to focus the homily, and this is essential if the preacher is to provide a word which brings the hearers into communion with Christ.

Sometimes when a biblical text has been selected and the preacher begins a careful study of that text, one occasionally wanders into a homiletic "no-man's land," a trackless waste separating the biblical text from the nascent homily. "How in the world," asks the desperate preacher, "am I supposed to get from the biblical text to my homily?" All too often this is the moment when the preacher approaches the biblical text from every possible perspective, asking a wide array of questions and getting a wide array of answers which provide no clear direction for the homily. It is like when a traveler is lost in a foreign city and he asks five people for directions to the train station. Each person gives him an accurate, albeit different, route to the train station, leaving the traveler not only lost, but entirely perplexed about which route he should take. Consulting biblical commentaries, studying the scriptural text in the original language, and reading other homilies can yield a great amount of data. While quality biblical data is essential for effective preaching, raw exegesis rarely reveals the proper direction for the homily. A seemingly endless sea of interpretations from one text provides nothing to guide the direction of the homily, nothing to chart its course. When a preacher simply "studies the text," the result can be like a child's "dot-to-dot" puzzle which has a thousand dots on a piece of paper with no numbers. It is completely unclear where one should begin, and where one should end. If quality and quantity of data were the sole qualification for effective preaching, then a preacher's task would be easy—simply carry one's favorite Bible commentary out onto the ambo and read a few pages to the faithful on Sunday morning. However, this is certainly not the case. In order for a preacher effectively and efficiently to craft a homily, the preacher must have some idea of the homily's form before the first sentence is crafted.

Form is an essential component of any artistic creation. Haiku and a limerick, a waltz and a march, a television sitcom and an episode from a miniseries all have distinct forms, and in order to be successful in creating any of these, one must possess a thorough knowledge of the particular form. The same holds true for the homily. From the very beginning, the preacher should have a good idea of the basic homiletic form which the homily will take. The homiletic form is immensely helpful as it serves as a kind of template for the preacher who can then "fill in the blanks," as it were. Moreover, a pre-established form focuses and guides the exegetical work of the preacher. For example, if one approaches the biblical text looking for "three points" (which has been one of the most popular homiletic forms), it is very likely that three points can be found, which neatly facilitates crafting a "three-point homily." Although the "three-point homily" is helpful inasmuch as it gives the preacher a definite form, preaching in the eucharistic liturgy requires a more poetic shape than the "three-points" model.

For preaching occurring in the eucharistic liturgy, it is not particularly helpful to think about "points." Simply put, the liturgy does not speak in the language of "points." The liturgy is a journey from suffering and death, through repentance, to new life in Jesus Christ, and the homily should have the same basic shape. As was earlier pointed out, the contemporary homily needs to be very particular, and it needs to address the concrete struggles of the faithful. Not only should it address the problems, but it also needs to point the way toward salvation. A perfect example of this can be found in the Holy Week liturgy of the Byzantine Rite. In nine days, the faithful are taken on a journey from the raising of Lazarus (Lazarus Saturday); into Jerusalem (Palm Sunday); through the Last Supper, the passion, crucifixion, and burial of Jesus (Great and

Holy Friday); with the journey culminating in the glorious celebration of Christ's Paschal resurrection. Holy Week is powerful because it tells a compelling story, and the hearers have an opportunity to participate in this Christian story. The liturgical celebration of Holy Week is powerful not only because of its narrative structure, but because it possesses a single trajectory. Every detail, every image, every piece of dialogue takes us one step closer to the Cross. Preaching in the eucharistic liturgy should have a single trajectory; it should take the hearers from sin, to repentance, and conclude with new life in Christ.

Eugene Lowry gives a wonderful description of this narrative form in his book *The Homiletical Plot*.[47] The homily begins by "upsetting the equilibrium" of the hearer, uncovering a particular tension which exists with the lives of the hearers. From here, the tension increases as the preacher explores the underlying reasons behind a particular challenge. A key to the success of this type of homiletic form is the use of the inductive method. The homily provides concrete examples of problems with which the hearers can identify, thereby inviting them to examine the tensions and conflicts in their own hearts and lives. The tension increases to a point at which the preacher reveals the solution, the moment at which we say, "Aha! That is it!" It is like the moment in a murder mystery when the true identity of the villain is revealed, or the moment when Nathan says to David, "You are the man!"[48] At this point the preacher reveals the root cause of the particular sin, and in revealing the cause, the preacher points toward the solution. From this point, the preacher provides concrete examples of a new life in Christ, showing the hearers what a life lived according to the Gospel should look like, and what they can expect.

Preaching within the eucharistic liturgy should be a form of spiritual corrective, it should address a particular sin or challenge and reveal the corresponding solution in the Gospel of Jesus Christ. Preaching should be a corrective because Holy Scripture is always a corrective. No prophet, patriarch, or apostle ever set ink to parchment for the fun of it. The Scripture was written to address a particular sin, to correct an abuse or a deformation of the community. For that matter, no secular author ever wrote a book unless the author was trying to solve a problem or make a difference in the world. Paul Scott Wilson, in his book *The Four Pages*

---

[47] Eugene L. Lowry, *The Homiletical Plot: The Homily as Narrative Art Form,* expanded ed. (Louisville: Westminster John Knox Press, 2001).

[48] See 2 Sam 12:1-7.

of the Sermon,[49] describes four questions which help a preacher craft a single-trajectory homily. The questions, slightly re-phrased, are (1) What is the sin in the text? What concrete error is being corrected in the biblical text? (2) What does that sin look like today? How is it manifested in the lives of the members of this parish right now? (3) What is the hope for salvation in the text? How is this corrective Good News, how does it bring new life? (4) What does that hope for salvation look like today? How can we expect to be transformed by Christ who is alive and active in our lives? By looking for the particular problems being addressed and looking for the solutions given, the preacher discovers sin/salvation pairs. The preacher is not dreaming up some conflict, or using psychology as the source of the homily. Rather, by asking these questions, the preacher allows the biblical text to chart the course for the homily and so the problem and the solution—the sin and the salvation—are defined by Holy Scripture. Furthermore, by asking how this particular sin/salvation pair is manifested today, the preacher can begin to discover how the Christian community, with its own struggles and sins, can benefit from and find salvation in Christ through the Holy Scripture. The reason the sin/salvation pair is so important is that it gives the preacher a definite beginning and ending for the homily. It begins with a sin, it examines that sin, and finally it points the way out of the sin and to communion with Christ.

This "four question" methodology reveals a number of possible sin/salvation pairs, a number of possible trajectories, which the homily could take. Then, just as it is necessary to choose one lectionary reading to begin with, the preacher must choose one problem/solution pair. More often than not, effective preaching is as much the result of good editing as it is of thorough research. When a preacher studies a text, prays about it, meditates on it, a veritable flood of ideas can be unleashed that can sometimes lead to a sort of homiletic paralysis. When a preacher faces the dilemma of "I don't know what to say" it is rarely due to a lack of ideas. More often than not, "preacher's block" is the result of too many ideas and no obvious way of presenting them in a coherent manner. By using the four question method the preacher distills a number of possible beginning and ending points for the homily.

Once a number of these sin/salvation pairs have been discovered, the preacher must select *one*. To do this one should ask, "Which pair means the most to me today?" At first glance, this may seem selfish on the

---

[49] Paul S. Wilson, *The Four Pages of the Sermon: A Guide to Biblical Preaching* (Nashville: Abingdon Press, 1999).

part of the preacher—shouldn't we preach the word for the community? The answer is a resounding yes; preaching is always done on behalf of the Body of Christ. However, while speaking from a position of leadership, the preacher is never to assume the role of God, who alone judges. Rather, the preacher is first and foremost a member of the community; so if the preacher selects the sin/salvation pair which is personally the most compelling, then the homily is guaranteed to be effective and meaningful for at least one member of the community. Furthermore, when the preacher delivers a homily which is personally meaningful, a homily which touches the heart of the preacher, calls the preacher to repentance, and gives concrete hope of salvation, it is almost certain that the preacher will deliver the homily with conviction and authenticity. By choosing the sin/salvation pair most meaningful on a personal level, and offering this particular path from sin to salvation, the preacher is most likely to achieve what Robin Meyers calls an "intentional act of self persuasion." However, as was noted earlier, choosing the sin/salvation pair most compelling for the preacher does not mean that the homily should become confessional. While crafting the homily, the preacher must always keep the community in mind. A helpful question to ask is, "How does this affect me personally, and in what ways do the members of my community face the same challenge?" For example, if the sin being addressed is anger, then think of the concrete situations facing the community which may elicit a sinful response of anger. Here, a number of different examples should be given to ensure that each member of the community (including the preacher) is given a chance to reflect on the temptations they face in their own lives. The goal is to craft a homily which personally touches the heart of the preacher and also touches the hearts of the hearers because it addresses the concrete challenges and temptations of daily life and offers the possibility of redemption and salvation in Jesus Christ.

This kind of preaching is like bypass surgery on the spiritual heart. When the surgeon looks directly upon the heart and identifies exactly which blood vessel is diseased and in need of repair, the work has just begun. What would happen if, halfway through open-heart surgery, the doctor said to the patient, "There you go, good fellow, you see, this artery is completely closed and if you want to live you have to open that thing up. Get to work, and see me in a week." Surely, the patient would die. Likewise, the preacher does little good and, in fact, inflicts more damage if only half of the lifesaving procedure is completed. Focusing concretely on a particular source of sin and despair, the preacher must also show

how Christ can work in our lives today and give us hope and courage to live according to the Gospel.

The homily should be viewed as a journey which begins with a concrete problem, leads us to consider the deep underlying reasons why we sin against God, and ultimately points the way toward salvation and new life in Jesus Christ. This kind of preaching assumes that when most people come to the eucharistic liturgy on a Sunday morning, they carry with them very particular burdens. A father yelled at his children as he was getting them ready for church; a grandmother spent another sleepless night caring for her bedridden husband; a teenage girl is nursing wounds from a particularly nasty fight she had with her boyfriend the night before; and a first-grade boy lives every day feeling sick to his stomach as he watches his parents' marriage disintegrate. Everyone bears the weight of their own particular sins, challenges, and tragedies. Yet, simply because people are suffering does not mean that they come to church in a particularly reflective state. While some may come to church looking for a miracle or for consolation, the preacher should always try to name the particular suffering and the sin, to pinpoint the occlusion which blocks the flow of divine mercy, so that the light of the Gospel can pierce, illumine, and heal the broken heart. The only way to accomplish this is for the homily to examine a particular aspect of life and reveal the sin, struggle, and suffering plaguing all of us. The hearer is invited to reflect on his or her own life through concrete examples the preacher provides. Rhetorically, this can be accomplished by asking questions such as, "Have you ever been left out of the group?" The preacher can ask the hearer to recall particular events: "Think of the last time you were caught in traffic, I mean a really bad traffic jam, where all the cars came to a dead stop; you were late for an important appointment and the rage of frustration boiled up inside you." Or the preacher can help the hearer imagine a situation: "Imagine if someone said to you, 'He who eats my flesh and drinks my blood has eternal life, and I will raise him up at the last day.' What would you think about a statement like that?" By asking questions such as these, the preacher puts the hearer in an active role of examining his or her own life, and coming up with honest answers to difficult questions.

The saying, "Show me, don't tell me" is a very important axiom for preachers. People don't want to be drowned by data or pushed around by moral arguments. Data and moral arguments make little difference to the person who is suffering and is doing his miserable best to keep his head above water. "Show me, don't tell me" is important because, contrary to popular belief, it does not mean "Shut up!" When Jesus preached, he did so mostly with parables—earthy little stories which led people to the kingdom of heaven. Preachers should always seek to accomplish the same thing through concrete examples and vivid images. This kind of language "shows" people something about themselves and about God; they can "picture" certain realities in their minds, and they can imagine (image) a new life in Christ. In preaching it is always better to *show* the hearers than it is to tell them. When we "tell" we report on our experience, but when we "show" we lead people to Christ.

The beginning of the homily should create tension in the mind of the hearer; it either reminds the people of a problem they are trying to re-solve or a challenge they are facing, or the homily questions a particular worldview or outlook. For example, a homily might begin by touching on the "good reasons" for why we are not comfortable with strangers. "Everyone has heard the admonition, 'Don't talk with strangers' and there is good reason for this because strangers can be dangerous. When we see someone who dresses differently, who smells differently, and who talks differently from how we do, it is only natural to keep our distance, isn't it?" A rhetorical question like this is almost impossible to disagree with; one can immediately identify with the gut response to flee from that which is different, unusual, and possibly frightening. Once the hearer has been "bought into" this particular idea, they have taken their first step on the journey of repentance.

Having inductively led the hearer into this familiar mindset, the preacher can begin to question the presuppositions. "After a while, we realize that everyone is different from us. Our family, our friends, our co-workers . . . they are all different, and it is just easier to keep our dis-tance than it is to live with strange and frustrating people. But, when we keep everyone at arm's length, where does that leave us? Where are we left when we even keep God at arm's length?" The homily should help them re-examine their surroundings. The preacher is like a guide who leads people on a tour of their own neighborhood, pointing out things they never noticed before, both the bad and the good.

Christian salvation, unlike any other saving act, can never be forced. St. John Chrysostom pointed this out in *On the Priesthood:*

> . . . it is necessary to make a [person] better not by force but by persua-sion. We neither have authority granted us by law to restrain sinners, nor, if it were, should we know how to use it, since God gives the crown to those who are kept from evil, not by force but by choice . . . [If someone] wan-ders away from the right faith, the shepherd needs a lot of concentration,

perseverance, and patience. He cannot drag by force or constrain by fear, but must by persuasion lead him back to the true beginning from which he has fallen away."[50]

Few people today can be brow-beaten into repentance and, more often than not, when a preacher speaks down to a community, demanding repentance, the reaction is anything but productive. However, by creating tension in the mind of the hearer, the preacher gives the hearer an opportunity to recognize the unrelenting hunger for salvation lying deep in the human heart. To use St. John's pastoral imagery, endowed flock of sheep won't return to verdant pastures unless they first realize that they are dying in the wilderness. When the preacher successfully upsets the equilibrium, both preacher and hearer say, "Yes, that is I! I suffer like that. I do those very things which hurt other people. I have cut myself off from the love of God! Now how do I get back home?"

When preaching in the context of the eucharistic liturgy, the preacher should preach the whole Gospel every Sunday. This means that for the faithful, the Good News of Christ's resurrection should be made even more concrete and vivid than the reality of sin and death which upset the equilibrium in the first place. Once the preacher has upset the equilibrium, and the hearers are hungry for salvation, then the preacher has to show the way toward salvation; the second half of the sin/salvation pair needs to be revealed. This turns out to be one of the most difficult tasks for the preacher because just about anyone, given enough time, can think of concrete examples of tragedies and disasters on a personal or corporate level. Hackneyed but true, all one needs to do is to look at a newspaper or watch the first five minutes of the evening news in order to find some pretty bad news. However, it is much more difficult to think of concrete examples of repentance, salvation, and new life in Christ. When it comes time to address the good news of salvation and leave the hearers with a hopeful message, the preacher fails by merely offering the "lettuce" ("let us") solution: "Brothers and sisters, *let us* therefore pray to God for strength and hope . . . . " While few could argue against praying to God for strength and hope, this type of message is like giving a cookie to a starving person. Certainly, there is some nourishment, but much more is needed. Furthermore, the eucharistic liturgy itself should never be used as an easy way out. Preachers who identify sins and challenges only to say, "And today, let us partake of the Holy Eucharist unto our salvation and redemption. Amen" tacitly imply that the sacramental

[50] II.2, II.4. Chrysostom, *On the Priesthood,* 56, 58.

Body and Blood of Jesus Christ is some sort of magic potion. In the same way that a celebrant would never dream of beginning the eucharistic liturgy if he did not intend on distributing Holy Communion, a preacher should never begin speaking to the faithful unless he intends on giving them a concrete vision of hope and salvation in the Gospel.

Just as the homily gives concrete examples of suffering, it should also give concrete examples of what it is like when we repent, and how our lives change when we open our hearts to Christ. Taking a cue from the parables of Jesus, the preacher could proclaim the hope by way of simile: "The kingdom of heaven is like a child who is lost in a department store, but then is reunited with his mother." Another possibility is to use images from the lives of saints—images of repentance, true joy, and unshakable peace. At some level there is a degree of ambiguity to the message of hope; in so many ways it is yet to be realized, and for each person it will come about in a different way. However, the preacher needs to show the faithful what life can be like if they are made strong in Christ. If the hope is to be found through fervent prayer, then describe the fruits of a life of prayer in the everyday world. If the hope is to be found through fasting, then present the faithful with the concrete reality of a life lived with greater and greater freedom from the cares, addictions, and passions of this world. If the hope is to be found through almsgiving, then show the hearers what the smallest act of kindness can mean to a child, a homeless mother, or a senior whose family has abandoned him on Christmas day. If Christ is risen, then hope and salvation are real and the task of the preacher is to reveal that heavenly reality.

CONCLUSION

Those who regularly attend the eucharistic liturgy are rarely the un- churched who wander in from off the street. Most come to church with some degree of faith and/or a sense of duty; without either of these they would surely find a better way to spend Sunday morning. The eucharistic liturgy is a remembrance of the teaching of Jesus Christ and a thanks- giving for the mercy God has shown to us through his only-begotten Son. Absurd as it might sound to many, we place all of our hope in this crucified first-century Jew from Palestine. It is a celebration of faith and thanksgiving which stands in stark contrast to the expertly crafted mes- sages which constantly encourage us to please ourselves, indulge our desires, and use other people as tools to get what makes us happy. The powerful arguments we hear and see daily tell us that life will be better for us if we buy the right products, live in the right homes, and drive the right cars. St. John Chrysostom claims that the Body of Christ is always in danger of being infected with the deadly disease of false doctrine, and that the only remedy available to the pastor is the spoken word.[51] While there are few advertising campaigns today promoting the Arian or Nestorian heresy, it is clear that Christians are under just as much pressure to adopt false teachings today as they ever have been. Ultimately, the preacher is challenged to show the faithful who have gathered to celebrate the Lord's Supper that living according to the Gospel of Jesus Christ, to place oneself under obedience to the teaching of Jesus, is the best way to live. The homily must present a concrete vision of the problems we face and the sins with which we struggle. And, equally important, it must offer a concrete vision of the hope and strength offered to us in Jesus Christ.

Preaching within the context of the eucharistic liturgy is a challenging opportunity. It requires the preacher to craft a word which functions within the ancient biblical language of the liturgy, while simultaneously resonating with the contemporary life of the faithful. It is a challenge because it is an act of poetic imagination requiring great precision and attention to detail. But it is also a wonderful opportunity because the celebration is one of such great importance and it lies at the very heart of the life of the church. As Charles Rice wrote, preaching in the eucharistic liturgy is an opportunity to proclaim boldly that "Life is more than one damn thing after another: Those who tell stories and celebrate the Eucharist make it so."[52]

REFERENCES CITED

Bradshaw, Paul. *The Search for the Origins of Christian Worship: Sources and Methods for the Study of Early Liturgy.* New York: Oxford University Press, 1992.

Chrysostom, Saint John. *Six Books on the Priesthood.* Translated by Graham Neville. Crestwood, NY: St. Vladimir's Seminary Press, 1984.

The Divine Liturgy according to St. John Chrysostom. Second edition. South Canaan, PA: St. Tikhon's Seminary Press, 1967, 1977.

Dix, Gregory. *The Shape of the Liturgy.* Fifth edition. Glasgow: Dacre Press, 1945, 1952.

---

[51] IV.2, Chrysostom, *On the Priesthood,* 115.

[52] Charles L. Rice, *The Embodied Word: Preaching as Art and Liturgy,* Fortress Resources for Preaching (Minneapolis, 1991) 100.

Halvorsen, J. Sergius. *Encountering the Word: From a Bipartite Understanding of Word and Sacrament towards a Holistic Perspective on the Eucharistic Liturgy.* Ph.d. diss., Drew University, 2002.

The Lenten Triodion. Translated by Mother Mary and Kallistos Ware. London: Faber and Faber, 1978, 1984.

Lowry, Eugene L. *The Homiletical Plot: The Homily as Narrative Art Form.* Expanded edition. Louisville: Westminster John Knox Press, 2001.

Meyers, Robin L. *Worship Amplifies the Voice of the Preacher.* Edited by David M. Greenhaw and Ronald J. Allen. St. Louis: Chalice Press, 2000.

Meyers, Robin R. *With Ears to Hear: Preaching as Self Persuasion.* Cleveland: The Pilgrim Press, 1993.

Wilson, Paul S. *The Four Pages of the Sermon: A Guide to Biblical Preaching.* Nashville: Abingdon Press, 1999.

Mary Ann Wiesemann-Mills, O.P.

PREACHING IN THE CONTEXT OF "DOING THE LITURGY"

I. HISTORICAL AND THEOLOGICAL DESCRIPTION OF THE ROLE OF PREACHING

The doing of the liturgy is to be for us the source of the true Christian spirit, and not one source among many, but the primary source and—in a strong and challenging word—the Indispensable source. Where do we put on Christ? In doing our liturgy. Where do we find little by little what a Christian life looks like? In doing our liturgy. Note, please it is not in studying our liturgy, in observing the liturgy, in being uplifted by the liturgy, but in *doing* the liturgy. Where are the deeds, the habits of the heart . . . to be learned by Christians, learned in the sense of made our own? Where do we learn to speak and move and look and act the way a Christian speaks, moves, looks, acts? In doing the liturgy. Are there other sources of the Christian spirit, other ways in which we learn to put on Christ? Certainly. But to say that the doing of liturgy is for us the primary and indispensable source is to plan an order, a discipline, on our formation.[1]

Gabe Huck's insightful words capture the essence of Roman Catholic preaching. The entire eucharistic liturgy forms Catholic Christians. The Table of the Word—the proclamation of the Scriptures and the preaching which flows from these texts, as an integral part of the liturgy—shares in the act of formation. What is begun in the faithful at the Table of the Word is brought to the Table of the Eucharist, confirmed and celebrated and sent forth. The homiletics team at St. Mary Seminary and Graduate School of Theology, which is composed of three diocesan priests and the author, build our classes on this understanding. Therefore, we who

---

[1] Gabe Huck, "Liturgical Spirituality," *Assembly* 14, no. 4 (June 1988) 402–03.

150

teach preaching at St. Mary's embrace the homiletic vision proposed in the American Bishops' document, *Fulfilled in Your Hearing: The Homily in the Sunday Assembly* (FIYH). In light of this document, we composed the following mission statement: We believe that the homily should break open the scriptural word so that the faith of the members of the assembly may be reintegrated and renewed in such a way as to lead each to name and to celebrate the presence of God in their life.

Each syllabus for the homiletics classes at St. Mary's opens with the above mission statement. This mission statement is followed by the following five foundational principles:

1. The homily, as a part of the liturgy, is addressed to an assembly gathered in faith to worship God.

2. The homily is to interpret people's lives by drawing upon the texts of the Bible as they are presented in the Lectionary.

3. The homily draws upon a preacher's capacity to listen to the people, pray the Scriptures, and recognize the action of God in his or her own life.

4. The homily requires order, clarity, and convincing delivery that uses language which is specific, graphic, and imaginative.

5. The homily employs the language of a poet and storyteller in order to invite the assembly to respond to God with heart and mind.

The mission statement with the foundational principles is threaded through each homiletics course. These elements give shape to individual classes within each course. Our object as preachers is to convince ourselves and others that God so loves us that we can only respond with our lives—at the Eucharist and in the world.

Such preaching assumes living faith. Homiletic preaching is neither evangelization nor catechesis nor exhortation nor witnessing. As homiletic preachers, we do not set out to instruct our listeners nor do we morally exhort them nor, heaven forbid, harangue! Nor does the homiletic preacher specifically witness to the wonderful works of God in his or her own life. We may do all or some of this incidentally, but this is not our purpose. Liturgical preaching—the homily—is not "liturgical" because it occurs during the liturgy. Liturgical preaching is preaching which is essentially of the liturgy. It is itself liturgy—in itself an act of worship. Our purpose is to plunge our listeners and ourselves into an experience of God, an experience which will naturally lead to a celebration which seeps into our bones and urges us toward change. Homiletic preaching is directed to deeper and deeper conversion of already faithful believers.

The homily is a moment in theology. The homily is a ritual event. The act of speaking, hearing, receiving, and integrating the word is an ecclesial action—the action of God's gathered assembly. A threefold approach is highlighted in the document FIYH: the assembly, the preacher, the homily. The experience of the assembly is the starting point for reflection on preaching. I have in mind a triangle, with God, the assembly, and the preacher at the respective points. Movement in the creation of the homily travels back and forth among these three points. "The Word was made flesh and dwelt among us"; the Word *is* made flesh and *dwells* among us. God is continually present and at work in the lives of the people as well as in the life of the preacher. The latter serves as an interpreter, one who through the lens of the Scripture texts names the grace present, enabling both the preacher and the assembly, in the light of that truth, to praise God for God's mighty deeds on behalf of God's people. The goal of the liturgical preacher is not simply interpretation of a text of the Bible (as would be the case in teaching a Scripture class) but to draw on the Lectionary texts of the Bible to interpret people's lives in such a way as to lead to action for the sake of God's kindom.[2]

As Christians, we are believers in the Word made flesh. We believe that God's truth was embodied in a human being—a human being who grew tired and hungry, who was elated and downcast; a human being who suffered and died and rose again; a human being whose risen Body is still at work in the world. We are people of the Word Incarnate—Emmanuel, God-with-us. Believing this, we can say that the homily doesn't need to solve problems but to give us a way to face the problem in the company of Jesus Christ. Receiving insight and strength in the word preached and proclaimed, we approach the eucharistic table for the sustenance which enables us to be living presences of reconciliation and healing in our daily lives.

II. PREPARATORY STEPS

The course Theologies and Models of Preaching serves as the introduction to the ministry of preaching. The purpose of the course is fivefold:

---

[2] The author purposely uses the word "kindom" rather than "kingdom" to emphasize the unity of all God's people and to de-emphasize the masculine and military tone signified by kingdom.

1. To explore theologies of preaching within the Christian tradition in order to arrive at a personal theology of preaching;

2. To examine several models of preaching through which to articulate a theology of preaching;

3. To learn different methods of constructing a preaching event in order to preach more effectively;

4. To employ these methods in the writing and proclaiming of homilies. All homilies are designed to be preached within the eucharistic liturgy.

5. To apply basic principles of communication to the preaching event.

The *course outcomes* are threefold: cognitive, behavioral, and affective. Cognitive outcomes involve the learning of the knowledge of the particular discipline, including the key theories, concepts, and applications. Behavioral outcomes involve the ability to employ the specific skills or abilities presented throughout the course. Affective outcomes speak to the attitudes, beliefs, and values related to the specific discipline. Listed below are the respective outcomes of the course Theologies and Models of Preaching.

A. Cognitive Outcomes
    1. Students will recognize deductive and inductive movements in preaching.
    2. Students will know the components of Buttrick's moves; of Long's focus, function, and form; and of Lowry's homiletical plot.
    3. Students will understand key components of a theology of preaching.

B. Behavioral Outcomes
    1. Students will create a homily
        a. With one focus
        b. Logically and clearly developed
        c. Drawn from the scriptural texts of the Sunday liturgy
        d. Having sound theology
        e. And a tensive quality.
    2. Students will create a homily based on
        f. Buttrick's moves
        g. Long's focus, function, and form
        h. Lowry's homiletical plot.

3. Students will demonstrate the skills learned in LIT 371: Oral Interpretation and Proclamation through the proclamation of homilies.

4. Students will demonstrate skills learned in LIT 371: Oral Interpretation and Proclamation and LIT 373: Theologies and Models of Preaching by effectively critiquing their own and their colleagues' preached homilies according to the coaching method.

C. Affective Learning Outcomes

1. Students will have an appreciation for the homily as integral to the liturgy of the Eucharist.

2. Students will become aware of their own strengths and areas for improvement in writing and proclaiming homilies.

3. Students will develop an appreciation for a vital spiritual life from which springs sound preaching, as developed in the text *Spiritual Life: The Foundation for Preaching and Teaching* by John Westerhoff.

This course is a requirement for seminarians in the Second Year of Theology. The course Oral Interpretation and Proclamation is a prerequisite and is taken by seminarians in the First Year of Theology.

The core textbooks around which the course is built are two: *Fulfilled in Your Hearing: the Homily in the Sunday Assembly* and *An Introduction to the Homily*.[3] Portions of other texts are used as well as various pertinent articles. As the students read the assigned material, they are encouraged to apply the following prescriptive:

- Purpose: What is the hidden question which prompted the writing?
- Point: What is the answer to the hidden question?
- Presuppositions: What is the author taking for granted?
- Praxis: So what? What difference is this going to make to anyone? How will what you have read make a difference in your life?

A. A Spiritual Life—Prayer

John Westerhoff's *Spiritual Life: The Foundation for Preaching and Teaching* and Chapter 2, "The Life of Grace" from Richard Gaillardetz' *Transforming Our Days* are foundational to the course. A life rooted in prayer

---

[3] The Bishops' Committee on Priestly Life and Ministry, *Fulfilled in Your Hearing: The Homily in the Sunday Assembly* (Washington, DC: United States Catholic Conference, 1982); Robert P. Wazmak, *An Introduction to the Homily* (Collegeville, MN: Liturgical Press, 1998).

is an essential preaching element. Shallow living produces shallow preaching. A healthy spiritual life flows from our image of God.

Since preaching is a moment in theology, preachers influence, for good or for ill, the image of God of their respective listeners and they often do so unintentionally. The more aware preachers are of their own understanding of God, the better they can lead their people to form healthy and mature images of God. Both Westerhoff and Gaillardetz offer new ways of encountering and probing the mystery of God. The preacher is invited into new ways of imagining God, the church, and human life. From the onset of the course, the preachers are challenged to think prophetically and to form a prophetic heart so that they can discern the workings of God in the movements of today's culture. A deep spiritual life is a day-by-day process. Faithfulness to prayer and a contemplative stance in life leads to a gradual embodiment of the Gospel which overflows into the preaching act. No. 23 in *Fulfilled in Your Hearing* states:

> The preacher is thus called, above all, to be prayerful. The prayer we speak of is not prayer alongside the preparation for preaching, or over and above this preparation, but the very heart and center of the preparation itself. Unless the Word of God in the Scriptures is interiorized through prayerful study and reflection, it cannot possibly sustain the life-giving, love-generating words that preachers want to offer their people.

Throughout the course, text exegesis, preaching methods, and homily composition are approached in an attitude of prayer. Frequently, *GOD* is writ large on the board, with all subsequent class material written over the word to remind both professor and students that God is both the focus of and gives the grace for the preaching. The students are often reminded that the specific aim of every homily is to enable an encounter with the living God.

One Scripture text taken from the Sunday on which the students will base their first preaching is prayerfully proclaimed, slowly and aloud, during the second class of the course. This text is proclaimed twice, employing a different translation the second time it is proclaimed. The students are asked to spend a minute or two silently praying through the text, in light of the following question: What is the movement of God in this text? After some discussion, the students are asked to identify in one word this movement of God.

They are directed to pray this word over the next week and to be alert to God's movement within themselves. In the subsequent weeks, this procedure is followed for the other two readings for the particular

Sunday chosen for the first preaching. In such a way, the students can begin to live the praying of the Scriptures that is being asked of them as the first preparatory step for the homily.[4]

B. Analysis of the Assembly

The U. S. Bishops' document *Fulfilled in Your Hearing: The Homily in the Sunday Assembly* (hereafter referred to as FIYH), published in 1982, is the definitive Catholic document in the United States on the priestly ministry of preaching. FIYH specifically addresses "the intimate link between preaching and the celebration of the sacraments, especially of the Sunday Eucharist"[5] The document succinctly explores the nature and characteristics of (1) the assembly, (2) the preacher, and (3) the homily. The latter chapter is followed by discussion of a homiletic method.

FIYH considers first the assembly—those gathered to receive the preaching. The preacher must know well his or her congregation. "Unless a preacher knows what a congregation needs, wants, or is able to hear, there is every possibility that the message offered in the homily will not meet the needs of the people who hear it" (no. 3). The assembly is the People of God, the true temple in which Christ dwells. The preacher must always keep in mind that the Spirit of Jesus is alive within the assembly. He or she does not so much bring the word of God to the people as draw forth the present action of God in a particular culture for a particular people in a particular time.

The preacher names the grace or dis-grace present.[6] To do this, he or she must be familiar with the economic, social, and cultural milieu of the congregation and the big questions which arise from these. Bishop Robert Morneau suggests that our contemporary audience is dealing with eight crises:

1. Disconnection
2. Radical individualism
3. The widening gap between the haves and the have nots
4. Escalating violence
5. Loss of story (crisis of imagination)
6. Consumerism

---

[4] As far as possible, the author attempts to provide lived experience of the methods and procedures presented and discussed throughout the course.

[5] *Fulfilled in Your Hearing,* Introduction, no. 1.

[6] See Mary Catherine Hilkert, o.p., *Naming Grace: Preaching and the Sacramental Imagination* (New York: Continuum, 1997).

7. Spiritual amnesia—forgetting of being
8. Denial of suffering.[7]

Do these issues impact the congregation? Which ones? How? In light of these issues, the homiletics class takes a brief look at the characteristics of the pre-modern, the modern, and the post-modern worlds and what preaching looks like in each. Consideration is given to the characteristics of an oral culture, a literate culture, and an electronic culture and the characteristics of preaching in the respective culture.

At this time as well, the students are introduced to the two basic patterns of movement in preaching: deductive and inductive. This study is done in light of the revolution in the field of homiletics instigated by Fred Craddock. The deductive style, originating in Aristotle, reigned for centuries and became normative for preaching. In the Catholic Church, the medieval and post-Tridentine stress was on doctrinal preaching in the deductive style. Biblical texts were used solely to embellish the doctrine. This style begins with a general truth which leads to specific applications for a particular situation. It employs propositions followed by points and exhortations. Structurally, it looks like this:

- Statement of thesis
- Explication of the constitutive points
- Illustration of sub-theses drawn from the points
- Application to life situations.

Fred Craddock, with the publication of *As One Without Authority*,[8] took issue with the deductive style. He called for use of inductive movement in sermons. Such an approach begins with particulars of human experience and moves toward unexpected conclusions, inviting the listeners along on the journey. The entire sermon is grounded in both concrete experience and in the Gospel. The sermon is so constructed that the listeners find themselves plunged into the experience, surrounded by the Good News, with no other choice but to make a choice!

The students are presented with the question: Is one movement to be preferred to the other? This question can best be answered by first answering the question, What is the purpose of liturgical preaching? The homily, like the rest of the liturgy, is to draw the assembly into the

---

[7] Bishop Robert Morneau, "The Audience: Who's Out There," keynote address delivered at the National Conference of the Catholic Coalition on Preaching (September 15–18, 2002, in Philadelphia, Pennsylvania).

[8] Fred Craddock, *As One Without Authority* (Nashville: Abingdon Press, 1979).

paschal mystery—to make the mystery of Christ "present and active within [them]" (The Constitution on the Sacred Liturgy, no. 35). Either method of movement could effect this. However, preaching following the deductive method is more prone to point-by-point explication. Sheer exposition of doctrine or listings of moral *dos and don'ts* do not usually draw people into the experience of mystery.

The preaching is always to a specific people living in a specific time with specific experiences and needs. The eucharistic celebration is a trysting place where God, working in the twenty-first century, engages his twenty-first-century people. The inductive pattern of movement, with its emphasis on concrete experience, enables the listeners to better identify with the preacher's message, more easily allowing them to "come along" on the journey to God. Everything that we do as preachers is for the sake of allowing God to shine through, breathe through, speak through that God may draw us all into the divine embrace.

The preacher must be aware, too, of individual issues: who is going through a divorce, who is dealing with a debilitating illness, who is recently unemployed, and the like. He or she must walk among the congregation in order to hear the faith questions arising from individual lives. The opening line of FIYH is no. 4 of the Vatican II document, the Decree on the Ministry and Life of Priests: "The primary duty of priests is the proclamation of the Gospel of God to all." Today's congregations are increasingly diverse. To know the mindset of his or her people, the preacher must, as far as possible, become familiar with their day-to-day life and God's working therein.

Consideration is given to the specific use of the word "homily." The bishops intentionally chose the word based on its Greek root, *homileo,* which translates *a personal and conversational form of address* as opposed to the holding forth of a Greek orator. No. 63 in FIYH emphasizes that the New Testament usage "suggests that a homily should sound more like a personal conversation, albeit a conversation on matters of utmost importance, than like a speech or a classroom lecture." The homily is to be preached in such a way as to bring the assembly into the conversation. The preacher is to avoid moralistic preaching, which merely points out the sin and offers specific remedies. To simply tell people how God expects them to behave, then to apply such behaviors to their lives is like whitewashing a fence. The inherent condition of the fence is ignored and the whitewash will eventually wear away. Moralizing ignores the inherent human condition and the action of God's grace already present in the lives of the assembly.

C. Text Exegesis—Preaching and the Experts

The first move in text exegesis is reading the text in several translations; for example, the *New American Bible,* the *Jerusalem Bible,* and *New Revised Standard Version* of the Bible, noting the differences. These differences can jump start the flow of ideas for the preaching. The students are then directed to read the text several times, at first silently then aloud, paying attention to the movements within. Scriptural texts are dynamic; they were constructed to move the reader to action. The preacher asks: "What is going on within me? How am I moved? How is the text alive within me?"

To facilitate such awareness, the preacher does a structural analysis of the text; that is, the preacher "walks through the text," word for word, line by line, writing either by hand or computer, paying close attention to punctuation as well as to wording. Before laying out the text line by line, the preacher considers the text from a narrative viewpoint, asking how the text is plotted. The preacher next determines an *Introduction* and a *Conclusion* to the text. Noting these, she or he asks how the writer leads us on the journey from "start" to "finish," then begins to plot the journey line by line (see Figure A, p. 186). The author calls this "doing a structural analysis of the text."

In performing this exercise, Scripture scholar Dianne Bergant, c.s.a., cautions against reading into the text what may not be there, advising the homilist to let the text speak only what is present. In such a way the text communicates what it "wants" to—allowing sole primacy to the text.[9] Frequently, new and surprising insights come to light. Such "walking through" the text allows the text to settle within the preacher, leading her or him to the focal truth around which the homily will be shaped.

The above is done before consulting the experts—commentaries and homily aids such as *Homily Service* (The Liturgical Conference). In *How to Preach a Parable,* Eugene Lowry stresses the importance of staying out of the driver's seat, allowing the text to confront the preacher. To assist the confrontation, he directs the preacher to "look for trouble in, around, with, and about the text." Often consulting the verses which both precede and follow the chosen Scripture text reveals "the trouble" or what does not quite fit.[10] In fact, consideration of the preceding and following

[9] Dianne Bergant, C.S.A., "Interpretation and Preaching," oral presentation at the First Conference of the Catholic Coalition on Preaching, *Lord Your Servant Is Listening: Sunday Preaching Today* (September 23–26, 1993, in Schaumburg, IL).

[10] Eugene Lowry, *How to Preach a Parable: Designs for Narrative Sermons* (Nashville: Abingdon Press, 1989) 32–33.

texts is recommended. The writers intentionally ordered the texts in their respective book, gospel, or epistle (1 and 2 Corinthians is an exception). The meaning of a text is often related to its specific placement. A good example of this is found in Matthew 5–7. Matthew 5:3-16—the Beatitudes and being salt and light—set the tone for all the rest that follow. The bulk of Jesus' teaching in these chapters is revelations about how to be salt and light for the world.

As the above exercise yields particular textual issues, the preacher turns to the commentaries and other exegetical helps to confirm suspicions/assumptions, to clarify what puzzles, and to deepen insights.

D. The Lectionary

Prior to Vatican II, liturgical preaching was left to the discretion of the priest who generally focused on the feasts of the day or season and/or doctrinal or moral issues. Scripture texts were used to illustrate or to shore up the preacher's point. Very often the "sermon" preached was unrelated to the liturgy in which it occurred. Vatican II ushered in the era of the Lectionary. The Council Fathers, desirous of restoring the homily to its inherent place in the liturgy, called for the creation of a lectionary so that "the treasures of the Bible [would] be opened up more lavishly that a richer fare may be provided for the faithful at the table of God's word" (The Constitution on the Sacred Liturgy, no. 51).

The Lectionary committee changed the emphasis given to the Scripture readings. The core of the Lectionary is the life, death, and resurrection of Jesus Christ—the paschal mystery. "The new system of readings must contain the nucleus of the apostolic preaching about Jesus as 'Lord and Christ' (Acts 2:36) who fulfilled the Scriptures by his life, his preaching, and above all, his paschal mystery. . . ."[11]

The homiletics class on the Lectionary centers the discussion on the material found in Chapter 3, "The Lectionary: Richer Fare or Lesser Choice?" in Robert Waznak's *An Introduction to the Homily.* In this chapter Waznak addresses the following: (1) The history of the Lectionary, (2) Structure of the Lectionary, (3) Problems and suggestions, and (4) Some conclusions. Under (3) he considers six issues: (a) Difficulty of preaching on three readings, (b) The psalm response, (c) The second reading (out of sync with the first reading and the Gospel), (d) Devaluation of the Old Testament, (e) The exclusivity of the Lectionary, and (f) A straightjacket

---

[11] Godfrey Diekmann as quoted in *An Introduction to the Homily,* Robert Waznak (Collegeville, MN: Liturgical Press, 1998) 74.

for creativity. He concludes that, in light of the above six issues, the Lectionary, though not perfect, preserves the focus of God's word in the formation of the assembly and, for this reason alone, it deserves its primacy of place in liturgical celebrations. This author concurs with Waznak. Too often in the past, the focus of the preaching has been a hammering on, for good or for ill, the favorite topics of the preacher. Many of these were unrelated to the liturgical season or the liturgy of which they were a part.

III. THE PROCESS OF CONSTRUCTION

A. An Operative Theology of Preaching

As stated in FIYH, "the homily is preached in order that a community of believers who have gathered to celebrate the liturgy may do so more deeply and more fully—more faithfully—and thus be formed for Christian witness to the world" (no. 43). Every homily is to bring the meaning of God's saving action to bear upon the present moment, evoking a response for the kingdom of God. Every homily shapes, in some way, the theology of each member of the assembly. What the preacher believes about God, the human condition, and the church leaks through each homily. Because preaching is a moment in theology,[12] it is critical for each preacher to be aware of his or her theology of preaching. The first class of the course is devoted to a working definition of preaching and discussion of the meaning and content of a theology of preaching. Excerpts from writings by several noted preachers[13] are explored in light of the following questions: (1) What is the image of God conveyed? (2) What does each say about the way the word of God is received? About people's relationship with/to the word of God? (3) What does the preacher reveal about his or her belief of the human condition—sin and grace?

At this time, the students are asked to write, on a five-by-eight index card, their responses to the following questions:

1. How do you feel about the ministry of preaching?
2. What do you already know about preaching?
3. What do you most want to know about preaching?
4. What is the aim of preaching?
5. What are your fears around this ministry?

[12] See the article "Preaching as a 'Moment' in Theology," William J. Hill, o.p., *Homiletic and Pastoral Review* 77 (1976–1977) 10–19.

[13] Specifically, Archbishop Oscar Romero, Frederick Buechner, Walter Brueggemann, Mary Catherine Hilkert, o.p., and Thomas Troeger.

Considerable class time is given to the sharing of and discussion around their responses to these questions. It is important, from the first, to articulate feelings and expectations around the ministry of preaching so that positive understandings may be strengthened and expanded and negative understandings forthrightly addressed, for what is hidden governs us.

In the actions of both composing and proclaiming the homily, the preacher becomes the living word. In the Liturgy of the Eucharist, after the words of consecration, Jesus commands "Do this in memory of me." The preacher is to realize that he or she is the first to offer the bread and wine of his or her own life. The preacher must "walk the talk." Is the preacher a medium through which God works, enabling the assembly to realize that they live now in the presence and providence of God? Does the preacher realize that he or she is the first to be "body broken and blood outpoured" for the sake of the kindom? That he or she is charged with living the Eucharist before preaching this to others? What, ultimately, does the preacher hope for his or her preaching? The students are encouraged to compose each course homily against the backdrop of these questions. At the end of the course, the student is asked to submit a five-page double-spaced reflection paper articulating a personal operative theology of preaching incorporating the elements discussed in the introductory class. This reflection paper is written with the understanding that the thoughts expressed are but the beginning of a personal theology of preaching.

Consideration is given to the difference between preaching and teaching. *Teaching*—derived from the Greek *didache*—is the explanation of the rudiments of faith, moral guidance, and the social and ethical implications of the Gospel. Teaching is subservient to the proclamation of the Good News. *Preaching*—derived from the Greek *kerygma*—is the announcement of the Good News: the life, death, resurrection, and expected Second Coming of Jesus the Christ. Teaching and preaching have distinct purposes and affect the assembly differently, each eliciting a different response. Teaching addresses more the intellect of the assembly who respond to the teacher with agreement or disagreement. Preaching is to appeal more to the total person—intellect, heart, imagination, gut—not merely with ideas and logic, but principally with evocative language in league with the power of the Holy Spirit inherent in the proclamation of the Good News. Teachers teach *about* Jesus; preachers, hopefully, preach Jesus. The response to preaching is not to ideas but to Jesus himself, leading the assembly naturally into the posture of praise and thanksgiving before the living God as expressed in the eucharistic rite. There is no denying that the homily may contain some teaching in order to expand understanding. But teaching about God and the kindom is never the sole end of the homily. The differences between preaching and teaching as well as the appropriate employment for each are highlighted throughout the course. Chapters from John Westerhoff's *Spiritual Life: The Foundation for Preaching and Teaching* are assigned reading throughout the course and serve as the springboard for these discussions.[14]

B. Buttrick's Moves

David Buttrick, Professor Emeritus of Homiletics and Worship at Vanderbilt Divinity School, Nashville, Tennessee lined out his homiletic method in *Homiletic: Moves and Structures*. His is a *phenomenological approach* to preaching. He sees the task of preaching as the forming of a world in consciousness so that God is named. The preacher assists in creating a worldview for the assembly—a faith-view which announces God's new order, what Jesus calls the reign of God, incarnationally present within our lives. How can a preacher best achieve this? Buttrick studied the phenomena of how language forms in consciousness and then applied his learning to homiletic structure. After carefully poring over Scripture passages, Buttrick discovered that there is movement of thought or event or image by some logic on the part of the writers—a "theo-logic"—by which the author chooses the sequences of the episodes in the plot.

Buttrick insists, therefore, that the biblical text is not a static thing from which we distill an idea, like plucking an apple from a tree. Biblical passages are more like a film; they display movement of thought, event, or image. Not only does the language of Scripture *say* something; it intends to *do* something as well. Biblical passages "travel," creating movement within the reader. If the homilist can replicate that same movement, the truth of the homily will form in the consciousness of the assembly.

Furthermore, according to Buttrick, ideas are formed in consciousness through conversation, both formal and informal. He studied the interaction between the way we speak and the way in which consciousness grasps and understands. There is certain logic in normal conversations. One begins with Point A and goes all the way to H, and by the time one reaches H, it appears to have nothing to do with A. But, actually, there is logic to the flow of the conversation. If, then, a homily is written according to logical "moves" of a conversation, then the focal truth of the

---

[14] John H. Westerhoff, *Spiritual Life: The Foundation for Preaching and Teaching* (Louisville: Westminster John Knox, 1994).

homily settles within the listener, evoking a response to God which is the aim of the eucharistic celebration.

The students experience this phenomenon before an explanation is given. Professor and students engage in a conversation as the students gather for the class that day. At the appropriate moment, the conversation model—from the conversation held earlier with the students—is put on board. Professor and students move through the conversation, point by point, noting the "illogic logic" which ties together the conversation (see Figure B, p. 187). The conversation begins with the grandmother's illness and ends with the Indians' baseball team—two unrelated topics yet tied together through a certain "illogic logic" of the conversation. Something in the previous move triggers the subject of the following move. Buttrick patterned his homiletic "method of moves" on this conversational phenomenon.

To begin the process, Buttrick directs the preacher to ask of the passage what it intends or wants to do. The challenge for the preacher is to replicate the logic of that movement within the mind of the hearers so that the homily comes alive within each listener. Good preaching, according to Buttrick, creates movement within the listener that enables the assembly to enter wholeheartedly into the praise and thanksgiving of the eucharistic prayer. As the preacher does the structural analysis of each Scripture passage, described under Text Exegesis, he or she keeps in mind the following questions:

1. What am I feeling?
2. To what am I drawn in this passage?
3. What is moving within me?
4. Is one truth beginning to come forward?

It is critical that the student be alert for the one truth which resonates within him or her, a truth informed with God that impassions the preacher. A homily focused on one truth drawn from the text or texts has a better chance of settling within the listeners. Homilies which focus on two or more truths overload the listener to the extent that no truth settles within.

Thomas Long says that "breathing through the passage is a living memory, a living truth always pressing into the present as a demand and a resource."[15] A large circle is drawn on board; within the circle is written

---

[15] Thomas G. Long, *The Witness of Preaching* (Louisville: Westminster John Knox, 1989) 52.

that one truth—such as God's gracious mercy; God's persistent presence in our lives; God's call to be love for one another—which the students have gleaned from the Scripture texts (see 1 in Figure C, p. 187). The student now turns to the construction of the homily.

The preacher is to compose the homily in a set of "moves." Recall that Buttrick's creation of moves came from the realization that all human conversation, unless it is nothing more than a brief exchange of small talk, moves in an ordered sequence. These conversations have a certain logic to them in that there is a natural flow from idea to idea. These ideas move the conversation along, to the extent that the idea with which one starts may not be the one with which one ends, but the middle indicates the relationship, the natural logic which ties the first with the last. Homilies are more effective the more they imitate this natural flow. Writing in moves helps to ensure this logical progression. Buttrick defines a move as a "bundle of words" formed around an idea which the preacher wants to form in the consciousness of the listeners. A homily is a sequence of moves carefully designed to form in group consciousness according to the "theo-logic" of the biblical text.

Within the large circle drawn on the board and superimposed over the words naming the one truth are drawn boxes representing the moves of the homily (see 2 in Figure C, p. 187). The one truth on which the homily is focused must "bleed through" each move. Every word in the homily is to serve that one truth to facilitate its formation in the consciousness of the assembly, always with the intent to lead the assembly to praise and thanksgiving to the living God at the eucharistic table.

The students study and critique several sets of sample moves. The following criteria guide their critique:

1. Does each move have a central idea that is well developed?
2. Do the moves follow an ordered logic, causing the homily to flow?
3. Do the moves transition into each other? Does the last line of each move serve as the transition?
4. Is every sentence in the move pertinent to the central idea?
5. Does the one truth bleed through each move in some way?
6. How is God and God's world named through these moves?

C. Long's Focus and Function Statements and Sermonic Form

After the students have composed and preached their first homily based on Buttrick's moves, they are introduced to another method of distilling the one truth from the Lectionary texts for a given Sunday, namely, the *focus statement* and the *function statement* developed by Thomas Long in *The Witness of Preaching*. A focus statement, according to Long, "is a concise description of the central, controlling, and unifying theme of the sermon."[16] The student is to state in one brief sentence the core thought, revealing what the homily aims *to say.* Its companion is a function statement, defined by Long as "a description of what the preacher hopes the sermon will create or cause to happen for the hearers."[17] The function statement speaks to the tensive quality of the homily. The student, in as brief a sentence as possible, states what the homily *intends to do.* Both focus and function statements (1) grow directly from exegesis of the Scripture texts, (2) are related to one another—what the homily intends to do flows from what it intends to say, and (3) are clear, unified, and relatively simple.

After struggling with composing their first homily, the students are more receptive to both the understanding and the importance of employing focus and function statements. After studying and discussing sample focus and function statements, the students are directed to write their own statements based on the homily they preached the previous week. This exercise enables them better to perceive areas of their homilies that were unrelated to the one truth each aimed to call forth within the assembly. The struggle to compose these statements disciplines the students to clarity of purpose. In line with FIYH, which stresses that the homily is to enable an assembly "to recognize God's active presence and then to respond to that presence in faith through liturgical word and gesture" (no. 81), the students are directed to constantly ask themselves the following two questions:

1. What truth do I hope will be evoked within the listeners enabling them to respond in celebration during the remainder of the liturgy?
2. Is that truth clear in the homily I am creating?

Next the students consider Long's insights into sermonic form. Long defines form as "an organizational plan for deciding what kinds of things will be said and done in a sermon and in what sequence."[18] Form is critical to the sermon, for it "provides shape and energy to the sermon and thus becomes itself a vital force in how a sermon makes meaning."[19]

[16] Ibid., 86.
[17] Ibid.
[18] Ibid., 93.
[19] Ibid.

The form of a homily shapes the content and vice versa. Neither can be considered apart from the other. The two are so woven together that they form two sides to one coin. Thus, form embodies the focus and the function of the homily. When the preacher is clear about the message and the aim of the homily, the form of the homily almost creates itself. The shape of the Gospel being proclaimed and the listening patterns of the assembly likewise influence the form of the homily. The students are advised to consider the liturgical season of the church year, the social setting of the assembly, the tenor of the assembly at the time, and, in light of these, to discern what the assembly most needs for Gospel living. What form will best transmit the Gospel truth in light of the setting and the needs of the particular Assembly?

D. Image, Kinds of Imagination, Narrative and Story

FIYH defines the homily as "a scriptural interpretation of human existence which enables a community to recognize God's active presence, to respond to that presence in faith through liturgical word and gesture, and beyond the liturgical assembly, through a life lived in conformity with the Gospel" (no. 81). Homilies built with prosaic words do not enable the hoped-for active response, nor will homilies strung with flat statements and exhortatory urgings. Only those homilies possessing a tensive quality—one that creates a pulling, a stretching, a roiling around within the person—will challenge into response.

Before coming to class, the students are asked to recall a personal experience of conversion, using the following questions:

1. What prompted the conversion?
2. What were the feelings experienced throughout the process?
3. What convinced you to initiate the needed change?

Discussion is jump started by the following quote from Walter Brueggemann:

> The event in preaching is an event in transformed imagination. Poets, in the moment of preaching, are permitted to perceive and voice the world differently, to dare a new phrase, a new picture, a fresh juxtaposition of matters long known. Poets are authorized to invite a new conversation, with new voices sounded, new hearings possible. The new conversation may end in freedom to trust and courage to relinquish. The new conversation, on which our very lives depend, requires a poet and not a moralist. Because finally church people are like other people; we are not changed

by new rules. The deep places in our lives—places of resistance and embrace—are not ultimately reached by instruction. Those places of resistance and embrace are reached only by stories, by images, metaphors, and phrases that line out the world differently, apart from our fear and hurt.[20]

The students examine their conversion experiences in light of Brueggemann's quote. Images, metaphors, and stories have the ability to plunge us into a different world. In doing so, they create the inner tension needed to effect conversion. Do the students experience this inner tension? What caused that tension? Was there resistance at first? What brought about the embrace?

Why is this so necessary to the homily? If, according to FIYH, the homily is to bring about a face-to-face encounter with God that leads to full participation during the Table of the Eucharist, which in turn is to overflow into daily living, it must employ a tensive element which alone can draw people in. Stories, images, and metaphors disarm us, soften us, open us, and render us vulnerable, enabling God's desired work within us. Barbara Brown Taylor accosts the preacher with the necessity for such language:

> Much of our direct communication from the pulpit is like a travelogue to someplace our listeners have never been. We may do a masterful job of telling them about the various points of interest in God's country—the architecture, the museums, the geography, the politics—but when it is all over and the lights go up, they have been on our trip, not their own. What is still lacking is something we cannot give directly, which is a sense of having been there for themselves. [We preachers must] learn how to describe God's country so that people recognize it as their own country not as a foreign land they may visit some day but as the place where they live right now in the presence and providence of God.[21]

The operative word is *telling*. So often preachers wax eloquently, describing just what it is their listeners need to know and do in order to serve God and make way for God's kindom, when what is most needed are simple words which bring them into the embrace of God. The words fall away, the preacher is forgotten because the listeners are caught up in God who opens up new possibilities within and before them.

---

[20] Walter Brueggemann, *Finally Comes the Poet: Daring Speech for Proclamation* (Minneapolis: Fortress Press, 1989) 109–10.

[21] Barbara Brown Taylor, "Chapter Eleven: Preaching the Body" in *Listening to the Word,* ed. Gail R. O'Day and Thomas G. Long (Nashville: Abingdon Press, 1993) 209.

1. IMAGINATION / IMAGE

Prior to the class on imagination and image, the students write their own definition of imagination before reading the assigned Chapter 2, "Preaching and Teaching in a New Day" in Westerhoff's *Spiritual Life*. The class begins with discussion around the following three questions:

1. Of what/whom is Westerhoff speaking when he says we are creating "unthinking, unimaginative followers of authority figures?"[22]

2. At what is he getting when he declares, "Too many preachers want to tell people what they already know?"[23]

3. How did you define imagination? What are your feelings about imagination?

There has been for centuries a distrust of the imagination. The word has conjured up such ideas as "fluff," "the irrational," "the unreal." Vestiges of these ideas are often present in the students. We now know that imagination is basic to human knowing. What is known is the springboard to the unknown. Webster defines imagination as *the act or power of forming a mental image of something not present to the senses or never before wholly perceived in reality.* Richard Kearney speaks of imagination as "the human power to convert absence into presence, actuality into possibility, what-is into something-other-than-it-is."[24] Imagination is the power to think metaphorically—to perceive a unity between two dissimilar ideas that produces a new identity. Metaphorical thinking is critical to preaching. God and God's reign can only be grasped metaphorically. To speak of God *as* something, we know creates a new reality—a new way of seeing which issues in a new way of being. Jesus, in speaking of his Abba, yielded a new experience of God *as* "beloved daddy." To preach metaphorically, then, is to "un-arrange" the mind of the assembly so that they see the familiar with new eyes and through such "in-sight" find themselves face-to-face with God and new understandings about God and God's kindom.

To preach in such a fashion is to preach to change images—to reach that place in us that responds "Ah-h-h!" or "Ugh!" There can be no changes in a person's life without a change of the images on which lives are staked. Women and men live out of the images they hold. These deep-seated images give rise to who they are and what they do.

---

[22] Westerhoff, *Spiritual Life,* 17.

[23] Ibid., 23.

[24] Richard Kearney, quoted in *Listening to the Word,* ed. Gail R. O'Day and Thomas G. Long (Nashville: Abingdon Press, 1993) 13.

The revolution Jesus brought was a revolution of the images which set worldview—images from which convictions spring. Transformation occurs when these images are affected—when one set of images is replaced with another which results in radical change. God, ourselves, our neighbors, the world—all are perceived differently. This is very much in line with David Buttrick's idea of naming a world. "By naming," he declares, "we think the world we live."[25] The world becomes real for us because of language used. Preachers through images name the world for God; they assist their assemblies to see the world through the lenses of God and through that seeing comes an encounter with the living God.

Poetic language serves image; it describes faith as process, not content. Disciples of Jesus are not those who only *believe* certain things; disciples *live* a certain way. Poetic language is short on concepts and long on pictures. It goes straight to that gut place in us—that place of embrace and resistance where change occurs. Poetic language educes a response of "Ah, yes!" or "Ugh! No!" when encountering God or a truth involving God. An effective homilist avoids flat academic statements. Rather, he or she colors the homily with poetic words which draw the listeners into God's presence.

Poetic language is different from the language found in the conventional imagination. The conventional imagination is formed by the givens of a culture—the beliefs and traditions inherited. These provide the norms by which the members live and form their identity. The church is steeped in conventional imagination and necessarily so. The conventional imagination holds the People of God in a web of meaning. However, the language expressing these beliefs and traditions, which make them come alive, must alter with the times. Meanings must be uttered afresh. The images of one century will not speak to another.

> Indeed, the word of God is living and active, sharper than any two-edged sword, piercing until it divides soul from spirit, joints from marrow; it is able to judge the thoughts and intentions of the heart. (Heb 4:12 NRSV)

The images employed to preach such a word must also be living, active, and sharp for the times in which they are spoken. If they reek of another century, they do not penetrate the hearts and minds of the assembly. "Neither the sounds of ancient Samaria nor the rhetoric of Rome or Rahner can pour forth from today's pulpit unchanged, unaltered, unconverted. Not if we intend to be heard."[26] The students consider such

---

[25] David Buttrick, *Homiletic: Moves and Structures* (Philadelphia: Fortress Press, 1987) 7.
[26] Walter J. Burghardt, s.j., *Preaching: The Art and the Craft* (New York: Paulist, 1987) 13.

conventional images as "sacrifice," "sacrament," "faith," "sin," "grace," "redemption," and "the Mystical Body of Christ." What is the truth contained in each term? How is that truth best imaged for the post-modern twenty-first-century listener?

Along with discussion of the conventional imagination, the students are introduced to two other types of imagination—dialectical and sacramental. These two types have to do with the manner in which the word of God is revealed. The *dialectical imagination* sees the word of God as an event breaking into our lives. The revelatory event of preaching is intended to confront the hearer with a crisis not so much of understanding as of a crisis begging for a decision. Walter Brueggemann, especially, approaches preaching from a dialectical stance. He speaks of a dominant culture which works to keep all others narcoticized and numb so that belief in the current way things are is the only way they can be. Brueggemann insists that the Gospel calls believers to live counter-culturally to the dominant culture. Preaching provides the "counter speech" for jump-starting the lively imagination needed to wake up and to give courage to live as a member of the kindom of God. Christians are called to be an alternative community to that of the dominant culture.[27]

The *sacramental imagination* sees the word of God present in the depths of creation, of the human person, of situations. Preaching arouses awareness of this presence already at work and names the grace. Theologian Karl Rahner best exemplifies the sacramental imagination. He understands creation and human existence as fundamentally graced. Human beings are structured as openness to God's offer of love. The sacramental imagination stresses the incarnational presence of God as consistent and passionate self-communicating love. Men and women are the *imago Dei,* even through wounded by sin.[28]

The students are led to realize that the dialectical imagination and the sacramental imagination are not in competition with one another. Neither one is preferred to the other. Both speak to the way God reveals God's self and the coming of God's kindom. Whether the homily approaches from a dialectical stance or a sacramental stance depends on the form and function of the particular homily. For example, a homily with a prophetic tone would most probably speak out of the dialectical imagination, with God's voice breaking in, shattering tightly-held expectations.

---

[27] See Walter Brueggemann's *Finally Comes the Poet* (Minneapolis: Fortress Press, 1989) and *The Prophetic Imagination* (Philadelphia: Fortress Press, 1978).

[28] See Hilkert, *Naming Grace,* for an in-depth exploration of the sacramental imagination.

2. IMAGE AND METAPHOR

Metaphor is more than a literary genre. Metaphor is necessary for life because it is the way into reality. New learning is grounded in what went before. The unknown is reached and understood by standing solidly in the known and then stretching up and away toward the unknown. Metaphorical thinking brings two seemingly unrelated things together in such a way that a new insight into reality results. Metaphor, in a sense, creates a collision between the two dissimilar ideas, creating a spark or a flash of new insight, producing a surprising reconciliation between the two. Consider the metaphor, "the night was black ink." "Night" and "black ink" are two very dissimilar things, seemingly irreconcilable. However, at a deeper level there is an immediate recognition of what is meant—a recognition which easily reconciles, in actuality, two very unlike things.

Belden Lane speaks of metaphor as playing with language—talking about something familiar in a crooked way so as to reveal or suggest something unfamiliar yet strangely related.[29] Metaphorical thinking is definitely needed for preaching the mystery which is God and God's kindom, for these two realities are, in the basic sense, most dissimilar from ordinary human experience. God is only touched through the metaphorical *as, as if,* and *is like.* Jesus exemplifies this in his stories and parables. Metaphor is indeed the language of faith—Scripture's preferred way of conveying the truth about God and the kindom of God.

Metaphor and image are often used interchangeably. The author prefers to distinguish between the two when applied to preaching. Metaphor is the *process* in which image is employed. Image is a tool which serves metaphor. The image is the concept or object brought into relationship with the mystery of God so that an aspect of God or God's kindom is strongly, sometimes surprisingly, revealed. Following is a portion of a homily preached on the Twelfth Sunday in Ordinary Time (year A) whose Scripture texts are (1) Jeremiah 20:7, 10-13; (2) Romans 5:12-15; and (3) Matthew 10:26-33.

> Life in the 90s isn't turning out to be what we expected. With all our technology, all the advances in the scientific and medical fields, all is not well. Our world has gone awry. New diseases we never dreamed of are born every day. Homelessness and violence abound. Daily the media bombards us with one disaster after another. We can, to some degree, understand the

---

[29] Notes taken from a lecture given to the Spring Core Homiletic Seminar at Aquinas Institute of Theology, St. Louis, Missouri, 1995. Dr. Belden Lane, an ordained Presbyterian minister, is professor of theological studies at St. Louis University in Saint Louis, Missouri.

awful consequences that befall a person who has done the wrong things. We feel some satisfaction that he or she got what was deserved. But . . . to a good person, to a child, to *us*? We can rightly say with Jeremiah, "You seduced me, God! You are too powerful for me, and you have prevailed. I have followed your way and still my life is fraught with difficulties and with pain. Many mock me. I see that so often the bad flourish while the good suffer. Just what is going on? And yet, Jeremiah, after complaining bitterly to God, moves into praise of God. After addressing God, he addresses himself. "But the Lord is with me like a dread warrior; therefore my persecutors will stumble, and they will not prevail." Something has shifted within Jeremiah. His perspective has changed. Why? What has happened?

What happened?
I thought it was dead.
It had been in the jar of water since February.
A bit of mold had formed around one of the holes made by the toothpick.
A few years back, I had successfully raised an avocado tree from sprouting
    a pit in a jar of water, just as I was doing with this one.
Back then, a root had shot out in no time, followed a week later by a sprout
    from the top of the pit.
But there seemed no hope for this current pit.
I nearly discarded it at the beginning of May.
I didn't; each time I reached to throw it away, something in me said wait.
On May 24th, three-and-a-half weeks later, a half-inch root protruded
    from the bottom of that pit.
Life out of seeming death.
The root continues to grow.
I now await the green shoot that will surely follow.
"Everything," promises Jesus, "will be made known—everything brought
    to light."
What is revealed in the dark must be shouted in the light and from roof-
    tops.
What is revealed in the dark!
Perhaps God does God's best work in darkness.
Perhaps that is what Jeremiah came to understand.
In the darkness that was his life, God was at work.
God is ever at work, whether in the darkness or in the bright light of day.
Jesus promises this.
If not one sparrow falls to the ground without God caring about it, then is
    not God with us in and through the darkness?
If God knows the number of our hairs, does God not then know every
    pain, even the slightest?
We seem to operate out of the belief that God is only with us when our
    life is going well.

We act as if difficult times signal that God has left.

Hope is a slender white root—a fragile thing yet paradoxically a strong thing.

A slender small root that says life is happening.

The seemingly dead brown pit of our lives contains abundant life because God is at work there.

Ultimately, it is a matter of looking and seeing.

Looking and seeing are not the same thing.

We *see* what we look for.

In this homily, the tensive image employed is the moldy brown avocado pit which un-expectedly puts forth a shoot of life. This image assists the metaphorical leap that God continually surprises us with faithfulness. God works mightily to bring about life within us and most especially does God work in the pit times of life. Metaphor undergirds as well as permeates the entire homily, which the image makes apparent. Dr. Belden Lane names five characteristics of how metaphor operates as we receive it:

1. Concreteness: felt in a bodily way as well as intellectually.

2. Incompleteness: there is a certain ambiguity. Things are intentionally left unsolved. Note that Jesus is intentionally vague; he teases the minds of his listeners in active thought. Preachers ought to leave gaps. Refrain from being exhaustively complete. Let the Spirit of God speak a variety of truths.

3. Shocking quality: makes strange the truth; shocks people into a new perspective of truth.

4. Indirection: allow truth to creep up on people sideways. In the story of David and Nathan in Kings, David gets caught by truth that won't let him go. Preach so as to ensnare the congregation into the story all unaware.

5. Provisionality: a high level of multivalence present. Metaphor only approximates one level of truth at a time.

The students discuss these five traits in conjunction with the homily they are either preparing or have just preached.

3. NARRATIVE AND STORY: IS THERE A DIFFERENCE?

Narrative preaching, as defined in *The Concise Encyclopedia of Preaching,* is "any sermon in which the arrangement of ideas takes the form of a plot involving a strategic delay of the preacher's meaning."[30] Plot involves

---

[30] William H. Willimon and Richard Lischer, *Concise Encyclopedia of Preaching* (Louisville: Westminster John Knox, 1995) 342.

movement—a moving from an opening conflict, which escalates to a critical point demanding a resolution, followed by a choice leading to catharsis. In the plotted movement of the homily, the Gospel is introduced at the crisis, pointing the way to resolution. A story may or may not be involved. What is critical to narrative preaching is the plotted movement.

Homilies with a narrative quality serve transformation of images because they are characterized by movement. Such homilies are not an enumeration of points strung together. Narrative preaching is interactive preaching, drawing in and calling for a response from the listeners. A profound truth so grasps the assembly that they find themselves in face-to-face encounter with God. A string of flat statements, no matter how brilliantly constructed, does not do this.

Narrative preaching is related to story because it imitates the same action found in storytelling—the narrative of a sequence of words, actions, events, and experiences. Like a story, it contains complications, tensions, or surprises which not only sustain interest, but pull the listener forward. Narrative preaching may or may not employ a story as its tensive vehicle.

Story preaching, a distinct type of narrative preaching, is that which encompasses an entire story. All elements of story are involved in the preaching—setting, characters, crisis, and resolution. The story itself becomes the tensive vehicle drawing the listeners into the action. Telling a story as part of the homily does not make it a narrative or a story preaching.

Willimon and Lischer list and describe the following as types of narrative preaching: (1) story preaching, (2) inductive preaching, (3) episodal preaching, and (4) phenomenological move preaching.[31] Any of these is conducive to engaging the assembly through a felt tension demanding a resolution or response, a response further drawn forth by the continued celebration of the Eucharist.

E. Eugene Lowry's Homiletical Plot

Eugene Lowry describes his method of preaching as a narrative sermon that is "an event-in-time" which moves from opening disequilibrium through escalation to surprising reversal into closing denouement. According to Lowry, events deal in movement rather than thought. He challenges the preacher to create a homily which is an experience

---

[31] Ibid., 342–44.

rather than a collection of ideas. To do this, the preacher approaches the Scripture text alert to the movement contained therein. The students are encouraged to consider the homily as a journey experienced by both preacher and assembly. The preacher is to focus more on the "how" of reaching a destination, gleaned from the biblical narrative, rather than on "what" is getting said.

Look to the plot, directs Lowry. Resolution, the reaching of a destination, belongs to plots. A homily is intentionally plotted; that is, there is some kind of sequential ordering of events involving conflict, escalation of the conflict, a redemptive experience shedding light, which then leads to a resolution. This sequential ordering of events is a call to journey from problem to resolution. According to Lowry, a homily formed in such plotted moves is more apt to settle within the listeners, moving them to response during the liturgy that will, in turn, result in response through their daily lives. Lowry's method well serves the double-feasted tradition. The assembly, steeped in a problematic situation, wrestles with the tension and welcomes the resolution brought about by the Good News. Such Gospel relief moves the assembly into the praise and thanksgiving of the eucharistic feast which, in turn, sends the members forth to proclaim the truth of the encounter.

Lowry's method, with its emphasis on upsetting the equilibrium and reversing expectations with Gospel insight, naturally leads to the consideration of prophetic preaching. Drawing on the class SC312: Prophetic Literature, which the students are taking concurrently, they reflect on the nature of prophecy and the characteristics of a prophet. Material from Megan McKenna's *Prophets: Words of Fire* is also brought into the discussion as well as the following two questions:

1. What is prophetic preaching?
2. What current issues call for prophetic preaching?

McKenna declares that "the prophet speaks, acts, lives, and breathes from inside—inside God and inside the people's pain, knowing both "divine pathos" and intimacy with God as well as involvement with the people."[32] In light of the multitude of suffering and injustices proliferating the world today, is the call to the preacher in the twenty-first century to be, above all, a prophetic voice? God, through the prophet Jeremiah, emphatically reminds us that God's word often burns and breaks us before it comforts and heals. "Is not my word like fire, says the LORD,

---

[32] Megan McKenna, *Prophets: Words of Fire* (Maryknoll: Orbis Books, 2001) 7.

and like a hammer that breaks a rock in pieces" (Jer 23:29 NRSV)? The eucharistic liturgy commissions the faithful to go forth to proclaim the Good News received and celebrated, though that Good News may at first appear as bad news. Prophetic preaching assists this commission, alerting the assembly to prepare the way for the coming of the reign of God by bringing the hope of the Good News through word and deed. The opening words of the Vatican II document The Pastoral Constitution on the Church in the Modern World ratifies this charge: "The joys and the hopes, the griefs and the anxieties of the men *(sic)* of this age, especially those who are poor or in any way afflicted, these too are the joys and hopes, the griefs and anxieties of the followers of Christ. Indeed, nothing genuinely human fails to raise an echo in their hearts" (no. 1). Living these words often calls the faithful to firmly address those systems of oppression causing anxiety and grief. For their final preaching practicum, the students are asked to compose a homily based on Lowry's method and addressing a contemporary issue prophetically; that is, in a tone that both stirs up and comforts. In other words, prophetic preaching afflicts the comfortable while comforting the afflicted.

F. Critique—The Coaching Method

The homiletic team of St. Mary's Seminary employs the coaching method for critiquing homilies preached at the practicum sessions. This method makes a conscious effort to reduce the power equation which produces defensive postures. The coaching sheet is divided into four areas (see Figure D1, p. 188):

1. The left column reflects the preacher's insights; the right column, the evaluator's.

2. In the top left quadrant, the preacher records his or her positive comments about the homily just preached; in the top right, the evaluator records his or her positive comments. Both preacher and evaluator write those preaching elements done well and that should be repeated.

3. In the bottom quadrant, the preacher records those areas needing improvement; the evaluator records improvement areas in the bottom right quadrant. The preacher and the evaluator write what might be done differently if given a chance.

Preacher completes the same form on his or her own performance and begins by enumerating those things that he or she would do again, if given the chance. When finished, the class adds to that positive list. The preacher then moves to those things he or she would do differently, if given the chance. The class adds to this list.

After the first student completes his or her evaluation, the subsequent evaluators begin by saying "I affirm all that has gone before," adding only unvoiced insights. An insight is repeated only if the evaluator disagrees.

The preacher remains silent during the feedback of the evaluators, neither explaining nor defending elements of his or her preaching.

The following rules always apply:

1. Everybody needs to know what the rules are.
2. The preacher (the one being evaluated), speaks first.
3. Nobody else in the room gets to react while the one being evaluated is speaking. Nonverbal responses are to be kept to a minimum.
4. The preacher lets the evaluators know when he or she is finished so that they might begin.

See Figure D2, page 189, for Coaching Criteria. The bolded areas are those emphasized during the course.

This method has proved to be most beneficial. The students learn the vocabulary for critiquing. Awareness of both strengths and weaknesses is heightened. They learn to accept humbly the weakness critique without arguing or defending themselves, and begin earnestly to address those areas needing improvement. Emphasis on strengths as well as on weaknesses encourages rather than disheartens students. Since no point of critique is repeated, the method is efficient and timesaving. Students speak to the point with little or no embellishment.

Generally, the entire process—the preaching and the critique—takes twenty minutes, allowing for six homiletic experiences in one preaching practicum. In classes larger than six students, each fills out a coaching sheet but only the preacher, two students, and the professor give feedback orally. There are four preaching practicums during this basic homiletics course.

G. Homiletic Conversations

1. THE TRINITY: A BOTH/AND GOD RATHER THAN AN EITHER/OR GOD

Does God deal in polarizations? In dualisms which inflict injury? Or do polarizations and dualisms originate out of broken humanity? Careful studies of the Scriptures reveal that God is about wholeness, about abundance of life which comes about only when the organism is unified and at peace with itself and its environment. Jesus' entire life was a reaching out to those who were excluded, about a healing-to-wholeness of those who were broken. In Galatians we read that in Christ "there is no longer Jew or Greek, there is no longer slave or free, there is no longer male and female; for all of you are one in Christ Jesus" (Gal 3:28 NRSV). There are to be no more divisions; diversity, yes, but no divisions. "For just as the body is one and has many members, and all the members of the body, though many, are one body, so it is with Christ. For in the one Spirit we were all baptized into one body—Jews or Greeks, slaves or free—and we were all made to drink of the one Spirit" (1 Cor 12:12-13 NRSV). Humanity has lived for a long time with dualistic thinking. Such thinking has spawned many of the *isms* with which we are afflicted today: racism, militarism, nationalism, sexism. Because of this dualism we think too much in opposites pitted against each other. Dualism savors one-upmanship and deals in *either/ors:* one way is right and healthy and the other way is wrong and diseased. Dualism has created stereotypical imaging and labeling.

Hierarchies of being came into play, resulting in *power over* ruling relationships rather than *power with* and *power for service.* For centuries, humankind has taken for granted the sorting of creation into a hierarchical pyramid with the level(s) above dominating the level(s) below. In our day, various sciences, such as ecology and quantum physics, have toppled that theoretical pyramid, pointing out the communion between all creation, living and non-living. Our universe is one of vast, elementary connectedness, involving every created entity in a relationship of interdependency, suggesting the metaphor of a web. Movement on one part of the web affects the entire structure. No one place on the web is dominant. In the interrelatedness of the universe, each entity influences the whole. Every place on the web experiences the actions of the rest.

Jesus minced no words about the kind of power operative in the reign of God. Such power is intimately bound up with service in the liberation of others. Dominance of others is foreign in God's reign. "But Jesus called [the disciples] to him and said, 'You know that the rulers of the Gentiles lord it over them, and their great ones are tyrants over them. It will not be so among you; but whoever wishes to be great among you must be your servant, and whoever wishes to be first among you must be your slave'" (Matt 20:25-27 NRSV).

This issue of dualistic thinking is raised early on in the course in connection with the preacher's operative theology and, in greater detail, in connection with the class on prophetic preaching. The students are challenged to scrutinize their own beliefs and biases because, unexamined, such beliefs and biases can seep through their homilies as well as their day-to-day interactions. If Jesus did not dominate, did not coerce, did not lord it over others, how can we, his disciples? If Jesus entered into communion with humankind, shattering, through his incarnation and his lifestyle, the barriers which divide and keep apart, must not we do the same? Do the students intentionally operate from the image of the trinitarian God—a God of communion—revealed by Jesus?

In light of this question, the students consider briefly the following historical points:

1. Early in the history of the Church, the doctrine of the Trinity was relegated more to the inner life of God and, in a sense, separated from the economy of salvation. The early Church set out to preach the dying and rising of Jesus. Through their experience of the resurrection, the disciples understood that, through Jesus in the Spirit, God was at work to bring all people to salvation. They did not remain a community closed in upon themselves but were Spirit-impelled to bring the Good News of salvation to all peoples. Thus did the neophyte church expand into the Hellenistic Gentile world. In so doing, they discovered that the language and thought of the *kerygma,* originally based in liturgies, in oral Jesus stories, and in the evolving New Testament canon were insufficient for proclaiming the Good News in a Hellenistic world.

2. The early apologists, and some who preceded them, saw a connection with the Greek world through understanding Jesus as *logos.* In the Christian-Jewish context, *logos* was the Wisdom Word present and operative with God at creation, in the prophets, and in the Wisdom literature. For the Greeks, *logos* was bound up with reason and truth, the controlling principle of the universe. Thus could Jesus the Christ be preached to the Greek world as the Wisdom Word of God, fullness of life and truth bringing salvation to the world.

3. This expansion into the Greek world led to the inevitable struggle for universal meaning. Speculative theology grew from the Church Fathers' move into another order of language; this move, through the centuries after, stretched into scholasticism. Scholasticism with its penchant for high organization, specialization, and minute detail led to the separation of theology into precise compartments. A new dualism was inadvertently created: the separation of

God's inner life from God's salvific acts in history and the ordinary life of the Christian. Catherine Mowry Lacugna, in her definitive book on the Trinity, *God for Us,* describes this circumstance as "the defeat of the Trinity."[33] Although we have no actual access to the inner life of God, nor can we, with any accuracy, specifically explain the substance of God, speculative theology theorized on this inner life. Speculation which relegated God more and more to the great beyond, yielding a rumination upon the inaccessible and ineffable essence of God, served its purpose. But for the postmodern world of the twenty-first century, a detached speculative theology is no longer serviceable.

4. In a world characterized by the web metaphor of interconnectedness, God can no longer remain locked up within God's self and remain a believable God. The essence of God is unnameable. Continued speculation on the substance of God reinforces the separation of the relationship of the Trinity from the context of our lives. As the early church risked and expanded into another language and its consequent thought patterns, so must the church today. We must re-appropriate God-with-us as revealed in Jesus, the Parable of God, and in the Spirit of God.

5. Through the Incarnation, we know that human experience is profoundly revelatory of God. We only know about God from what we see in God's deeds and in Jesus, God's greatest Deed. These reveal the Father as the unbegotten One (the unoriginate Origin) from whom come all things—the Son, the Spirit of Jesus, and the world. Anything we say about God in Godself must be said in the light of God's revelation in Jesus and the Spirit of Jesus. We move from Christ and the Spirit to the Trinity, not vice versa and, even in doing this, we cannot make a one-to-one correspondence with God's self-expression in the history of salvation and God's self-expression in the Trinity. Lacugna, however, emphatically points out that we must make it perfectly clear that there are not two Trinities. There is only one God and one self-communication—"one begetting of the Son, one breathing forth of the Spirit, with both eternal and temporal aspects."[34] The inner life of the mystery of God-as-love-outpoured is communicated in Jesus the Christ and the Spirit of Jesus. The mystery of God is the mystery of God for us.

---

[33] Catherine Mowry Lacugna, *God for Us: The Trinity and Christian Life* (San Francisco: Harper, 1991) 8ff.

[34] Ibid., 224.

Retrieval of the doctrine of the Trinity from the realms of speculative theology reestablishes trinitarian life as our life, which greatly impacts preaching and preaching in the context of the eucharistic liturgy. We—all creation—have been included as partners/co-creators in this abundant life. Our lives are not separate from the life of the Trinity but bound up with it. The doctrine of the Trinity is not revelation about God but about God's life with us and our life with each other. The call of the Eucharist is to unite ourselves to this great self-gifting God and then go and graciously do likewise for one another.

In light of the above, the students wrestle with the following two questions:

1. How can the retrieval of the trinitarian God as the pattern for living bring healing to the world of the twenty-first century?
2. What obstacles challenge us in the living of trinitarian mutuality?

2. HOMILETIC METHOD

Section IV in FIYH is devoted to homiletic method, emphasizing that "a regular daily pattern of activity for the preparation of the Sunday homily is likewise often the key factor in effective preaching" (no. 82). In light of this directive, student preparation for the first homily preached is spread over the four classes in order to give a lived experience of a week-long preparation. At the conclusion of each class, the students are given a directive to pursue during the coming week; discussion of the directive opens the next class.

For example, for the first week, the students read the three Scripture texts for the assigned Sunday in various translations, noting differences in wording. They are to read these translations aloud several times, jotting down movements within themselves as they engage the texts. The second week, the students do a structural analysis of the texts, again noting the movement within. The third week, the students declare the one truth rising within them about which they can speak passionately; they then compose focus and functions statements around this core truth. The final directive is to compose the homily.

The first part of the class following the preaching practicum is devoted to discussing the experience of the students in both preparing the homily and in the preaching event. Focus is given to the three-week preparation, emphasizing that what took place over the course in three weeks actually occurs over the course of one week amidst the hustle and bustle of parish ministry. The students are asked to note, as they lived each step of the preparation week by week, what from their daily lives impacted the preaching? What added richness or changed perspective?

Throughout the course, the students are reminded of the necessity of establishing a weekly discipline of preparation and writing of the homily—a discipline they must stick to as far as possible even in the busiest of weeks.

3. THE ART OF PROCLAMATION

Since the course Oral Proclamation and Interpretation is a prerequisite for Theologies and Models of Preaching, no specific class is devoted to the art of proclamation. However, points pertaining to such are discussed as they arise in class and are a facet of the critiquing during the preaching practicum. See Figure E for specific criteria.

4. BEGINNINGS AND ENDINGS

Midway through the semester, one half of a class is devoted to composing an introduction and a conclusion to the homily. Prior to the class, the students are assigned to read in Buttrick's *Homiletic* and Waznak's *Introduction to the Homily* material relevant to beginnings and endings. Discussion of the criteria for effective beginnings and endings revolve around the following:

a. Introductions
  • Introductions give focus to the homily.
  • They maintain the attention of the assembly, preparing the folks to listen intelligently.
  • The first two or three sentences of an introduction cannot bear much weight because people do not easily attend to the first few sentences of any public address.
  • Initial sentences are to be kept short, uncomplicated, and without adjectives, if possible.
  • The last sentence of the introduction must stop the action. The end of the introduction and the start of a first move must be clearly separated.

b. Conclusions
  • Conclusions are meant to conclude! No new ideas introduced at this point.
  • Conclusions fix consciousness, enabling the homily to live in the hearts and minds of the Assembly, and then quit.

• The last sentence is short and free of many adjectives.
• Conclusions are spoken directly to the Assembly, with eye contact.
• Conclusions are concrete—what cannot be visualized will not be done.
• Though direct, conclusions are open-ended, leaving the Assembly to wrestle with the word of God in their own circumstances throughout the week.

Both strong and weak samples of introductions and conclusions are presented in class via overhead projector.

5. MAKING A HOMILY LEAN

A section of the first class after the first preaching practicum is devoted to the "paring" of a homily. An effective homily is lean, every word counting. Consideration is given to the following:

a. Eliminate "junk" words such as *and so, and then, very, really, truly, thus, therefore, just.*

b. Eliminate sentences beginning with *this, these, those, that* unless they modify a noun. These words work well in written compositions but, orally, their reference is lost. Buttrick says that sentences beginning with these words are instantly erased.

c. Avoid beginning sentences with "it." Do so only immediately after a sentence to which the "it" refers.

d. Avoid bulky phrases like "actually we can see," "we can see however that," "it is clear that," "it is evident that," and the like.

e. Beware of using too many adjectives; adjectives clutter oral language. Use them sparingly when it is necessary to define or to distinguish. Make sure that the adjectives used give punch to the thought.

f. Polish verbs. Excitement in preaching is usually created by verb color and precision. For example, for "look" use peer or scan; for "realize" use grasp or discern.

Listeners appreciate a homily which doesn't waste their time with unnecessary verbiage. Homilies which are concise, spare, and clean bear the word of God more effectively.

6. PREACHING POSTILS

Save for the first class of the course, each class begins with a student preaching a postil based on the readings of the day. This preaching is followed by five to seven minutes of critique in accordance with the coaching method. A postil is a brief interpretation of one truth gleaned from the readings of the day whose length is no longer than three minutes. Thus, preparation for the postil is minimal compared with that for a Saturday or Sunday homily. The practice of preaching a postil is begun in the course Oral Interpretation and Proclamation.

7. THE LIFE OF THE PREACHER

Since preaching extends beyond the pulpit, the quality of the preacher's life is stressed throughout the course. Indeed, the life of the preacher influences for better or for worse what is communicated from the pulpit. Even one's most private beliefs, feelings, and attitudes can leak through at any given time, and especially in unsuspecting and surprising ways. The way one answers the telephone or opens the door to an unexpected knock, the places one frequents for shopping or entertainment, the books found in the office preach. Hence the necessity for the preacher to be "all of a piece" and growing in self-knowledge.

Throughout the course, the students are reminded that the call of all the baptized is to live the Eucharist. With the words, "Do this in memory of me," Jesus is directing us to do as he has done: to be broken and poured out for the sake of the kindom. Certainly those blessed with the charism to preach the living Word of God are called to lead the way. They, through their preaching ministry, offer the bread and wine of their lives weekly in disciplined and faithful preparation of the homily. Parish ministry is hectic, mostly unpredictable. The discipline for this faithful preparation begins now. Working homily preparation into their busy student lives week in and week out readies the students for the busy days of ministry—working the homily preparation into the flesh and bones of their lives.

The course both opens and closes with Paul's sacred charge to Timothy and to all blessed with the preaching charism:

> In the presence of God and of Christ Jesus, who is to judge the living and the dead, and in view of his appearing and his kingdom, I solemnly urge you: proclaim the message; be persistent whether the time is favorable or unfavorable; convince, rebuke, and encourage, with the utmost patience in teaching. For the time is coming when people will not put up with sound doctrine, but having itching ears, they will accumulate for themselves teachers to suit their own desires, and will turn away from listening to the truth and wander away to myths. As for you, always be sober, endure suffering, do the work of an evangelist, carry out your ministry faithfully (2 Tim 4:1-5 NRSV).

Figure A

STRUCTURAL ANALYSIS

Second Sunday of Easter (B)   April 26/27, 2003

GOSPEL: JOHN 20:19-31

Introduction: On the evening of that first day of the week, when the doors were locked, where the disciples were, for fear of the Jews, Jesus came and stood in their midst and said to them,

- "Peace be with you."
- When he had said this,
- he showed them his hands and his side.
- The disciples rejoiced when they saw the Lord.
- Jesus said to them again, "Peace be with you.
- As the Father has sent me,
- so I send you."
- And when he had said this, he breathed on them
- and said to them, "Receive the Holy Spirit.
- Whose sins you forgive are forgiven them,
- and whose sins you retain are retained."
- Thomas, called Didymus, one of the Twelve,
- was not with them when Jesus came.
- So the other disciples said to him,
- "We have seen the Lord."
- But he said to them, "Unless I see the mark of the nails in his hands
- and put my finger into the nailmarks
- and put my hand into his side, I will not believe."
- Now a week later his disciples were again inside
- and Thomas was with them.
- Jesus came, although the doors were locked,
- and stood in their midst
- and said, "Peace be with you."
- Then he said to Thomas, "Put your finger here and see my hands,
- and bring your hand and put it into my side,
- and do not be unbelieving, but believe."
- Thomas answered and said to him, "My Lord and my God!"
- Jesus said to him, "Have you come to believe because you have seen me?
- Blessed are those who have not seen and have believed."

Conclusion: Now Jesus did many other signs in the presence of his disciples that are not written in this book. But these are written that you may come to believe that Jesus is the Christ, the Son of God, and that through this belief you may have life in his name.

Figure B

CONVERSATION MODEL

A. Student A, arriving to class at the last minute, relates that his grandmother, to whom he is close, was rushed to the hospital the night before and his mother called as he was leaving for class informing him of his grandmother's condition.

B. As the professor and students express their sympathy at Student A's distress, one student comments that Student A looks tired.

C. Student A responds that he didn't get much sleep since he was worried about his grandmother.

D. Another student asks if Student A heard the thunderstorm that moved through around 3 A.M., commenting on the powerful winds accompanying the storm which kept him awake for a good while after.

E. Still another student stated that he hadn't slept much either; his sleeplessness was the result of disappointment at the poor playing by the Cleveland Indians at last night's game.

F. Several students commented on the state of the Indians team, noting that the team lacks unity. "They don't know yet that they are a team."

Figure C

THE HOMILY WRITTEN IN MOVES

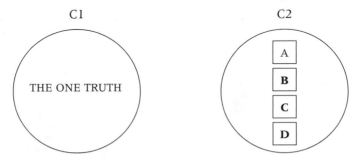

Figure D1

COACHING FORM FOR PREACHING

Event:_____

Name	Preacher Recognizes	Coach Recognizes
Preacher's Strength	A. Agree and reinforce	B. Identify, illustrate and point out importance
Preacher's Improvement Opportunities	C. Agree and reinforce	D. Identify, illustrate, and point out importance

Figure D2

COACHING CRITERIA:
THEOLOGIES AND MODELS OF PREACHING

one focus. . . . . many foci

focus clearly discernible. . . . . fuzzy focus

well-developed focus . . . . unfinished focus

clear progression of ideas. . . . . scattered, unlinked ideas

rooted in Scripture text . . . . unrelated to Scripture text

liturgical context . . . . little or no reference to liturgical context

theologically grounded . . . . theologically questionable

names grace . . . . passes judgment

imaginative/tensive . . . . steno

engaging. . . . . disinterested

evocative . . . . flat

integrity of preacher. . . . . false persona

genuine presence . . . . artificial presence

pastoral in approach . . . . self-righteous in approach

animated presence. . . . . little or no enthusiasm

proclamation of the word . . . . instruction about the word

reflects life experience of assembly. . . . . . little or no consideration of assembly

respect for freedom/dignity of assembly. . . . . badgering and haranguing
the assembly

concrete language . . . . abstract language

relevant language. . . . . jargon, slang

effective introduction. . . . . nondescript introduction

effective conclusion . . . . abrupt or weak conclusion

pace measured and natural. . . . . pace jerky and erratic

Figure E

COACHING CRITERIA:
ORAL INTERPRETATION AND PROCLAMATION

Coach's Name: _____

Proclaimer's Name: _____

Date: _____

COACHING GRID
The "Ways" It Came Across

Check off one of these seven boxes for each pair of words.

stiff								sloppy
distracting moves								robotic movement
straining to hear								bombastic
expressionless								pasted-on smile
preachy voice								uninspiring tone
drudgery								rapid fire
glaring								shifty eyes
intimidating								uninteresting
ran words together								dragged
intense								indifferent
read to								casual chat
sing-songy								monotone
harsh								sugar-sweet tone

Comment on one thing to keep and one thing to do differently.

Proclaimer	Coach

ANNOTATED BIBLIOGRAPHY

Allen, Ronald J. *Interpreting the Gospel: An Introduction to Preaching.* St. Louis: Chalice Press, 1998. A comprehensive and practical hands-on guide for the beginning preacher. The first chapter alone is worth the purchase of the book. This chapter offers a random collection of anxieties common to beginners with responses by the author.

————. *Patterns of Preaching: A Sermon Sampler.* St. Louis: Chalice Press, 1998. A companion to the above-cited *Interpreting the Gospel,* this book is a collection of both contemporary and classical styles of preaching. Each sermon is annotated with comments about the purpose of the sermon and the setting in which it was preached.

Brueggemann, Walter. *Finally Comes the Poet: Daring Speech for Proclamation.* Minneapolis: Fortress Press, 1989. A fine resource for the homiletics professor. Brueggemann considers "preaching as a poetic construal of an alternative world . . . whose purpose is to cherish and open the truth" for contemporary culture. He challenges preachers to dare to be a voice which shatters settled reality in order to create alternative ways of living.

Buttrick, David. *Homiletic.* Philadelphia: Fortress Press, 1987. One of the most influential books on homiletics in the twentieth century. Buttrick's approach is phenomenological in nature. He places strong emphasis on preaching in a way which is consistent with the way people process information and amply describes each step in the creation of a sermon. Part 1, "Moves," is a detailed study of the components of sermons; Part 2, "Structures," he devotes to his structural theory. The best part of the latter are the chapters he devotes to the structuring of sermons according to "moments" in consciousness, which he names (1) moments of immediacy, (2) moments of reflection, and (3) moments of being in the world because of new understanding. Three modes of preaching correspond to these three moments: (1) the mode of immediacy, (2) the reflective mode, and (3) the mode of praxis. Buttrick suggests specific scriptural texts befitting each preaching mode.

Eslinger, Richard. *A New Hearing: Living Options in Homiletic Method.* Nashville: Abingdon Press, 1987. A great resource for the teacher of homiletics. Eslinger succinctly describes the work of five eminent preachers who are part of the revolution in the field of homiletics: David Buttrick, Fred Craddock, Eugene Lowry, Charles Rice, and Henry Mitchell. He details each one's technique, shows how it differs from the traditional "three points" sermon, presents one sample sermon, and then offers strengths and weaknesses of the respective method.

Hilkert, Mary Catherine. *Naming Grace: Preaching and the Sacramental Imagination.* New York: Continuum, 1997. Another must for the preacher's library. This book deals with the art of preparing and delivering a homily in a Catholic liturgical setting. Steeped in the theology of Karl Rahner, s.j., and Edward Schillebeeckx, o.p., Dr. Hilkert invites the preacher to employ skills inclusive of both sacramental and prophetic imaginations. She also challenges the church to take seriously the preaching of women and other different voices. Especially helpful to the beginning preacher is the chapter on doctrinal preaching.

Long, Thomas. *The Witness of Preaching.* Louisville: Westminster John Knox, 1989. The book is Long's theology of preaching. For him, preaching is "bearing witness to the Living Word of God." He stresses the preachers do not come *to* the Church with the word. Rather they *are* witnesses to the word coming *from within* the church itself, which is a dwelling place of the Word. He adeptly provides theoretical and practical advice for building the sermon. I find especially helpful his chapters on focus and function statements and the basic form of the sermon.

Lowry, Eugene. *How to Preach a Parable: Designs for Narrative Preaching.* Nashville: Abingdon Press, 1989. This book is not so much about how to preach parables; rather, its emphasis is on how to do parable preaching—preaching which does not necessarily involve a parable per se. After describing the elements of parabolic preaching, Lowry offers, in clear step-by-step fashion, four options of narrative design for homilies: running the story; delaying the story, suspending the story, and alternating the story.

———. *The Homiletical Plot: The Sermon as Narrative Art Form.* Atlanta: John Knox, 1980. An introductory-level textbook. Lowry begins with an in-depth study of the revolution in homiletics over the past twenty-five years and then goes on to carefully develop his understanding of the sermon as an event-in-time—a kind of temporal sequencing or plot that creates disequilibrium followed by Gospel insight which brings resolution with a challenge to live differently. Describes in detail his "oops," "ugh," "aha," "whee," and "yeah" approach to the sermon.

National Conference of Catholic Bishops. *Fulfilled in Your Hearing: The Homily in the Sunday Assembly.* Washington, DC: USCC, 1982. The chief

Roman Catholic document on liturgical preaching. This document is a summary of the Catholic approach to the homily based on the teachings of conciliar and post-conciliar documents from Vatican II. It also incorporates primary insights of the leading Protestant homileticians. In the words of Robert Waznak, it "offers a fresh understanding of the homily since it shifts its meaning from instruction to interpretation" (*An Introduction to the Homily,* 14).

O'Day, Gail, and Thomas Long. *Listening to the Word.* Nashville: Abingdon Press, 1993. Twelve scholars versed in the field of homiletics pay tribute to Fred Craddock. Each focuses on one of the themes central to Craddock's homiletic. These themes are organized under three headings: (1) Turning to the Text, (2) Turning to the Sermon, and (3) Turning to the Listener. Particularly helpful to an introductory preaching course are Chapter 5, "The Revolution of Sermonic Shape" by Eugene Lowry; Chapter 7, "Beyond Narrative: Imagination in the Sermon" by Paul Scott Wilson; and Chapter 11, "Preaching the Body" by Barbara Brown Taylor.

Waznak, Robert P. *An Introduction to the Homily.* Collegeville, MN: Liturgical Press, 1998. A basic for homiletic professors. This book offers a firm foundation in liturgical preaching. From the jacket of the book: "A work that leads to a practical understanding of what the homily is and what it is supposed to do. Its purpose is to demonstrate how new homiletic scholarship from the various Christian churches, the insights found in normative church documents, contemporary theological, liturgical and biblical studies, plus the lived experiences of preachers and people can help us understand the function of the homily in the liturgical tradition of the Roman Catholic Church."

Westerhoff, John H. *Spiritual Life: The Foundation for Preaching and Teaching.* Louisville: Westminster John Knox, 1994. Westerhoff wrote this book as a resource to help preachers and teachers revitalize their lives and their ministries. Though he clearly delineates the difference between preaching and teaching, he stresses that both effective preaching and teaching are based in a sound spiritual life. He invites the readers to open their imaginations to new ways of knowing that will lead to a fuller relationship with God.

Linda L. Clader

THE FORMATION OF A EUCHARISTIC PREACHER

FIRST, PRAYER

Almighty God, unto whom all hearts are open, all desires known, and from whom no secrets are hid: Cleanse the thoughts of our hearts by the inspiration of thy Holy Spirit, that we may perfectly love thee, and worthily magnify thy holy Name; through Christ our Lord. Amen.[1]

I have been hearing this prayer every Sunday since I was a baby. Long before I became a priest myself I could say it by heart, and for me it was a favorite part of the eucharistic liturgy. Now, in the Episcopal Church's current version of the *Book of Common Prayer,* the rubrics tell us this prayer may be said, and sometimes it isn't. I understand the thinking of the liturgists who explain that the prayer is properly said prior to the real start of the liturgy, in preparation before the entrance. Perhaps that is more correct. I am only reporting here that I am certain this prayer has made a profound impact on who I am as an Episcopalian and as a priest.

Think about it: every Sunday, for fifty-eight years, I have been acknowledging that my heart is open to God, asking God to enter my heart and purify it, and recognizing that my purpose, at least at this moment, is simply to love God and offer God glory. Of course the words of the prayer have sometimes simply washed over me. Of course I have not always held them in mind either as the liturgy progressed, or as I

---

[1] BCP, 323.

walked out of the church and into my daily activities. But you don't pray a prayer like this over and over without it working on you.

That may be why when I think about what preaching is in the context of the Episcopal liturgy, the first thing that comes to me is prayer. I do not say that as an exclusive definition of what preaching is, but perhaps to broaden the range a bit beyond what we most often seem to hear: preaching for formation, preaching for instruction, preaching as prophecy, preaching as evangelism, preaching for sanctification, preaching for conversion. I say yes to all of those; but first, I say to remember the prayer.

The *Book of Common Prayer* of the Episcopal Church divides the Eucharist into two parts: the Word of God and the Holy Communion. Usually, I think, when we imagine the "Word of God" half of the service, we think of the biblical readings and the sermon. But our Prayer Book does not limit it that way. The "Word of God" portion includes songs of praise and the recitation of the Nicene Creed, and it ends with the exchange of the Peace through the congregation. It also includes as many as three collects, the intercessory Prayers of the People, and the prayer of Confession and Absolution. The "Word of God' portion of the celebration of the Eucharist is not just an instructional period before the real prayer of the church.

The Collect for Purity printed above emphasizes openness to God, openness to the inspiration of the Holy Spirit. Certainly it is appropriately prayed at the very start of this gathering for common prayer to God. But the sermon, as I see it, intends to continue the work of that prayer. During the time of preparation, the preacher has invited the Spirit to enter her heart and direct the process of exegesis, invention, and formation of the homily. When the preacher begins preaching the actual homily, part of her prayer must be that the Spirit will also enter the hearts of the faithful and move them to receive the truth of God's word.

I am not sure whether I am guided by an unusually strong theology of the work of the Spirit, but I do know that it is a conscious and constant dimension of the way I talk about preaching with my students. My outline for exegesis of Scripture begins with prayer for guidance.[2] My discussion of attention to the congregation includes prayer for them as part of a preacher's preparation. And when I talk about the authority of the preacher, I also talk about the mysterious movement of the Spirit in a group of people who pray and work together.

Whatever else a preacher does, in studying a text and crafting a message, this prayer for openness keeps the preacher honest, and the prayer

[2] See An Approach to Exegesis, p. 221.

for the congregation keeps the preacher connected with the people, so that an authentic, holy conversation among them may be possible. Later on, it will also be seen that this intention about openness influences the form of the individual homily itself.[3]

THE MUSIC OF PREACHING

No, I'm not referring to the hymns, although they are still ringing in the air around the preaching. I am referring to breath, and bodies, and the intentionality of playing a musical instrument. For that is what we preachers are, aren't we? We are living, breathing musical instruments—a kind of reed instrument, in fact. And at times, the breath which makes the music is the Spirit.

My choral director in high school used to start rehearsals saying, "Put your flat feet on the floor!" It has been stunning to me, over the years I have been teaching preachers, how many of us don't start with that. We twist and we turn; we put all our weight on one hip; we hang our heads and stare at the manuscript. I am no expert on vocal training, but I do know a few things, and one of them is that if our feet aren't flat on the floor, we're probably not really breathing.

We must stand with our feet about as far apart as our shoulders. Now, take a deep breath without raising our shoulders at all. Which parts of our body move? Raise our head so our chin is parallel to the floor, and proclaim "The Word of the Lord" in a voice like thunder. Can we bring it up from the floor on which we're standing?

If we are afraid to take a really deep breath, and to really broadcast our voice, how effectively are we going to be able to proclaim the Gospel? Did John the Baptist bury his chin under his collar? Did Mary Magdalene? Did Jesus?

My hunch is that this reticence really to breathe comes from ambivalence about our "right" to be proclaiming the word at all. Perhaps it is even influenced by childhood experiences in a church where loud speech was a no-no. It might require a bit of therapy to get past these old messages. It might take the equivalent of Demosthenes placing pebbles in his mouth and declaiming to the sea. Go into the preaching space and make noise. Shout, and whisper, and hum. Listen to the way our own body feels when we make each kind of sound. Feel what vibrates when we speak, when we sing. Can we feel our ribs? Can we feel the bridge of our nose? Laugh—ha! ha! What happens to our body when we do that?

[3] Ibid.

It is absolutely necessary for a preacher to be aware of and in control of her voice. Does it tend to crack? Then figure out when, why, and how. When we preach three homilies in one morning, do we get husky? Then we probably need to exercise our voice more, and warm up like a singer before we preach. Do people tell us they can't hear us, no matter what? Work on preaching with amplification (and get a good setup!). Do we drop our voice at the ends of phrases or sentences? Learn not to do that. The point is to be heard, and that's only for starters. Beyond that, the point is to be able to sing the music of the Gospel. Our use of our voice proclaims to the world the dimensions of our faith.

BEING THERE

None of what I have just written is really about "technique" in preaching. It is not about the art or the craft of our vocation. It is about presence.

Although we do sometimes talk about "spiritual presence," in the context of preaching, presence is about bodies. Perhaps this is especially true when we preach at a eucharistic celebration. Our liturgy is filled with embodied prayer. We kneel, sit, and stand at different points in worship. The sacred ministers carry objects and move around the building. Candles are lit, hands are washed, food and drink are blessed, and sacraments are experienced through touch, taste, and smell. It is ironic that so often the matter of preaching is thought of simply as words hurled into the air, as disembodied as any electronic recording pumped through a speaker. Eucharistic preaching, like the rest of the liturgy, must be an incarnational event.

Our bodies are not just vehicles used to transport the mind we apply to our studies and the voice with which we speak. Our bodies are also instruments of our proclamation. I am not arguing for broad gestures when they aren't warranted by the content of the homily. I am simply trying to stress that preaching includes everything we are, and makes use of everything we have. If we want to engage in a kind of communication which is in any sense a conversation, then we must allow ourselves to be fully present to our listeners in the moment.

Beginning preachers are usually quite concerned about presence, but their concern is often focused on technicalities such as eye contact and the graceful use of a manuscript. These are important aspects of delivery, but they are more symptomatic than they are truly involved in real preaching. Beginners think of eye contact, for example, as a means to control the attention of their audience. If I connect with someone visually, I am likely to keep him or her "with" me for another moment or two, because he or she experiences a kind of communication. More important, however, is not the aspect of control, but the aspect of attention. In an arrangement where I am the only speaker, really looking at the congregation before me is a way to "visually listen" to them. When I am having an intimate conversation with one or two friends, I can observe my listeners' response and repeat myself, or say something another way, or change my voice to be sure I'm being heard. Think about it: can there be a kind of conversation more intimate than sharing our faith in God? Shouldn't I be taking care in the best ways I know how to pay attention to the other parties in that conversation?

Similarly, beginners are usually overly concerned with how well they use a manuscript. The point is not whether we use a manuscript or not; the point is whether we can tell the story we have to tell in a voice that is authentic to us and to our faith. Anything we need to make that happen is "legal." No one is going to look at that manuscript but us, and we can print it or scribble it or embellish it any way we want. Much more central to the event itself is having a manuscript or notes with which we are so thoroughly familiar that we can step away from them and come back again without getting lost. No one will think us a bad preacher if we have to check where we are now and then. They will only think we are a bad preacher if we have nothing important to say, if our faith never shines through us, and if we do not care about the kind of relationship we are building with those who hear us.

OUR LITURGICAL DIALECT

All preaching is contextual, since all speech is contextual. I have to know to whom I'm talking in order to know what kind of language to use, how much of my own story to divulge, whether a joke will be understood, what I can assume about shared experience. I have to know whether our conversation is bounded by a particular set of customs, whether there is a time limit on our interaction, who else may be listening in. I need to be aware of our surroundings, in order to predict distractions or include what we see, hear, and smell in the way I explain myself. If I am making plans to hold a conversation with someone, I may very well think about the arrangement of furniture, the level of light, and the clothes I put on, and I may think about the comfort of the person with whom I expect to converse.

If I am truly intending this to be a two-way conversation, I will situate myself, one way or another, to be able to hear that other person's responses and questions to me, just as I take care with the words I offer to the other. My concern with lighting or our seating arrangement is not based on how best to present myself, but on how our context for conversation makes hearing one another and picking up one another's visual cues most natural. If I am truly intending to participate in a two-way conversation, I attend to all the ways communication happens, whether through words, gestures, or unconscious cues. If I am preparing in advance for such a conversation, I consider what I know about the other person in order to be as certain as I can be that when he or she speaks, I am hearing what the other person intends for me to hear.

Preaching in the context of a celebration of the Holy Eucharist is an invitation to think about all these dimensions in a very particular way. I am aware of furniture, lighting, music, sound, and ceremonial garb— not only as they enhance the aesthetic dimension of common worship, but also as they create or reduce distance between me and those who hear me. Will the congregation be able to see and hear me clearly? (Usually, dealing with these questions is a "given.") Will I be able to see and hear the congregation? (This is an element often ignored.) How do the vestments I wear set me apart from others, and what messages do they convey? Is my homily "set off" from the rest of the liturgy by music, an elaborate Gospel procession, or a prayer? How does that "setting off" affect the relationship between me and the congregation, and between my homily and the texts on which the proclamation is based?

Perhaps the most significant aspect of the liturgical context, however, is the language in which the Eucharist is conducted. No matter how informal or idiosyncratic my preaching style may be, the context within which I preach is largely "scripted" and formal. The implications of this reality for preaching are not primarily about whether my own style "fits" or "contrasts" with the language of the liturgy. Rather, traditional ceremonial language has its impact on preaching by creating a specialized "dialect" with loaded, often highly metaphorical language which is familiar to the community through frequent repetition. Like the images and stories of the biblical record itself, the language of the liturgy can "bend" our preaching to tune itself to the worship tradition.

How does this work? I remember preaching, one evening, about space exploration (the homily was actually about idolatry and pride, based on a reading from Exodus, but "space" was my vehicle). It was easy enough to throw in a clip from one of our eucharistic prayers:

". . . the vast expanse of interstellar space . . . " or ". . . this fragile earth, our island home."[4] I did include that language, and I did ask the presider at that Eucharist to be sure and use that particular prayer. At times, I have been quite intentional about finding specific, loaded words which connect one part of the liturgy to another. But in this case, the echo of the prayer was already in my head before I began working on the homily. Did the idea of playing around with a "space" story come to me *because of* the prayer I knew might be an option? And when I think about space at all, don't those words often pop into my head?

A liturgical preacher is influenced not only by the language of the prayer texts, but also by the language of the hymns. I am sure we have all heard ourselves quoting from familiar songs—hymns or popular music— in casual speech. The language of our hymnody is rich and we hear favorite hymns repeated many times, so the images and metaphors live deep in our bones, and are likely to come into our heads whether we intend them to or not. In fact, I have heard it claimed that our hymns represent a compendium of the "real" theology of our tradition—they are the vivid form of shorthand our community often uses to convey theological truth. That is why, in the Episcopal Church at least, discussions over the texts to be included in official hymnals can be long and occasionally a bit bloody.

Many of our prayers and hymns draw on theological statements needing explication. What might it mean, for example, if we echo an expression like, "I crucified thee," or "humbly I adore thee," without nuancing the implied guilt of the first or the meaning of humility in the second? It has been amply attested how the traditions of the church have served to keep the disadvantaged subordinate, because the language of oppression has echoed the language of Christian values (humility, submission, forbearance, etc.). There is also the language of triumphalism which can support aggressive and arrogant behavior. If we use a phrase like "trampling Satan under his feet," for example, can we be sure about how our listeners would read that expression? How about all the talk of victory, the language of kingship, overcoming the Evil One, and so on? If we tend, in our preaching, to call upon the theological shorthand of our tradition, it is imperative that we train ourselves to be aware of how it could be mistranslated according to contemporary vernacular, and adjust our use of the terms accordingly.

More generally, if we are thinking about preaching as a form of conversation, we need to take seriously the fact that we are operating

---

[4] BCP, 370.

in a specialized liturgical and denominational dialect. If we allude to hymn texts or familiar phrases from our liturgy, are we inviting our congregation to be "in on" the connection, or are we using it as a way to cement our authority? Newcomers to the Episcopal Church often note the plethora of specialized "church" words they find alienating—words like "narthex," "undercroft," "reredos," "thurifer" (I note with some satisfaction that my automatic spell-check just underlined all four of those terms). I suspect that our preaching is not often laced with such terminology, but those of us who live every day with the jargon of our denomination need to be particularly sensitive to our use of it, for it can create a barrier or set us apart in a way we claim we would not choose. That is not to say, by the way, that we should "dumb down" our church jargon; for learning the specialized dialect of a community can be an entertaining, even if challenging, activity for a newcomer. But the jargon should not be used as a barrier to understanding the Gospel; rather, it should be offered as a gift for incorporation into the Body.

With these dangers and challenges in mind, the preacher can use the language of the liturgy in the service of integrating the homily into the rest of the Eucharist, without making a gesture or an awkward statement that "turns toward the Table." I am not one of those professors of homiletics who maintain that every eucharistic homily *must* make an overt reference to the Sacrament to follow. I do believe, however, that if we preachers are attentive to the language, the images, and the general context of the liturgy as we prepare, the connections will be made. They may be as overt as my echo of the "vast expanse of interstellar space," or they may be much more subtle, referring to a community gathered, or a feast, or sacrifice. The actual eucharistic references are far less important, to my mind, than references to God's action in human history, to forgiveness, to the love of Christ. If the homily whispers one of those themes, it sounds loud and clear when the Absolution is said, or when the Thanksgiving over the Gifts is spoken.

THE CONGREGATION

If it is, indeed, a conversation we're having, of course we'll be anxious to know the people we're having it with. This dimension to preaching is obvious enough, but there are certainly many examples of preachers who have not taken the time to get to know who is listening to them.

We know the signs: a church more than half-full of women hears a preacher extolling the ministry of women, and saying things like, "We need to support and give thanks for their ministry among us." A seminary chapel full of families and friends of the students hears a preacher talk about "When you get ordained . . . . " An ecumenical gathering hears a sermon laced with the kind of denominational jargon I referred to above. We all make assumptions like this when we talk; of course we have a location, a point of view, a finite circle of experience. But a preacher is called to be especially careful about his or her familiarity with the congregation.

We call this a part of our process of exegesis. Although we are still likely to make blunders now and then, we can take on a regular program to minimize our insensitivity. When I am planning a homily for a particular group, I tend to visualize the faces I know in that group as I work. Sometimes I pray for them. It helps me keep real people in my mind.

Suppose, though, we don't know the people who will hear us? A visiting preacher, or a new preacher in a particular congregation needs to be asking a lot of questions. Will there be children present? Of what ages? What are the most important "stories" of this congregation? For example, did a central member of the community recently die? Why is the regular preacher not preaching today—is there a story we need to know? What is the general economic bracket of the members, and are there some who fall at the extremes of the spectrum? What kind of town is the church located in, and what are the hot topics in the local political scene?

Beyond specifics such as these, I can simply remind myself of general truths: in the congregation with whom I will be speaking someone will be grieving a death; someone has recently been diagnosed with a life-threatening physical ailment; someone is struggling with mental illness; someone is addicted to drugs or alcohol; someone is abusing or being abused by a spouse; someone carries a load of old mistakes and shame; someone is facing retirement; someone is caring for an elderly or ill family member. And so on. It isn't a mistake to write down statements like these early in the process. Or, once we have a homily worked out to a stage close to complete, it isn't a bad idea simply to go back through it, looking for places where someone in one of these specific situations might misconstrue what we are trying to say.

We can't foresee every "hot button" we are going to push with our preaching. There will always be secrets which have not been shared with us, pitfalls we can't discern. But if we have built a prayerful relationship of trust and honesty between us and our listeners, we are more likely to be sensitive in the first place, and they are more likely to respond with gentle criticism if we say something difficult to hear.

SCRIPTURE

Our exegesis of the scriptural texts appointed for a given occasion takes place at the same time as our exegesis of the congregation. As we gain familiarity with a given congregation, the two processes are likely to become more and more tightly bound together. Our very reading of a biblical passage may call up images of people we know, just as a visit to a particular parishioner may remind us of an episode in the Scriptures. This kind of confusion, in a sense, is exactly what we are aiming for, not only in our own homiletical process but in the lives of the faithful among whom we preach. One of our goals is that the biblical story be firmly entwined with our own.

If we begin our preparation for a homily with a wide-open reading of the lections, these connections are more likely to find a way into our imaginations. When I am working on a homily, I normally begin my process a week before the day I am to preach. I begin reading the assigned passages, without reference to any of my handbooks or commentaries. I pray with the lections, asking God to make known to me what the word will be for this particular occasion and these particular people. And normally I maintain this kind of distance from secondary sources until about halfway through the week. This schedule keeps me from being influenced too early by what the scholars have to say, and makes it more likely that what appears to be an "unconnected thought" may occur to me and begin to work in the back of my mind.

When I advocate this approach to my students, I encourage them to write down the ideas which come to them during this early stage of their preparation.[5] Once we begin delving into the commentaries, it is easy to discard our own reflections in favor of what the "experts" have to say, so we need to take care that those "naïve" reactions don't get lost. But I am also a champion of word-studies and other kinds of exegetical research. Exploring the Hebrew and Greek underpinnings of our translations of the Bible often suggests new avenues we might pursue in our preaching, as we discover the implications of a particular word or a social custom. As we dig deeper into the cultural background of a text, we still need to keep its narrative or artistic context in mind, too, and so it is helpful to be making notes all along the way. Most of them won't find their way into the final homily, but the confidence with which we preach reflects the fact that we have "steeped" the homily in research as well as meditation.

[5] See An Approach to Exegesis, p. 221.

Part of my exegesis of a congregation entails considering how much they know of the biblical story, how attentive they have probably been to the reading of Scripture during the Service of the Word, what they have actually taken in. As I work with the readings assigned, I need to pay attention to how easy they are to "hear." Is there a bold, familiar story, such as the tale of Noah or the parable of the Good Samaritan? Is there an element which is likely to disturb the listeners or be misunderstood, such as teachings on divorce or references to arcane customs? In practical terms, can I assume the Scriptures will be read well, so they can even be heard? And once they are heard—returning now to my exegesis of the congregation—how will they be interpreted?

In some ways, those were the easy questions. It is far more difficult to assess how much of the biblical story we need to re-tell, one way or another, before we try to interpret it or relate it to the lives of our congregation. I wish I knew who first said it is as if we preachers have seen the whole movie, but our listeners only have a box full of slides, all mixed up. One of the challenges of using a lectionary is exactly that: the Scriptures are presented in bits, and much of them—notably the Hebrew Bible portions—are never read in order in our worship context. I remember the day, sometime in the first semester of seminary, when it dawned on me that for awhile there had been two kingdoms in ancient Palestine. My knowledge of the history of Israel had been mostly a blur, with a few sharper images of events like the Exodus or the Sacrifice of Isaac which got read in church now and then. Suddenly, now, I began to experience something about the political and social realities in which the ancient stories and prophecies were embedded. We have to keep reminding ourselves that for many of the people hearing us preach, "Scripture" is still simply disconnected tales.

Questions like these lead logically to the greater question of how much of our preaching is intended simply to expose our congregation to the ancient story. This is a profoundly important issue in a post-Christian society. If our congregations are not familiar with the stories—and the Great Story—which undergird our faith, then they are likely to consider Christianity something like a set of precepts they can memorize and attach to their bumpers right beside "No war on Iraq" or "Dare to Keep our Kids Off Drugs." There is no question that Christianity and its Hebrew mother are deeply ethical religions, but those ethics are rooted in a narrative, and that narrative is rooted in a people with a history and a worldview.

It is obvious that there is more than one way to read the Bible. The results of our various ways of reading it are in the newspaper almost daily. Consider the battle over having the Ten Commandments in front of a courthouse, or the quotations which are flung by both sides over gay and lesbian rights. It is possible to consider the Bible to be a compendium of rules for behavior, and it is possible, as we all know well, to pick and choose which rules we think apply to our lives and culture today.

Preaching in the context of the eucharistic liturgy, however, almost dictates a way of reading the Scriptures different from that. The liturgical event itself has a movement through time, a kind of narrative structure. We prepare, we pray, we gather at the Table, we depart. Something happens. There is a kind of plot.

More centrally, the focus of this event, the climax of the narrative, if you will, is the rehearsal of salvation history in the eucharistic prayer, culminating in the realizing of God's saving action in the very Presence of Christ in the community gathered for the Breaking of Bread. We do not simply say a short blessing over the Gifts and distribute them; we bless them through and with the recounting of the whole story of God's interactions with God's people. We experience God's acting in time, in history, both in the past and right now. The liturgy presents our faith explicitly in terms of events, told in stories.

As we struggle with how to manage the biblical material for those who hear us preach, it is important to stay conscious of that liturgical story line. This is not an argument for a particular "form" for our homily, although I confess that I gravitate to a narrative shape to my homilies most of the time. But if we keep the overarching movement of the Eucharist in mind throughout our preparation, I believe we are likely to stress the sweep of the biblical narrative, rather than bumper-sticker-type rules and regulations—a reading of the biblical record that is more true to its origins as well as to its place in the Christian tradition.

THEOLOGY

One of the things that baffles people about the Anglican tradition is how indirectly we "teach" our theology. The classic formulation is the vignette of someone asking what Anglicans believe, and hearing the response, "Come and worship with us." Indeed, the English Reformation was conducted largely through the establishment of a *Book of Common Prayer:* worship conducted in English, the language of the people, conveyed the theology of the Church as it was being redefined, independent from Rome. Ours was not a confessional Reformation, but a liturgical one.

Although we do offer Sunday School for children and study groups for adults, Episcopalians generally expect people to "pick up" the peculiarities of our tradition not by being explicitly catechized, but by being immersed in it. This approach has the advantage of respecting individual differences, and exhibits the theological inclusiveness Anglicans endorse when they call their path the *"via media."* The disadvantage is that learning by osmosis is a slow process, and especially adult converts may come to the Anglican tradition with preconceptions which don't "fit" well and which may not be explicitly challenged for years. The recent controversies in the American Episcopal Church ignited by the election of an openly gay bishop illustrate the deep divisions in how Episcopalians understand Scripture and how they base their ethical decisions. Perhaps more disturbing, the controversies have revealed that Episcopalians are not just divided, but also confused.

From its beginnings, Anglicanism has been defined contextually. The foundational belief that worship is to be conducted in a language the people understand has been extended to include many dimensions of "language" beyond simply the words we use. The Anglican liturgy adjusts itself to be a living expression of the culture in which it enables worship. The cultural adaptations are particularly obvious in terms of music, but there are more subtle differences, as well.

Anglican theology in America has been profoundly influenced by the church's involvement in American culture. Although there is still ample evidence of a leaning toward our English roots, the Episcopal Church is clearly American. Ideas and attitudes which had their birth in the evangelical church of the western frontier have been embraced by many Episcopalians because of their prevalence in the cultural context we inhabit. Seminary-trained clergy may have a fairly clear understanding of the bases for Anglican theology, but the people who hear us preach most certainly do not.

Anglicanism's preference for operating inductively has been reflected in a tradition of preaching that leans toward a pastoral emphasis. This does not mean that Episcopal preachers ignore theological foundations or the Scripture of the day, but that they tend to begin with the issues facing their congregation, and bring the Scripture to bear on them, rather than the other way around. The circular process of exegeting congregation and Scripture at the same time supports this kind of preaching.

A weakness of this preference is that theological issues not related to the immediate concerns of the community (or demanded by a major feast such as Easter) may never come up. More subtly, perhaps, if a preacher consistently applies Scripture in an indirect manner, the community may never realize what kind of hermeneutic the preacher is using. It may have been possible at some time in the past to claim that explicit instruction about how to read the Bible belonged in adult education classes. Today, however, it is obvious that for most adults, the homily is the only Bible class they ever attend. The same goes for instruction in the principles of the faith. Preaching must carry these burdens, whether they fit comfortably in the context of "liturgical preaching" or not.

The implication for preachers at the Eucharist is that although it is important to focus on the liturgical narrative and integrating the homily into the greater movement of the liturgy, there are times when the ideals of liturgical integrity may need to give way before the need to educate the community explicitly in the theological tradition. The Lectionary may be a flawed set of snippets from the Holy Scriptures, but it offers no shortage of material from which to draw for presentation of the church's teachings. Indeed, at their ordination, Episcopal deacons, priests, and bishops declare they believe the "Holy Scriptures of the Old and New Testaments to be the Word of God, and to contain all things necessary to salvation."[6] Our vocation demands that we speak from that belief, that we share with our community how the tradition has given us a place to stand as we struggle with issues related to corporate living as well as private devotion.

THE CALL TO PROPHESY

We read and we preach the Holy Scriptures because we believe that somehow they still have something to say to us. They are the first foundational text of our preaching, and the second is the liturgy of which our preaching is a part. The third text is that protean entity called the "current situation," made up of the small stories of every person present; the composite story of our preaching community; and the unmanageable, multidimensional story of the greater culture and world.

What do we do when those three texts clash in some way? What is the function of the preacher?

It goes without saying, one hopes, that the point of holding the Scriptures up against current human life is to induce a realignment. Sometimes, the ancient story judges us and condemns our behavior. Sometimes it offers us a way to reframe our current situation so as to suggest a new direction or solution. Sometimes it shocks us with glory. In

[6] BCP, 526.

any of these cases, the meeting of Scripture with experience requires and effects movement of some sort. And as we preachers underline the places where our texts diverge or clash, we participate in that movement.

I believe that the contrast we sometimes draw between "prophetic" and "pastoral" preaching is artificial. Rhetoricians claim that all human speech is persuasive, and much preaching is perhaps intentionally so. A preacher may cry out at injustice or whisper comfort; both of those homiletical modes are persuasive in nature. Both intend to encourage a movement toward alignment with the will of God. It is just as "prophetic" to invite a fearful parishioner to open up to God's love as it is to denounce the current occupant of the White House.

And perhaps more appropriate to the Eucharistic celebration, I return to that opening collect of our Episcopal liturgy: the first call, as I understand it, is to be open. Although there are certainly times when a preacher must speak out about a particular social or political situation, I believe that our primary prophetic responsibility is to invite openness.

This is not to back off on the need to tell the truth, to name the dissonance we perceive between God's word and human activity. But if we have a solid relationship with those who listen to us, we respect them enough to allow them to make up their own minds about issues. Our task as preachers is to acquaint our congregation with how the Scriptures or our tradition reflect on the kind of issue at hand. It is not out of line, within the proper bounds of our relationship and our authority, to express our own opinions, as they represent our theological reflection on a situation. But we do not give orders to our listeners about what they are to think or do. Rather, we show them how to hold up the current context against the great narrative of God's interaction with God's creation, and allow them to draw their own conclusions. This implies a long process, an approach which does not wait until a critical issue confronts us, but which is continually aimed at the spiritual and ethical formation of the worshiping community.

It would be dishonest not to admit, too, that the community in which I and my students most often preach is also identified with "the Establishment." I once sat in on a course taught by a colleague who is both a professor of preaching and the pastor of a large Baptist congregation. The course was on preaching in the African American tradition, and more than half the students in the class were white. One day, an enthusiastic young white seminarian was commenting on Dr. J. Alfred Smith, Sr.'s teaching about preaching liberation. She said something like this: "It's inspiring to think about preaching liberation to the children of

Israel. But the people I'll be preaching with are more like the Egyptians. How do you preach to the Egyptians?"

With a twinkle in his eye, Dr. Smith replied, "I don't know how to preach to the Egyptians. But fortunately we have Professor Clader among us. She's an Episcopalian. She can tell you how to preach to the Egyptians!"

Not all Episcopalians are wealthy, Anglo-American, or highly educated, in spite of the caricatures members of other denominations sometimes like to draw. But there is usually a grain of truth beneath a stereotype, and there is more than a grain of truth to this one. The denomination in which I serve as a religious leader is generally identified more with the economically and politically powerful than with the disenfranchised and oppressed. If I am called to prophesy, it is as a privileged member of a privileged community, challenging that community to relinquish power and to open their doors to include people on the margins of their experience.

In general, people in power are not inclined to listen to someone berating them for their sinfulness. I recall Aesop's fable about the contest between the Sun and the Wind, arguing about which was stronger. They determined to prove it by seeing which of them could make the traveler remove his cloak. The Wind, of course, blew with all his force, but the traveler only pulled the cloak more tightly around him. When it came time for the Sun to try, he simply shone gently, and eventually the traveler removed the cloak to bask in the warmth.

Perhaps it is only that I am a coward, but when I think about a prophetic voice which is appropriate to the community I serve, I lean away from the image of John the Baptist. After all, my students and I are "insiders," paid by the community among whom we preach. The image of the fool seems much closer to the approach I take. In fact, the desktop on my computer displays Polish artist Jan Matejko's wonderful painting of the court jester Stanczyk grimly reflecting on news of a Polish military defeat while members of the court dance in the next room. Some fools feign madness in order to be able to speak the truth; some are simply playful. While I do not exactly advocate madness to my preaching students, I do encourage a playful spirit. A non-threatening presentation is more likely to be received by a powerful listener. In addition, when we approach our preaching with a lighter touch, we are more likely to allow the Holy Spirit to shape our proclamation and to enter our own hearts with surprises and with grace.

When I talk with my students about the call to be prophetic, I stress the action of the Holy Spirit. If we find ways to loosen the hinges a bit, we can invite people to "think outside the box," which I think is another way of saying they can allow the Holy Spirit to enter and direct their hearts. My version of prophetic preaching emphasizes imagination and allowing our listeners to rattle around a bit among ideas or images before nailing down something absolute. Not only does this approach offer new thoughts on a troubling subject, but it gifts our listeners with the knowledge that we respect them to rely on their own relationship with God.

OPENING WINDOWS TO THE SPIRIT

I am still talking about the formation of a preacher, rather than technique. I am talking about the development of an attitude, intentionally accepted and shaped by prayer. One word for it might be "humility."

Humility isn't about considering ourselves worthless or inept. In fact, it's the opposite—it's remembering that we are God's creatures. When we expend enormous amounts of time and energy crafting a homily, wanting to make it as good as it possibly can be, it is all too easy to become obsessed with polishing and perfecting an artifact, or to fall into the trap of thinking of our preaching as self-expression. But preaching is not self-expression. It is proclamation of God's word. And although it is appropriate for us to take care in making our speech understandable and engaging, in the end we are not called to create a work of art, but to utter a word of faith.

It is in that vein that we seek to offer our listeners an experience of the presence of God. Because what really matters in the preaching event is not what we preachers say but what our community hears, we conceive of our proclamation in terms of offering a gift rather than making a point. Possibly the very best thing we can do is to step back and allow our favorite idea to remain unsaid, in the hope that our listeners hear that word on their own. That intent, with its requisite restraint, is what I call the goal of opening windows for the Spirit.

Here is precisely where techniques of composition and organization come into play. Books, tapes, presentations, and casual conversations have covered them better than I can. I wish simply to expand a bit on the spin I give to some of the topics, with a particular intent to remain alert to how these aspects of our art are peculiarly applied to preaching in the context of the Eucharist.

FORM: TREES AND RIVERS

When we contemplate finding a prophetic voice—one which can invite rather than cajole, and suggest rather than pontificate—one of the dimensions we must consider is the form our speech takes. In general, the approach I have advocated is ill-suited to a deductive sermon—one beginning with statements of received truth or propositions and proceeding to deduce from them appropriate responses of faith or action. A deductive process is also rather foreign to Anglican theological thought. Instead, we are likely to begin with questions or observations, and draw conclusions after a mixture of theological reflection and attention to our worship context.

Nevertheless, once we have planned the homily we are going to preach, we need to determine a direction in which it will grow or move. In his classic textbook on preaching, H. Grady Davis advocates thinking of a sermon under construction as a tree, with branches emanating from the central trunk.[7] Other homileticians, in one way or another, have described "construction" of a sermon with building blocks. All of us have, at times, imagined a theme or question with a series of illustrations. But the sermon-construction metaphor which works best for me is the image of a river.

I ask my students to imagine the Mississippi River watershed. We begin our journey in Minnesota, where we can literally hop across the trickling Mississippi on a few rocks. We launch our canoe and start to float downstream. Now, we know that our ultimate destination is the Gulf of Mexico, and we keep that destination in mind for the rest of the trip. But after some miles it occurs to us that there are these hundreds of tributaries into the great river, and we decide to explore some of them. We may jump over to Montana and follow the course of the Missouri for awhile—but we know that ultimately that water winds up in the Mississippi, and then in New Orleans. Or we take a detour over to the southern end of Indiana and catch a ride on a barge on the Ohio. And so on. We might explore numerous smaller streams, but still the destination remains the same—and our listeners are able to follow our progress if we ourselves keep that destination clearly in mind.

The result of imagining the structure of our homily this way is to give it a skeleton, or perhaps a dominant musical theme, but still to allow our listeners to fill in the gaps between discrete moments in the preaching.

---

[7] H. Grady Davis, *Design for Preaching* (Philadelphia: Muhlenberg Press, 1958) 15–16.

We may only follow the Missouri River through Montana before we hop to the Ohio, but if the downstream movement has been established, our listeners will make the leap on their own to another part of the watershed. They fill in the missing steps themselves, and in general are induced to stick with us because that kind of imagining is pleasurable and a compliment to their engagement and intelligence.

Eugene Lowry has described the creation of suspense in preaching in terms of the development of plot.[8] While in my own preaching I tend to the kind of narrative approach he advocates, and while I agree that a narrative structure is effective in maintaining interest on the part of the listeners, I am not exactly echoing him in my Mississippi model. One slight difference, I believe, is that the conclusion toward which Lowry's suspense is aiming is either contained within the scope of the sermon itself, or at least is suggested primarily by the combination of the Scriptures read and the sermon preached and heard. When I imagine the metaphor of the river, it helps me stay in touch with the fact that the water keeps flowing after we have all reached New Orleans. The homily I am preaching takes on a life which first involves itself in the gathering around the Table, before (one hopes) it flows out the door of the church building and into our activity in the world. Suspense is built with the leaps between tributaries, or with the suggestion that the river has a long path to travel beyond the end of the homily time. I believe my model is a little less tightly controlled than Lowry's, although I assign his book to my students and refer to it often in my teaching.

A SAMPLE—WITH HOLES

The Mississippi River model for the form of a homily does not necessarily imply anything about what happens on the various excursions we take to oxbows and headwaters. Our listeners' attention is aroused by wondering just how we're going to get from downtown Chicago to St. Louis, but the attention is drawn only to our cleverness if our visits to those places do not provide memorable information. Normally, each one of those stops should be providing some kind of illumination for our listeners of the day's message, founded on the biblical narrative.

It occurs to me that my prevailing river metaphor may be implying that I advocate a pastiche of different illustrations. In fact, that is rarely

---

[8] Eugene Lowry, *The Homiletical Plot: The Sermon as Narrative Art Form*, expanded ed. (Louisville: Westminster John Knox, 2000).

the way I preach myself. Rather, I tend to move fairly methodically toward the goal I have identified for the homily. The leaps I take from one tributary to another are more about leaving gaps in the "argument" and allowing the welding of homiletical plates to remain leaky. But as I move from one to another "angle" on the overall proclamation, I am hopeful that the views from those angles are all clear, vivid, and, if possible, provocative.

I hazard a short example here. This is a homily I preached for a weekday Eucharist on the feast of St. Michael and All Angels. Structurally, I believe it is riddled with holes and logical gaps. Nevertheless, it was deemed "successful" by my congregation. In a sense, almost all the homily was a set-up for the final couple of sentences. That was New Orleans.

A Homily for St. Michael and All Angels

(LECTIONS: GENESIS 28:10-17; JOHN 1:47-51)

1. Did you actually hear that last line? " . . . you will see heaven opened and the angels of God ascending and descending upon the Son of Man." Think about that for a minute. Angels ascending and descending upon the *Son of Man*. Isn't that a little strange?

2. It seems clear that in his conversation with Nathanael, Jesus is intentionally looking back to the story of Jacob's dream. When Jesus sees Nathanael approaching, he says, "Here is truly a son of Israel in whom there is no deceit!" I wonder if that's a Johannine joke. Jacob was full of deceit. In the part of his story which comes right before the bit we just heard, Jacob has just deceived his blind old father Isaac with animal pelts on his arms and a savory stew, and he's ripped off his brother Esau, stealing the blessing reserved for the older son. Now he's on the run. If he has a conscience at all, it's probably guilty. He's afraid, too. Afraid that Esau will come after him to take revenge.

3. But Jacob gets tired, and it's night time, so he curls up to sleep with his head on a rock. And then he has this dream of angels ascending and descending on a mighty ramp running between earth and heaven. You might be tempted to think this is one of those hyper-active dreams brought on by Jacob's fear and guilt feelings. But then the Lord himself comes to stand beside Jacob, and speaks directly to him. And what the Lord says doesn't sound like the kind of thing a man with a guilty conscience would make up for himself. It's not about retribution or punishment, and it's not a call to Jacob to clean up his act or go home and apologize to his brother. Instead, God promises Jacob a future he could never have imagined.

4. God says, "You and your offspring will inherit the land on which you are lying." And God says, "Your children will be as numerous as the grains of dust on the earth, and will fill all the earth with blessing." And God says, "Know that I am with you and will keep you wherever you go, and will bring you back to this land; for I will not leave you until I have done what I have promised you."

5. God's promise to Jacob offers him a change in course. When Jacob wakes up, he marks the place as holy, as the gate of heaven. And he accepts the promise God has given him, and he affirms that Yahweh will be his God.

6. A vision with angels. A voice with a promise. A change in course. A recognition and celebration of God's steadfast presence and guidance. When Jesus echoes the story of Jacob, he reminds Nathanael of all that.

7. "You will see heaven opened and the angels of God ascending and descending upon the Son of Man," says Jesus. You might say it's a bit of a stretch for Jesus to be comparing himself to a ladder. But remember, this is the same Gospel where Jesus also calls himself a Gate, not to mention the true Vine, the Way, and the Bread of Life. A ladder—a mighty ramp connecting heaven and earth—that's not such a far-out metaphor in the Gospel of John.

8. But what then do we do with those angels, especially since it's the angels we're supposed to be celebrating today?

9. Remember, in the story of Jacob, the vision of the angels is really only the precursor to Jacob's encounter with God—an encounter which changes his course, and indeed, his life. It isn't the vision of angels that changes things, but the promises offered by God.

10. The angels are like the warm-up act for the real feature. They're the trumpets before the parade begins. "Watch out," says Jesus to Nathanael. "This is not just about magic tricks." Angels are a signal for an inbreaking, a warning to look out for the kind of heaven-quake that happens when God takes a hand in the history of the human race, or in the great story of Jesus, or in the private story of one insignificant human being like Jacob, or like Nathanael, or like you, or like me.

11. I got a catalog from a gift company the other day, and since it's now only eighty-one shopping days until Christmas, the catalog was full of angels. And most of them were cute and cuddly, with childlike faces and soft white feathery wings.

12. But the angels who signal major changes in human life are almost never cuddly. Like the three strangers who dropped in for dinner

with Abraham and Sarah, it's easy to mistake them for regular folks. In fact, sometimes you don't recognize them for what they are until later, when the change they have signaled has begun to take shape.

13. I bet you know what I mean. I remember one who appeared to me, a long time ago. I was in the midst of tremendous upheaval in my life. I was struggling to grow up, and to be honest with myself, and to get sober, and to listen to God. I was with a friend, and we were actually talking about messengers who signal God's steadfast presence, who signal God's offering us direction, taking a hand in our lives.

14. And I remember that for a second, everything seemed to get a little brighter around my friend. And I said, "You're one of them, aren't you?" And he said, "No, I'm just a humanoid."

15. I think at the time I just shrugged and smiled. But today, many years and a long journey later, I know that he was wrong. It's just possible that God's messengers don't themselves always know that's what they are. Which would mean it's also possible that you're one yourself. For someone, sometime. Think about it. They used to try to calculate how many angels could stand on the head of a pin. It might not be a totally crazy thing to try meditating on how many angels could be sitting right now, on September 29, 2003, in the chapel at CDSP.

Notice the gaps between ideas. The first paragraph asks a question based on the last thing the congregation has heard, the very ending of the Gospel. It underlines an absurd sort of statement which might just have gotten past the listeners. But right away, instead of answering the question posed, the homily veers off to a discussion about Jacob's dream. It gets there through a short riff on the idea of "deceit," as a trait missing in Nathanael and richly present in Jacob. Jacob's deceitfulness is sketched in contemporary terms, such as "ripping off" his brother, and being "on the run," and I liken his vivid dream to the kind of anxiety-dream most people have had. I also sneak in a little exegetical information, noting that the "ladder" was really a "ramp." The image in my listeners' minds shifts at that moment from angels climbing the paint ladder on their back porch to a procession on a middle-eastern ziggurat.

Paragraph 6 offers a synopsis which foregrounds the elements of the story I want people to "get," ending with a connection back to the Gospel and Nathanael. This is followed by a re-statement of the original question, about Jesus calling himself a ladder/ramp, and another little bit of exegesis. Then comes the biggest leap, the logical hole that could sink my canoe. We drop Jesus and Nathanael, and switch to a discussion of angels. From the Wisconsin Dells we have just jumped to Great Falls, Montana.

The homily began basically as an exegesis of two typologically related scriptural passages. Now it has changed focus to a thematic exploration of who or what angels may be. From here on, scriptural references come in as illustrations of the central "what is an angel?" question, and no longer really function as narratives on their own. But the language I used in this section (paragraphs 10–12) is intentionally colorful, to give the thematic exploration the flavor of narrative. The angels are "like a warm-up act for the real feature" and "trumpets before the parade." Jesus says, "Watch out, this is not just about magic tricks," a statement which would remind a biblically literate listener of a recurring theme in the Gospel of John.

Paragraph 11 begins still on angels, but taking off from a new starting place. The angels in the catalog ("only eighty-one shopping days until Christmas") are "cute and cuddly," an image I suspect resonates with anyone who has experienced the holidays in the U.S.A. And of course the "cute" angels set the homily up for a contrast with the kind of angels most of us encounter.

These three paragraphs also create the explicit bridge to our own experience that will make the biblical story "matter" to us. "Angels are a signal for an inbreaking, a warning to look out for the kind of heaven-quake that happens when God takes a hand in the history of the human race, or in the great story of Jesus, or in the private story of one insignificant human being like Jacob, or like Nathanael, or like you, or like me." The *function* of the angels is now laid out in a way suggesting we might be involved. But the matter of who or what angels actually *are* is still left hanging.

The hint comes in paragraph 12, carried by another familiar biblical story of an angelic visitation: "Like the three strangers who dropped in for dinner with Abraham and Sarah, it's easy to mistake them for regular folks. In fact, sometimes you don't recognize them for what they are until later, when the change they have signaled has begun to take shape." And it's a fairly easy ride from there, through a specific personal experience, to the goal I had in mind: to alert us all to the presence of angels in our very midst.

When I asked my listeners what they had heard in the homily, every one of them noted the importance to them of the "point," the provocative conclusion we had reached. One or two specifically remembered the expression, "heaven-quakes" for moments of angelic visitation (this expression, of course, has particular poignancy in the seismically active area where our seminary is located). Some expressed appreciation for the tidbit of my own story I shared. Not one single person mentioned Jacob, or Nathanael, or Jesus, or John, or even ramps or ladders. What they *heard* was that God takes a hand in their lives, that God's messengers are among us every day, and that, indeed, we ourselves could be messengers to others, unawares.

Not inconsequentially, too, I think they heard that their homiletics professor and the academic dean of their seminary believed in angels, and her life had been changed by what she identified as the hand of God. It was a small stroke in the homily, and not very personally revealing. No one mentioned it when they spoke to me afterward. On the other hand, more people spoke to me than usual. Could there have been a connection?

The exercise I have just engaged in is a pretty fair example of the way I teach. I find it extremely difficult to lay down rules about form, imagery, language, the use of Scripture, and how one relates one's own experience. Rather, I offer examples, and then ask students what techniques or emphases they can identify. A primary goal of my teaching is to encourage students to find their own authentic voice for preaching. It seems appropriate, therefore, to share with them as candidly as I can how I have found and keep discovering my own.

DETAILS AS PRAYER

In the homily I analyzed above, my intent was not to use imagery or vivid language as decoration, but as elements which grew organically from what I was attempting to say. I do not pretend, however, that I use them unconsciously. I have taught expository writing long enough to have taken in some of my own advice, such as finding verbs with real coloring, or using a specific picture or story when a generalization might have sufficed.

There is a dimension to this kind of attention, though, that goes beyond trying simply to write lively prose. The details in my preaching are a reflection of my own spiritual rule of life. In my preparation for preaching, I spend considerable time taking walks, and while I am walking, simply noticing things. At times, I watch with the kind of attentiveness Simone Weil identified with prayer.[9] I am a bird-watcher and a nature-

---

[9] Simone Weil: "The key to a Christian conception of studies is the realization that prayer consists of attention." She makes this statement at the beginning of her "Reflections on the Right Use of School Studies with a View to the Love of God" in *Waiting for God*, trans. Emma Craufurd (New York: Harper and Row, 1951). I apply her concept of school "exercises" to observation of objects and events while meditating.

watcher, and at times also a people-watcher, and my observations wind up shaping my prayer life. Occasionally, the observations themselves find homes in my homilies; more often, the practice of attention in general results in imagining details I have not observed recently at all. They could be memories of events or pictures long past. But when the details pop up in preparing a homily, the context of the prayer still clings to them, like a fragrance, maybe, or objects in a gravitational field.[10]

If we make preaching a focus of our rule of life, we find ourselves observing the world in a particular way. We observe the way individual drops of a waterfall shimmer in the sunlight, and we ask ourselves whether that might be a metaphor for something we are thinking about for Sunday. Eventually, we find we are observing everything more closely. Our preaching makes the world jump with life.

A sensory sort of prayer—and a sensory homiletical language arising from it—is entirely appropriate for the supremely "materialistic" context of our sacramental liturgy. In fact, using a significant proportion of concrete imagery in our preaching may even help alert our listeners to the concreteness of the rite we are celebrating. When it seems appropriate in our preaching to make overt reference to the physical elements of the eucharistic meal—or of a baptism or of a funeral—it is not so long a stretch, not so abrupt a turn, as it would be if the homily were filled with abstract concepts.

WITHIN BOUNDS

When we discuss how to bear witness in our proclamation, offering our own experiences and faith in conversation with the faith of our congregation, we naturally run into the question of just *how much* of our own experience is appropriate to share. Probably all of us have at some time or another experienced a preacher we judged to have crossed a boundary, telling us so much we began to squirm uncomfortably. Sometimes, our nervousness was about confidential information the preacher appeared to be sharing. More often, the preacher was confiding his or her own weakness—or touting his or her own success—in a way which called too much attention to the preacher and forced the congregation into a role it hadn't signed on for.

Without trying to duplicate what has been written on this subject elsewhere, let me just try to engage it from the perspective of preaching

---

[10] I have explored these ideas more fully in my book, *Voicing the Vision: Imagination and Prophetic Preaching* (Harrisburg: Morehouse, 2004).

in the eucharistic liturgy. In the formal, structured context of the Eucharist, the preaching moment is perhaps an anomaly. Although we may be dressed in a style setting us apart, when we preach we often attempt to bridge the distance created by our role and our appearance. We adopt a more conversational style of speech than one hears in the rest of the liturgy. We may stand down from the raised chancel area, "among the people." We may use a microphone so we can speak in our "natural" voice instead of having to project in a more theatrical style.

All of this is appropriate for liturgical preaching. The homily is a place in the liturgy where the daily, pastoral issues of the community can be brought together with the great story of our tradition, where the mundane can be blessed along with the homely elements of bread and wine. It is right and good that "normal" human conversation, as it is encapsulated in the preaching, be a participant in the sacred dialog.

Nevertheless, whatever steps we may take to bridge the gap between the formality of ritual to the informality of a coffee shop, we are still operating within the ritual. We have been singing together, praying together. And that activity has made the members of our congregation vulnerable, as they may not be in their lives "outside" the liturgical context.

This vulnerability could actually be physical in nature. A study has been done, for example, which suggests that very deep organ tones ("infrasound," inaudible to the human ear), may induce "religious feelings" in people unaware of what they are hearing. In a controlled experiment run by scientists in England, people exposed to the sound of a very large organ pipe reported shivering, an increased heart rate, feelings of anxiety, and "a sudden memory of emotional loss."[11] Perhaps we can recall having similar feelings ourselves. There is no question that many religious (and other) traditions have made use of controlled breathing and music to stimulate response in a crowd. The effect of deep bass music and drums is familiar to anyone who has attended a rock concert. We need to take seriously the fact that even if our congregation has been singing quietly, a cappella, the experience of simply breathing in concert has made an impact on forming a gathering into a unity, and of readying individuals to be stirred by something from outside themselves.

The vulnerability I have just described could be awakened by any kind of music, any kind of common prayer (or chanting, or rhythmic noise-making). In our eucharistic context, that vulnerability is combined

---

[11] This study was described by Jonathan Amos, "Organ Music Instills 'Religious Feelings,'" BBC News, September 8, 2003, http://news.bbc.co.uk/1/hi/sci/tech/3087674.stm.

with the congregation's awareness, even upon entering the sanctuary, that they are in the presence of the Holy. Their prior experience with this rite has taught them that openness to God in this place, for this time, is desirable, and so their vulnerability is first *willed*, and then enhanced by the musical and other sensory dimensions of the liturgical event. Emotionally and psychologically, the worshipers who listen to us preach have already, to some degree, offered us open hearts. As we try to cross the divide between chancel and nave, we need to view that space as holy ground. It is not to be danced upon disrespectfully.

Rhetoric has gotten a bad reputation among some homileticians, who are uncomfortable with the idea that preaching is a form of persuasion. But as I said earlier, I am of the school that maintains all speech is intended to be persuasive. It is far better, I believe, to understand clearly that we are engaged in a form of persuasion, whether we will it or not, than to operate blindly.

As we study and mature in our craft, we obtain more and better tools to move our listeners. We may learn, for example, that a particular kind of story is likely to "touch" people; that "quoting" directly the voice of God has particular force; that using particular kinds of metaphors "speak" especially to the congregation with whom we are familiar. It is useful to be aware of such dynamics. But it is also essential, always, to be grounded in the knowledge that the *goal* of wielding our homiletical tools is not movement for its own sake—in order to prove to ourselves, perhaps, that we have such power. We are called, most of the time, to exercise a gentle rhetoric, a rhetoric of suggestion rather than trumpeting truths.

The liturgical context within which we preach hardly ever persuades overtly. Music may stir us in mysterious ways, but at the same time we may be singing *words* whose meaning grows on us as we sing the same hymn again and again. The very words of the ordo may not strike us with their meaning for years—they could just as well be said in Latin or Greek. And then, one day, we realize that we have been formed by the great salvation narrative, just as I suggested at the outset my preaching has been formed by the words of the Collect for Purity. Our preaching, Sunday after Sunday, also forms people in that subtle way. Our task is to do the best we can to be faithful to the Gospel and respectful of our listeners. The message we preach grows quietly, like that seed Jesus talked about that sprouts while the farmer is asleep.

AN APPROACH TO EXEGESIS
(handed out to beginning students on the first day of class, the first assignment of which will be a homily from the Gospel of Mark)

Introductory Comments

In preparing for your first homily, your first task is to do some exegesis—on the text and on the congregation. There is more than one way to go about exegesis for preaching, but the following is a suggested approach. The order of some of the steps is arbitrary: for example, you should really be thinking about your preaching context at the same time that you are digging into the scriptural passage.

Steps to Be Taken

1. Read the pericope several times.
   • Read it in several translations, and in Greek (if that is possible for you). Read it aloud. Read it "naïvely"—that is, don't try to get scholarly at this early stage.
   • Pray it. Ask God, in whatever way is natural to you, for guidance in hearing the Good News, and hearing the hard things.
   • Pay attention to immediate questions, reactions, likes and dislikes, irritations—these are most likely the responses your listeners will have had to the reading of the Gospel just before you preach—but pay attention also to possible "hot buttons" of your own.
   • Write down your reactions and ideas, but don't analyze them yet. Overall, were there any surprises?

2. Re-read (skimming is ok) the entire Gospel of Mark.
   • Pray it.
   • Make an outline, or pay attention to the outline your version of the Bible offers you. Review what you think Mark's Gospel is doing, as a whole.
   • Look at parallels with other Synoptic Gospels.
   • Write down your answers to the following questions:
       Where does your pericope fit into the overall story?
       What rhetorical reasons might there be for the author's placement of this part of the story?
       Does Mark use your episode differently from Matthew or Luke? Why?

Watch out especially for loaded vocabulary that might be used differently in one or another Gospel. What is its effect on the import of the pericope?

3. *After* the above steps, you may turn to your tools and commentaries.
   • Poke around! Use complete commentaries like the *Jerome* or *Harper's*, but please dig deeper into works devoted just to Mark.
   • Look up vocabulary in a concordance or theological dictionary (for example, Kittel, *et al.*).
   • Write down:
     What do various commentaries point to that you find particularly compelling or troublesome?
     Keep references to sources for these insights.

4. Force yourself to pay attention to sections you may want to avoid.
   • One approach: try writing out the passage for memory. What did you leave out? Any clues why?
   • Is there anything that bears another look?

5. Consider your congregation.
   • Who are they? Make a demographic sketch, including categories like age, sex, denominational affiliation, year in seminary, place in respective ordination paths or academic program.
   • What else do you know about them? What is going on in their lives—as individuals, as a group? How well do you know them?
   • What is your pastoral or peer connection with them? When you imagine the congregation seated before you while you preach, what do you see? Do any faces stand out? Why?
   • Pray for your congregation several times as you prepare your homily.
   • Write down your questions, analysis, speculations, reflections.

6. And what about the world?
   • What are the big issues pressing on everyone at this time? Are there any social/justice/greater church connections which you see in the pericope you are studying?
   • Write down any implications you draw from the Scripture regarding issues confronting us.

7. Preaching in the context of the Eucharist.
   • Are there elements in what you have uncovered in your exegesis

of the text that particularly connect with your congregation in a liturgical context? Why?
- Write down:
  What hymns or prayers do your explorations evoke for you?
  What directions might those poetic texts take you that are/are not relevant to the message which is beginning to emerge?

8. Remember, the above is only the beginning of your process.
Once you have opened the text for yourself and reacquainted yourself with the context for your preaching, you still need to bring it all back to a focus, a direction, a word. This process takes time, and the whole process outlined above should take about six days. The longer, the better—don't rush! Take walks, or meditate, or find some other way to give your brain some down time in between the steps. Try praying for wisdom before a down time, and open your heart to the direction of the Holy Spirit.

ANNOTATED BIBLIOGRAPHY

Avis, Paul. *God and the Creative Imagination: Metaphor, Symbol and Myth in Religion and Theology.* London and New York: Routledge, 1999. A provocative and readable theological exploration of imagination, not explicitly focused on preaching.

Childers, Jana L. *Performing the Word: Preaching as Theatre.* Nashville: Abingdon Press, 1998. A witty and concise treatment of what preachers can learn from the techniques and experience of acting. Pays explicit attention to the body as the instrument of our vocation.

Clader, Linda L. "Preaching the Liturgical Narrative: The Easter Vigil and the Language of Myth," *Worship* (April 1998). This article explores the place of the homily in the overall liturgical narrative, with special emphasis on how our language can make implicit connections with mythic structures from Christian and pre-Christian traditions.

_____. *Voicing the Vision: Imagination and Prophetic Preaching.* Harrisburg: Morehouse, 2004. An exploration of formation for imaginative and prophetic preaching, with practical suggestions and illustrations.

Countryman, L. William. *Interpreting the Truth: Changing the Paradigm of Biblical Studies.* Harrisburg: Trinity Press International, 2003. Although this book is not explicitly aimed at preachers, everything Countryman says about "interpreters" of Scripture applies. Takes seriously the "triangular conversation" among text, interpreter, and community, and the fact that a classic text tends to "open space for reflection more than to close it."

Davis, H. Grady. *Design for Preaching*. Philadelphia: Muhlenberg Press, 1958. Some credit this book with beginning the "New Homiletic." It is still a classic, and takes the form of the sermon seriously.

Daw, Carl P., Jr., ed. *Breaking the Word: Essays on the Liturgical Dimensions of Preaching*. New York: Church Publishing, 1994. A collection of essays explicitly about preaching in the Episcopal liturgy. See especially the articles by Daw and Dozier.

Eisner, Will. *Comics and Sequential Art*. Tamarac, FL: Poorhouse Press, 1985. This classic discussion of how comics are constructed has influenced me in paying attention to what happens in the "gaps" between "frames" in a comic book or a sermon.

Gelpi, Donald L., s.j. *God Breathes: The Spirit in the World*. Wilmington, DE: Michael Glazier, 1988. This little book is an accessible distillation of Gelpi's extensive scholarship on the Holy Spirit. His work has been deeply influential in how I think of the work of the Spirit in preaching.

Hethcock, William. "Preaching at the Eucharist." *Sewanee Theological Review* 39:2 (1996) 131–46. An explicitly Episcopalian take on liturgical preaching.

Hovda, Robert W. *Strong, Loving and Wise: Presiding in Worship*. Collegeville, MN: Liturgical Press. Fifth edition, 1983. Although this book is not focused on the preaching ministry, what it has to say about presiding at the Eucharist applies wonderfully to the presider-as-preacher.

Lakoff, George, and Mark Johnson. *Metaphors We Live By*. Chicago: University of Chicago Press, 1980. An introduction to a particular view of how metaphor permeates our language, whether we are aware of it or not.

Lowry, Eugene L. *The Homiletical Plot: The Sermon as Narrative Art Form*. Atlanta: Westminster John Knox Press, expanded edition, 2000. This is the classic presentation on narrative preaching.

_____. *How to Preach a Parable: Designs for Narrative Sermons*. Nashville: Abingdon Press, 1989. Examples of narrative preaching by a number of homileticians. Not about preaching *about* a parable, but about parabolic, provocative preaching.

Malina, Bruce J., and Richard L. Rohrbaugh. *Social-Science Commentary on the Synoptic Gospels.* Minneapolis: Fortress Press, 1992. This is the book I order for beginning students as a resource on historical context for preaching on the synoptic Gospels. The authors have produced other volumes on Revelation and the Gospel of John. Helpfully arranged as verse-by-verse commentaries, with cross-references to longer discussions of particular cultural issues.

Ong, Walter. *Orality and Literacy.* London: Routledge, 1982. I always recommend this book as the classic treatment of how writing has influenced the way we think.

Pollan, Michael. *The Botany of Desire.* New York: Random House, 2001. A delightful example of attention. Not a book about preaching, but full of whimsical reflection of the sort which brings a homily to life.

Rice, Charles R. *The Embodied Word: Preaching as Art and Liturgy.* Minneapolis: Fortress Press, 1991. A thorough treatment of liturgical preaching by an Episcopal priest and professor of both homiletics and worship.

Rose, Lucy A. *Sharing the Word: Preaching in the Roundtable Church.* Louisville: Westminster John Knox, 1997. A broadening of the inductive approach to preaching to include the voices of more people than just the preacher.

Schlafer, David J. *Your Way with God's Word: Discovering Your Distinctive Preaching Voice.* Cambridge, Eng.: Cowley, 1995. Some exercises and provocative suggestions on finding one's own voice.

Taylor, Barbara Brown. *The Preaching Life.* Cambridge, Eng.: Cowley, 1993. This book has been so influential on my teaching and preaching that I had intentionally chosen not to read it as I was preparing this chapter. Essentially, it is on the formation of a preacher. I assign it to every introductory class I teach.

Turner, Mary Donovan, and Mary Lin Hudson. *Saved from Silence: Finding Women's Voice in Preaching.* St. Louis: Chalice, 1999. Deals head-on with issues concerning authority in the experience of women preachers. Includes interviews with a number of women about challenges they have faced finding their voice.

CONTRIBUTORS

Rev. Linda Clader, Ph.D., is professor of homiletics and dean of the Church Divinity School of the Pacific at the Graduate Theological Union, Berkeley, California. Rev. Clader, an Episcopalian priest, completed her doctorate at Harvard University.

Rev. J. Sergius Halvorsen is a priest of the Orthodox Church in America who teaches homiletics at Holy Apostles College and Seminary in Cromwell, Connecticut, and at St. Tikhon's Orthodox Theological Seminary in South Canaan, Pennsylvania. He received his M.Div. from St. Vladimir's Orthodox Theological Seminary and his Ph.D. from Drew University. Fr. Sergius, his wife, and three children live in Middletown, Connecticut.

Father Michael Monshau, o.p., Ph.D., is a Dominican priest who earned the Ph.D. in homiletics and liturgics at Vanderbilt University. He is professor of homiletics and liturgical studies at the Dominican School of Philosophy and Theology at the Graduate Theological Union, Berkeley, California.

Rev. Mary Alice Mulligan, Ph.D., serving the Christian Church (Disciples of Christ), is director of the Chapel and affiliate professor of preaching and ethics at Christian Theological Seminary in Indianapolis. Rev. Mulligan completed the Ph.D. in homiletics and ethics at Vanderbilt University.

Sister Mary Ann Wiesemann-Mills, o.p., D.Min., an Akron Dominican Sister, is adjunct professor of homiletics at St. Mary's Seminary and Graduate School of Theology, Wickliffe, Ohio. Her Doctor of Ministry in Preaching was earned at Aquinas Institute of Theology in St. Louis, Missouri.

INDEX